PN
513
.S26
1965

PN513.S26 1965

A012335801

FINCH
COLLEGE LIBRARY

P9-CDU-982

Date Due

SENECA
FINCH
COLLEGE LIBRARY

SENECA
FINCH
COLLEGE LIBRARY

17.2

Situations

PLEASE
DO NOT WEED
OCT 0 5 2001
SENECA LIBRARY
NEWNHAM

Situations

JEAN-PAUL Sartre

PLEASE
DO NOT WEED

OCT 0 5 2001

SENECA LIBRARY
NEWNHAM

TRANSLATED FROM THE FRENCH BY BENITA EISLER

GEORGE BRAZILLER   NEW YORK

English translation, copyright © 1965, George Braziller, Inc.

Originally published in France as *Situations IV* © 1964, Editions Gallimard.

The single chapter, "Nathalie Sarraute," originally appeared as the Preface to *Portrait of a Man Unknown*, translated by Maria Jolas, © 1958, George Braziller, Inc.

All rights in this book are reserved.

For information, address the publisher:
George Braziller, Inc.
215 Park Avenue South
New York 3, New York

Library of Congress Catalog Card Number: 65-14602

First Printing

Printed in the United States of America

DESIGNED BY JACQUELINE SCHUMAN

Contents

All footnotes are the author's except where (*Trans.*) is given.

Situations

Situation.

The Prisoner
of Venice

The Prisoner of Venice

JACOPO'S WILES   Nothing. His life has been swallowed up. A few dates, a few facts, and then the cackling of ancient writers. But if we persevere, *Venice speaks to us*. This voice of a perjured witness, now strident, now whispering, broken by silences, is her voice. The life story of Tintoretto, a portrait of the artist painted in his lifetime by his native city, betrays a relentless animosity. The City of the Doges informs us that she had taken a violent dislike to the most celebrated of her sons. Nothing is actually said. There are only insinuations, hints, and then the subject is changed. This inflexible hatred has the inconsistency of sand. More than a stated aversion, it is a cold sullenness, the insidious dispersal of rejection. But it is all we need to know. Jacopo waged a losing battle against a numberless adversary, grew weary, and died, defeated. And that is the essence of his life. We shall see it all, in all its dismal nakedness, if, for a moment, we brush aside the overgrowth of slander which blocks our way.

Jacopo Robusti was born in 1518, the son of a dyer, but immediately, Venice whispers to us that it was a bad beginning. *Around the year 1530, the youth entered Titian's studio as an apprentice, but after a few days, the illustrious painter of ninety discovered the boy's genius, and threw him out.* As dry as that. This anecdote appears in every account with striking insistency. It does little credit to Titian, we shall say, and we will be right. In our eyes, today, this does him no credit. But when Vasari told it, in 1567, Titian had reigned for more than half a century.

Fragment of a work in progress. Originally published in Les Temps Modernes, *November, 1957.*

Nothing is more respectable than a long period of impunity. Furthermore, according to the laws of the time, he was the Master, after God, in his own studio. No one would deny him the right to dismiss an employee. On the contrary. It is the victim who was presumed guilty; marked by misfortune, perhaps even contagious, he must have had the evil eye. In short, this is the first time that a cursed childhood figures in the golden legend of the Italian painters. No doubt there is a conclusion to be drawn from this, but we shall come back to it later. The Voice of Venice never lies, provided that we are able to interpret it. We shall listen again when we have learned more. For the moment, whatever the real truth may be, I shall only call attention to the improbability of the facts.

That Titian was not an easy man is well known. But Jacopo was twelve years old. At twelve, a gift is nothing, and anything can obliterate it. But time and patience are needed to transform a fragile skill into talent. No artist at the height of his fame, not even the most supercilious of them all, is going to feel threatened by a small boy. Let us even concede that the Master fired his apprentice through jealousy. This amounted to the same thing as murdering him. The curse of the nation's pride weighed heavily indeed, and all the more so as Titian lacked the honesty to admit his real motives. He was king, and at his frown, all doors were closed to the black sheep, and he was barred from the profession.

A black-listed child is something of a phenomenon. Our interest is aroused. How did he manage to overcome this ill-fated beginning? But the question is asked in vain. At this very moment, the same in every single book, the thread of the narrative breaks and we are confronted by a conspiracy of silence. No one will tell us what became of Jacopo between the ages of twelve and twenty. Some have thought to explain this gap by claiming that he was self-taught. But we know precisely that this would have been impossible. And contemporary writers knew it better still. At the beginning of the sixteenth century, the art of painting remained a complicated technique, more akin to a ceremony, weighed down by a mixture of recipe and ritual, skill rather than knowledge, a set of procedures rather than a method, professional rules, traditions and workshop secrets. All these contributed to making apprenticeship both a social obligation and a necessity. The silence of his biographers only betrays their embarrassment. Unable to reconcile the precocious notoriety of the young Robusti with his excommunication, they cast a veil of darkness on the eight years which separated the one from the other. We can take this as a confession; no one dismissed Jacopo. Since he didn't waste away, or die of contempt in his father's dye-works, he must have worked regularly, just as was normal, in the workshop of a painter about whom nothing is known save that *he was not* Titian. In all closed and suspicious organizations, hatred is retroactive. If the mysterious beginnings of this life seem a premonition of its mysterious end, if the curtain which is raised upon a miraculously arrested shipwreck falls upon a shipwreck bereft of miracle, it is because Venice rearranged everything after the fact to scar the child with his future old age. Nothing happens and nothing lasts. Birth is the mirror of death and between the two, there is only scorched earth. Everything has been consumed by the curse of bad luck.

But if we move through these mirages, the haze lifts on the other side, and we can see as far as the horizon. An adolescent appears, and starting at top speed, charges towards glory. In 1539, Jacopo left his patron to establish himself on his own. He was *past master*. This young employer conquered independence, a reputation, a clientele, employing other workers and apprentices in turn. But make no mistake. In a city flooded by painters, where imminent depression threatened to strangle the market, becoming a master at twenty was the exception. Neither talent, nor work, nor resourcefulness alone would have sufficed. He needed luck. And indeed, everything favored Robusti. Paolo Caliari* was ten years old, Titian sixty-two. Between the unknown child and the old man who would surely not be long in dying, were to be found many good painters, but only Tintoretto gave promise of excellence. In any case, he was unrivaled in his generation. Thus, the way was open. And in fact, he coasted along for some time on the impetus of his beginning. Commissions multiplied, he enjoyed the favor of the general public as well as that of the patricians and connoisseurs. Aretino deigned to congratulate him in person. This young man was blessed with the supernatural gifts which Providence usually reserves for adolescents destined for premature death.

But he didn't die, and troubles began. Titian showed all the signs of a horrifying longevity, continuing to shower all the attentions of hatred upon his young challenger. The old monarch was even so malicious as to appoint—as though there could have been any doubt who it would be—Veronese as his successor. Aretino's condescension turned to

* Veronese (1528–1588) (*Trans.*)

rancor. Criticism pinched, bit, clawed and shrieked; it became modern, in other words. None of this would have mattered, had Jacopo remained in the good graces of the public. But suddenly, the wheel turned. At thirty, sure of his talent, he asserted himself and painted *St. Mark Saving the Slave*, putting all of himself into this one painting. To astonish, shock, and impose himself on others by surprise—that was really his style. But for once, he was the first to be surprised. The work dumfounded his contemporaries but it also outraged them. He found impassioned detractors, but no defenders. We sense, in the background, the presence of a cabala. There was a sudden halt.* Face to face, united and divided by the same uneasiness, Venice and her painter stared at each other uncomprehendingly. "Jacopo," said the city, "failed to keep the promise of his adolescence." And the artist said, "I only had to reveal myself to disappoint them. So it wasn't even me that they loved." Misunderstanding degenerated into mutual recriminations. A thread had broken in the Venetian tapestry.

Fifteen forty-eight was the pivotal year; *before that*, the Gods were for him, *afterwards*, against him. No major misfortunes, just small troubles. But they would see to it that he choked on them. The Gods had smiled upon the child in order the better to bring about the downfall of the man. Jacopo suddenly became himself, the frantic, hounded outlaw, Tintoretto. We know nothing about him *before* this; only that he must have worked feverishly. How else could anyone make a name for themselves at twenty? *Afterwards*, the fervor turned to fury. He had to produce, and to pro-

* Ridolfi even claims that the Scuola di San Marco rejected the painting, and that Tintoretto was obliged to take it back.

duce unceasingly, sell, crush his rivals by the sheer number and dimension of his canvases. There is an element of desperation in this forcing of his powers. Until his death, Robusti raced against time, and it is hard to decide whether he was trying to find or to flee himself through his work. "Lightning-Tintoretto" sailed under the black flag, and for this driven pirate, all means were fair, with a marked preference for foul play. Disinterested whenever disinterest would pay, he lowered his eyes, and refusing to quote a price, repeated like the Italian porters, "It shall be as you decide." But porters should know better than anyone that luggage transportation has fixed rates. They count on the client to fleece himself, through generosity.

At other times, he offered the merchandise at cost to obtain the commission. This ruinous contract would bring him other, more profitable ones. On learning that the *Crociferi* were about to give a commission to Paolo Caliari, he feigned ignorance and offered them his services. They tried to dismiss him politely: "Nothing would delight us more, were it not for the fact that we want a Veronese." "A Veronese, splendid," he says, "and who is going to paint it for you?" Somewhat taken aback, they reply, "But we understood that Paolo Caliari has already been designated." And now it is Tintoretto's turn to reply in amazement: "Caliari? What an insane idea! I will paint you a better Veronese than he ever could, and for less money." The deal was on and the promise kept. He must have resorted to this trick twenty times over, "making" Pordenones, Titians, and always at bargain prices.

How could he cut the costs? That was the question which plagued him. But one day he found the appropriately inspired and stingy solution, one which was to upset an entire tradition. The masters were accustomed to having their works copied; replicas were executed in their workshop, and then sold at inflated prices, which amounted to the same thing as saying that the painter had two markets at his disposal. In order to corner the second market, Jacopo would offer them *better products for less.* Eliminating copies, he allowed his assistants to use his paintings but forbade their *imitation.* By using simple and invariable formulas, his assistants made originals without having to invent a thing. For example, they might reverse a composition, placing the left side on the right, or substitute an old man for a woman, who could then be used elsewhere. These operations required a certain amount of training, but took no more time than ordinary reproduction. Thus, Tintoretto was able to announce candidly: "In my studio, an original can be had for the price of a copy."

When people didn't want his paintings, he gave them away. On May 31, 1564, the president of the Confraternity of the Scuola di San Rocco decided to decorate the conference chamber by placing a painting in the central oval of the ceiling, Paolo Caliari, Jacopo Robusti, Schiavone, Salviati and Zuccaro were invited to submit preliminary sketches. By bribing the servants of the Confraternity, Tintoretto obtained the exact measurement of the space to be filled. I wouldn't preclude the possibility that he might have even had accomplices within the *Banca e Zonta.** On the appointed day, each painter presented his sketch. When

* *Banca e Zonta:* The governing board of the Confraternity, which would have jurisdiction over the treasury. *Zonta* is the Venetian form of *giunta* or ruling body. (*Trans.*)

Robusti's turn came, there was stunned amazement. He climbed on a ladder, and lifting away the sheet destined for the cartoon, to reveal, above the heads of those assembled, a dazzling painting, already in place. Furor ensued. He then explained: "A drawing lends itself to misinterpretation. While I was about it, I preferred to do a finished painting. But if my work doesn't meet with your approval, gentlemen, I will donate it. Not to you, but to your patron, San Rocco, who has shown me proof of his favor." He was forcing their hand, and he knew it, the fraud. The statutes of the Confraternity prohibited the refusal of pious donations. There was nothing left for them to do but enter the event in the records of the Scuola: "On this day, the below-mentioned Jacopo Tintoretto, a painter, made us the gift of a painting. He demanded no payment, agreeing to further complete the work if it should be so requested, declaring himself satisfied." And the undersigned wrote, in turn: *Io Jachomo Tentoretto pitor contento et prometo ut supra.*

Contento? I should think so! His offering threw his rivals into a state of panic. For it opened all the doors of the Scuola to him, abandoning its immense, barren walls to the fury of his brush, and finally, brought him an annual income of one hundred ducats. So satisfied was he, in fact, that he repeated the same ruse again in 1571, this time, at the Doges' Palace, where the *Signoria* had organized a competition of sketches for a painting to commemorate the Battle of Lepanto. Again, Tintoretto produced and donated his finished painting. And again, it was gratefully accepted. But this time, he sent them his bill shortly afterwards.

It is perhaps tempting to regard this infamous and charming double-dealing as more characteristic of the times than of Tintoretto's own character. He was not to blame, we shall say; it was his century. And if someone were to condemn him on the strength of these anecdotes, I know what the defense would say. First, the following and most serious argument in his behalf: no one, at that time, *could work for himself*. Today, the market is in paintings; at that time, it was the painters who were on the block. They stood in the public squares like the *braccianti* * today in the towns of southern Italy. The buyers came and, examining them all carefully, chose one whom they took home with them, to their church, their Scuola or their *palazzo*. Painters had to be available and advertise themselves, just as today, our stage directors accept any work they can get, in the desperate hope that any script, however bad, will still reveal their own talent. Everything was arranged by contract, the subject, number, rank, and sometimes even the pose of the personages. Religious traditions, as well as those of current fashion, imposed further restrictions on the artist. And the patrons had all the moods and caprices of our producers, and alas, their sudden inspirations, as well. At the slightest sign of displeasure, everything had to be completely repainted. While doing the frescoes for the Medici Palace, Benozzo Gozzoli was deliberately and interminably tortured by his idiotic patrons. And in Tintoretto's case, we have only to compare the *Paradise* in the Louvre with the painting of the same subject in the Doges' Palace, to imagine the pressures to which he must have been subjected. Intransigence, the refusal to compromise, the proud choice of poverty were impossible alternatives for an artist who had a family to feed and a workshop to maintain, which was like

* *braccianti:* farm workers, hired on a daily basis. (*Trans.*)

the machinery of today. In a word, they either had to renounce painting or paint to order. No one can blame Tintoretto for wanting to get rich. And in fact, by the middle of the century, he was never out of work, and money wasn't lacking. But the principle of this utilitarian was that nothing was done for nothing. Painting would only be a pastime unless it were financially worthwhile. Much later, as we shall see, he bought a comfortable, plebian house in the working-class district of Venice. There he was finally secure in his own home, whose purchase crowned his career. But all of his savings had gone into it and the Robusti children were left only the most meager inheritance to be divided among them; the contents of their father's studio, a diminishing clientele, and the house itself, which went first to the eldest son and then to the painter's son-in-law. Twelve years after her husband's death, Faustina bitterly recalled that her father had left his family in straitened circumstances. And she had cause for complaint. The deceased had always done just as he pleased. He had loved money, certainly, but he loved it the way Americans do, only as the exterior sign of success. At heart, this contract-chaser had only asked one thing; the means to practice his craft. Moreover, even his fraudulent practices were not without justification, for they would not have been remotely conceivable without his professional ability, capacity for work, and speed. It was this speed which gave him the real advantage, for he could complete a good painting in the time it took others to make bad sketches.

Further, if he plagiarized from Veronese, the latter repaid him in kind. We must view these reciprocal borrowings with contemporary eyes. To most people, then, the greatest painters were only social entities, legal and collective personalities. Whereas for us, it is *that* painting which we covet, at least, at first. Later, through the painting, we come to desire the whole man; we hang Matisse on our walls. But compare this attitude with that of the *Crociferi*. They couldn't have cared less about Caliari. They wanted a particular style which spoke straight to their souls, felicitous stupidity, agreeable and unproblematic splendor. They recognized a trademark or a slogan; they felt at ease with a painting signed "Veronese," and that was all they required. Caliari was capable of better things and he proved it by painting the terrifying *Crucifixion*,* but was far too good a businessman to squander his genius. In these circumstances, we would be unfair to blame Tintoretto for occasionally having appropriated a style which didn't belong exclusively to anyone. After all, he made an honest proposition: "You want something empty and lifelike. You shall have it!"

I am aware of all that can be said on both sides. But the problem is not one of judging him, but of determining whether he was the undistorted reflection of his age. And on this point, all accounts are explicit. His methods shocked his contemporaries, turning them against him. They might perhaps have tolerated a little disloyalty, but Tintoretto went too far. In all of Venice, there was only one cry, "He doesn't know when to stop!" Even in this mercantile city, this merchant, too clever for his own good, was considered an untrustworthy eccentric.

When he stole the commission at the Scuola di San Rocco, his rivals screamed so loudly that he felt obliged to appease

---

* Now in the Louvre. The irony is that it was inspired by the *real* Robusti.

them. The building had other walls and ceilings, the work was just beginning. For his part, once his offering was accepted, he would leave the field open to the most worthy among them. But his unfortunate colleagues soon discovered that he was lying like a heathen. The Scuola was to become his fief; for as long as he lived no other painter would cross its threshold. But they hadn't been waiting for this excuse to loathe him. It is still worth noting, however, that this scandal took place in 1561, and the first *Life* of Tintoretto appeared in 1567. The proximity of these two dates casts new light on the origin and meaning of the nasty rumors so assiduously collected by Vasari. Were they the calumnies of jealous rivals? But everyone was jealous of everyone else; why should these calumnies all be heaped upon Robusti alone, unless he was the "foul stench" in the nostrils of all artists, unless he represented to each and every one, the faults of the next, resumed and carried to extreme in one man. His clients, as well, appear to have been shocked by his methods. Not all, of course. But he made numerous and powerful enemies among them. His Lordship Zammaria di Zigninoni, a member of the Confraternity of San Rocco, had promised fifteen ducats towards the costs of decoration, with the sole proviso that the commission not be given to Tintoretto. Moreoever, the records of the Confraternity suggest that, after Jacopo's previous maneuver, the *Banca e Zonta* held several rather stormy meetings at the Scuola itself, on the sensitive suject of this alluring but restrictive donation. They finally reached an agreement, but his Lordship Zigninoni kept his ducats. Nor was the *Signoria* any more kindly disposed towards him. In 1571, Tintoretto presented them with his *Battle of Lepanto*, but the

painting was destroyed by fire in 1577. When the question
of a replacement arose, its author was secure in the belief
that they would once again turn to him. But not at all.
Deliberately passing him over, they gave the commission to
the mediocre Vicentino. It might be argued that the original
painting hadn't met with their satisfaction. But this is hardly
plausible. Jacopo always aimed to please when he worked
on an official commission. He painted "in the style of
Titian," effacing himself completely. And moreover, since
1571, the government had ordered several other paintings
from him. No, the Venetian government had no intention
of depriving itself of his services. It simply wanted to punish him for his outrageous conduct. In short, all were
agreed. He was a traitor to the profession, a renegade
painter. And indeed, there must have been something un-
savory about him, since he was without a single friend.

Oh you lofty, troubled souls, who use the dead to edify
the living, and above all, to edify yourselves, try, if you can,
to find in his excesses, the shining proof of his passion. The
fact remains that passions are as diverse as people. There are
passions that are devouring and meditative, dreamy and anxious, practical and abstract, lingering and precipitous. I
would call Tintoretto's passions practical, anxious-re-
criminating and devouring-precipitous. The more I reflect
on these ridiculous combinations, the more I am convinced
that they were born of a lacerated heart. What a viper's
nest it was! We find everything there; the delirium of pride
and the madness of humility, frustrated ambitions and unleashed confusion, harsh repression and persistent bad luck,
the will to succeed, and the dizzying urge to fail. His life is
the story of an opportunist gnawed by fear. It began briskly

and joyfully, with a well-launched offensive, and then, after the staggering blow of 1548, its rhythm quickens and goes awry, and it became a living hell. Jacopo struggled until death, but he knew that he couldn't win. Opportunism and anguish, these were the two largest vipers. If we really want to know him, we must come closer and scrutinize them.

THE PURITANS OF THE RIALTO   No one is a cynic. Punishing oneself for lack of other punishment is the diversion of saints: the chaste stigmatize their leachery, the generous denounce their avarice. But if they discover their real gangrene, saintliness, they search for justification, as do all the guilty. Tintoretto was no saint. He knew that an entire city condemned his conduct. If he persisted in behaving that way, it was because he felt that he was right and they were wrong. And let no one start telling us that he was aware of his genius, for genius, that stupid gamble, knows the risks but not its own worth. Nothing is more wretched than the sullen temerity that aims for the moon and dies in defeat. First comes pride, without papers or visa. When it disintegrates, you can call it genius, if you will, but I don't see what is gained thereby. No, Tintoretto didn't justify his piracy by the brief fulfillment of his skill, nor by the infinite yearning of his aspiration. He was defending his rights. Each time a commission was given to one of his colleagues, he felt that he had been wronged. Left to his own devices, he would have covered every wall in the city with his paintings, no *campo* was too vast, no *sotto portico* too obscure for him to disdain its illumination. He would have daubed every ceiling and passers-by could have walked upon his most beautiful paintings. His brush would neither have spared the façade of the *palazzi* on the Grand Canal, nor the gondolas, nor perhaps even the gondoliers. This man felt that he was born with the privilege of transforming his native city into himself, and, in a certain sense, he was right.

When he began his apprenticeship, painting was in decline. In Florence, the crisis was openly acknowledged. Venice, true to form, lied or remained silent. But we have formal proof that the authentic Venetian sources of inspiration had withered. At the end of the fifteenth century, the city had been deeply influenced by the sojourn of Antonello da Messina, and this had been the decisive turning point. After this, Venice had imported her painters. Not that she had to seek them very far afield, but it is nonetheless true that her most celebrated artists came from the mainland; Giorgione, from Castelfranco, Titian, from Pieve di Cadoro, Paolo Caliari and Bonifazio dei Pitati, from Verona, Palma Vecchio, from Bergamo, Girolamo the elder and Paris Bordone from Treviso, and Andrea Schiavone, from Zara, to name only a few. In essence, this aristocratic republic was primarily a technocracy. She had always had the audacity to recruit specialists from far and wide, and the good sense to treat them thereafter as her own. Moreover, it was at this time, when The Most Serene Republic was checked at sea and threatened by coalitions on the continent, that she tried to insure her power through conquest.

And the majority of these new immigrants came from these annexed territories. But Venice betrayed her anxiety by this massive importation of talent. When we recall that the artists of the *quattrocento* were born, for the most part, within the walls of the city, or in Murano, one can't help thinking that after the extinction of the Vivarini and Bellini families, and the death of Carpaccio, only a blood transfusion could have effected a resurgence of her generations of artists.

Painting was like all other crafts, in that it was the patricians who facilitated the immigration of skilled artisans. Evincing what could be called a cosmopolitan chauvinism, this class made the Republic of the Doges into a kind of "melting pot." In the eyes of this suspicious and jealous aristocracy, foreigners made the best Venetians. If they adopted Venice, it meant that they had fallen in love with her, and hence would be malleable if they hoped to be adopted by her in turn. But we may be sure that the local craftsmen viewed the newcomers differently, and why not? They were foreign competition. Not that the natives were so imprudent as to protest openly, but, while they made the best of the interlopers, there was conflict, constant tension, and the mutual recrimination of wounded pride. Forced to bow before the technical superiority of these aliens in his city, the native hid his humiliation, exalting it into a prerogative. He would allow his place to be taken by the more expert, the more skilled, but he transformed this usurpation into sacrifice for his country. Thus his rights remained intact. Only a native of the Rialto could claim Venice as his own; German craftsmen might be better glass blowers, but they would forever be deprived of this grace of birth. Before their death, the great *quattrocento* painters had the bitter experience of seeing public favor turn from them towards the young interlopers who had only contempt for their elders. Titian, for example, left the workshop of one Bellini for the other—Gentile for Giovanni—and always in pursuit of Antonello, another foreigner, that meteor who had rent the skies and waters of the Lagoon twenty years before. Finally, Titiano Vecellio had no need of Giovanni either. What he sought in him was a reflection, and the proof of this is the fact that he soon abandoned the master for the disciple, becoming a follower of Giorgione. Thus, a third alien appeared to the second as the *true* heir of the first. But Titian and Giorgione belonged to the same generation; in fact, the pupil may even have been older than the teacher. Did the Bellinis realize that on this day they had become outmoded? And what did the loyal disciples of Giovanni have to say? What did the others, those last representatives of the School of Murano, think? Many of them were still young men, or at any rate, in the prime of life. They had all been influenced by Antonello, but through the works of the Bellinis. Their color and light had come from Antonello, but Giovanni had acclimatized them; through him they became Venetian. These artists made it a point of honor to remain loyal, but their loyalty strangled them. Doing their best to adopt themselves to the requirements of the new techniques without abandoning the cruder ones which they had been taught, they condemned themselves to mediocrity. What bitterness must they have felt as they watched these two young intruders who, joining forces and breaking with local traditions, discovered the secrets of the Sicilian painter and carried painting effortlessly to its highest point of perfection? Notwithstanding, Giovanni still reigned supreme, and the reknown of this admirable painter spread through all of northern Italy. For the barbarian invasion was only to begin with his last years. But after his death in 1516, came the deluge.

Then, at the height of the invasion, in the heart of this occupied city, the greatest painter of the century was born, in an alley-way off the Rialto. Somber plebian pride, always humiliated and repressed, constantly lying in wait, seized its chance, and infiltrating the heart of the only native Venetian who still had any talent, incited and, at last, inflamed it. Remember that his origins were neither quite plebian nor quite bourgeois. His father had been a well-to-do artisan, the kind of *petit bourgeois* whose greatest pride lies in being self-employed. As a worker's son, Jacopo would have most likely remained the obscure assistant of another artist; as the son of a master craftsman, he had to become a master in turn, or admit failure. He would move up through the ranks, but the honor of his family and class would forbid that he ever stop on his way. We can now understand why he didn't leave pleasant memories behind him, in the workshop to which he was apprenticed. He entered it only to leave as soon as he could, in order to assume the place already reserved for him within the social hierarchy. And then, Schiavone (or Bordone or Bonifazio dei Pitati—it doesn't matter which one) undoubtedly regarded him as an interloper, but, by the same token, Jacopo viewed his master as an outsider, or in other words, a thief. The little dyer was a *native*, and Venice was his birthright. Had he been a mediocrity, he would have settled for external humility and internal resentment, but he was brilliant, and he knew it. Therefore, he had to triumph over all of them. In the eyes of a native of the Rialto, these resident aliens had no protection other than their professional value. If Jacopo proved their superior, they would have to go, even if he had to assassinate them. No one paints or writes without a sense of mandate. Would anyone dare if "*I* were not Another"? Jacopo had been invested by an entire working-class populace with the mandate of redeeming through his art the privileges of the purebred Venetian. This is what explains his clear conscience. In his heart, the grievances of the people became an austere passion for restitution. He had been given the mission of making their rights recognized. To one who upholds so just a cause, all means are fair. He would show no mercy, give no quarter. But it was his misfortune that his fight against the undesirables embroiled him in a struggle against the patricians themselves, as he attacked their policy of assimilation in the name of the indigenous craftsmen. When he shouted through the streets, "Veronese back to Verona," he was calling the whole government into question. As soon as he realized this, he started to recoil, but then immediately continued his march forward. This was the origin of that curious mixture of obstinacy and flexibility. As a wary citizen of a police state, he always gave in, or at least, pretended to. But as native-born citizen of the most beautiful city in the world, his arrogance exploded in spite of himself. He could even descend to servility without losing his *ankylosis* of pride. But all to no avail. The very intrigues which he plotted against the protégés of the aristocracy were destroyed by his impatience and by his irreparable errors in judgment; or else, they backfired. Now the rancor of the Republic is seen in a new light. This citizen only reclaimed what would have perhaps been conceded him eventually, but his belligerent submission infuriated the Authorities. They considered him a rebel, or at the very least, suspect as such. And, in essence, they were right. But where did his first great outburst lead him?

It led him, first of all, to that diligent and almost sadistic violence which I call the full employment of oneself. Born of humble people who bore the whole weight of a heavily hieratic society, he shared their fears and tastes. We find their prudence even in his presumption. His own kind, wary, courageous, with a tendency to be suspicious of outsiders, taught him that everything has a price and that life is dangerous. They taught him which hopes are permissible and which forbidden; specific, limited opportunities, a destiny whose outlines were traced in advance, a future, already visible and imprisoned like a tiny dried bouquet in a crystal paperweight—all these are killers of the dream. They only wanted what it was possible to have. This kind of moderation produces enraged madmen and incites rapacious, but short-lived ambitions. Jacopo's ambition was born suddenly; in all its virulence and diversity of forms, it was girded for war. But also, it had assimilated that merest thread of light, the possible. Or rather, that nothing is *possible*. There is the end, and the means, which is the prescribed task; one can rise above the heaviest, low-lying clouds to touch the taut luminous membrane of the ceiling. There will always be other ceilings, other membranes, more and more translucent, more and more delicate, until perhaps, at the very top, the blue of the sky. But Tintoretto wasn't interested in any of that. Each man has his own ascending force and his own natural habitat. He knew he had a gift, and he had been taught that this was capital. By proving his capabilities, his talent would become financially worthwhile, and he would find the subsidy he needed. There he was, totally mobilized for a lifetime, with nothing left to spare. He had become a vein to be exploited, until both miner and mine were exhausted. At about this same time, another glutton for work, Michaelangelo, grew disgusted, beginning a work, which he would abandon, unfinished. Tintoretto *always* finished everything, with the terrifying application of a man determined to complete his sentence, no matter what else he does. Even death waited for him at San Giorgio, allowing him to put the final brushstroke to his last painting, or at least, allowing him to give the final instructions to his assistants. Throughout his life, Tintoretto never allowed himself the luxury of caprice, not a moment of distaste, not a single preference, not even the repose of a dream. On his weariest days, he had to repeat this principle to himself: to refuse a commission is to present it to my rivals.

At any cost, he had to produce. And here the will of a man and a city were united. A hundred years earlier, Donatello had reproached Ucello for sacrificing creation to experimentation, and for carrying his love of painting to the point where he ceased to paint pictures. But this had happened in Florence. At that time, Florentine artists had just embarked upon the perilous adventure of *perspective,* and were trying to construct new plastic space by applying the laws of geometric optics to painted objects. Other times, other customs. In the Venice of Titian's reign, everyone believed that painting had reached its highest point of perfection. Art was dead, long live life. The great barbarism began with the idiocies of Aretino: "How alive it is! How real! *Who would believe it was painted?*" In short, it was time for painting to make way for *realisations*. Inspired merchants wanted useful beauty. The work of art should delight amateurs, spreading word through all Europe of the splendor that was Venice, and strike terror in the heart of the people. But it is the terror which has endured. Confronted by Venetian cinemascope, the rest of us humble little tourists murmur; "There is a film by Titian, a production by Paolo Caliari, a performance by Pordenone, a stage-set by Vicentino." Jacopo Robusti shares the preferences of his time, and the more sophisticated among us hold it against him. How many times have I heard people say, "Bah! Tintoretto, just like the movies!" And yet, no one in the world, either before or after him, carried a passion for experimentation farther. With Titian, painting suffocates under flowers, denied by its very perfection. Jacopo saw this death as the necessary condition of resurrection. Everything was just beginning, and everything remained to be done. We shall come back to this point later. But—and here is his major contradiction—he never permitted his experiments to halt his productivity. If one wall in Venice remained unpainted, the painter's task was to cover it. His morality forbade him to transform his studio into a laboratory. Art in its entirety was a serious business, and a hand-to-hand combat against the invaders. Like Titian and Veronese, Jacopo will deliver his exquisite corpses. But with this one difference; his dead men rave with fever, and one can't be sure at first whether this is a resurgence of life or the onset of putrefaction. And if you insist upon comparing him with our cinematographers, he resembles them precisely *in this respect;* he accepted imbecilic scripts, but unobtrusively charged them with his own obsessions. He had to deceive the buyer so as to give him his money's worth. The client would get his Catherine, his Theresa, or his Sebastian; for the same price, Tintoretto would even put him in the painting, with his wife and brothers too, if he insisted. But beneath and behind the scenes of the sumptuous and banal façade of this *production,* he pursued his own experiments. All of his great works have a double meaning. His strict utilitarianism masks an endless interrogation. Fitting his research within the framework of the paid commission, he was forced to turn painting inside out, while respecting the stipulations of the client. This is the profound explanation behind his furious productivity, and it was later to be the cause of his downfall.

He still felt a need to corner the market, and we have seen how he set about doing this. But let us re-examine his methods, for they are now seen in a new light. Tintoretto's rebellion next struck at the roots of the system. In revolt against the policy of the melting pot, he then felt compelled to infringe upon the regulations and practices of the guilds. Unable to eliminate competition, whose advantages it acknowledged, the government tried to channel it by means of organized contests. In the final analysis, the taste of the rich and powerful would save public order by constituting a more flexible form of protectionism. Regulated competition. Were they sincere? They undoubtedly were, and all would have been perfect, had we any evidence of their abilities. But we have to take them at their word. Sometimes they were lucky, and then, at other times, they chose Vincentino. But Tintoretto always managed to avoid these competitions. Was this to deny the judges any competence in such matters? Certainly not. He simply denied them the right to treat a native of Venice as they did an intruder. The competitions continued, notwithstanding. But in refusing to take part in them, our rebel was deliberately setting out to destroy protectionism. And there he was cornered. Since the officials laid claims to value judgments which he refused to recognize, he either had to renounce painting, or impose himself by the quality of his painting. When that didn't work, he found other ways. He outdistanced his rivals by his speed, placing a *fait accompli* before the juries, and put all his own skill and rapidity, as well as the diligence of his assistants at the service of a mass-production which broke all records, but which only allowed him to sell his paintings at starvation prices, and sometimes, just to give them away. On a Roman street, I once noticed two second-hand shops which faced each other. The owners, I imagine, had agreed among themselves to simulate a merciless price war, unless (which is more than possible) both shops had only one owner, a tragic-clown who delighted in confronting the two aspects of his nature in an eternal duel. On the one side, the window was lined with mournful announcements: *"Prezzi disastrosi,"* and on the other, a glass covered with gaily colored signs proclaimed: *"Prezzi da ridere! da ridere! da ridere!"* This has gone on for years now, and I can never pass those shops without thinking of Tintoretto. Did he choose laughter or tears? Both, I think, depending upon the client. One might even imagine that he occasionally chortled, when alone, and saved his laments for his family, crying that the others were cutting his throat. But it was always bargain day in his workshop, where clients succumbed to the lure of carefully calculated liquidations. They would come to order a medallion, and end by surrendering every wall in their house to the painter. It was Tintoretto who was the first to break the already weakened ties of guild brotherhood. To this Darwinist before the fact, a colleague was a mortal enemy. Before Hobbes, he had discovered the slogan of all-out competition—*Homo homini lupus*. Venice was in a turmoil. If a vaccine were not found against the virus of Tintoretto, the splendid corporative order would be destroyed, leaving in its place only a few motes of antagonism, a few molecules of solitude. The Republic condemned these new tactics, calling them felonies, and speaking of slipshod work, bargain sales, monopoly. Later, much later, other cities, in another language would glorify these same practices under the name of "struggle for life," "mass production," "dumping," "trusts," etc. But for the moment, this notorious man lost on one painting everything that he might have made on another. He carried off commissions at sword's point, but he was ostracized. By a strange inversion, the native, one hundred per cent Venetian seemed an interloper, almost a pariah, in his own city. Inevitably, he would have starved to death, if he hadn't produced a large family. If only to strangle rivalry in the heart of his own workshop, this champion of liberalism reversed the biblical precept, making sure that others would never be able to do unto him as he had done unto them. Moreover, he needed approval. Outside helpers were likely to be easily intimidated, or discouraged by the air of scandal surrounding him. Cajoling them into loyalty wasted too much of his time. But the thunder of disapproval would die down. What need had he for disciples? He only needed other pairs of hands and arms, that was all. From all-out competition to familial exploitation was the road he took. In 1550, he married Faustina dei Vescovi and began to produce children immediately, the way he produced paintings—without respite. This fine brood-hen had only one defect—a tendency to hatch daughters. No matter, he would put all but two in a convent: Marietta, who always remained at his side, and Ottavia, whom he married to another painter. "Lightning-Tintoretto" would fertilize Faustina as many times as it would take to produce two sons, Domenico and Marco. And he hadn't even bothered waiting for them, as he had taught his craft, meanwhile, to his eldest daughter, Marietta. In Venice, a woman painter was something of a rarity. He must have been impatient indeed. Finally, around the year 1575, his project was completed, and he had a new staff, consisting of Sebastian Casser, his son-in-law, Marietta, Domenico and Marco. And the symbol of domestic association was the *domus*, which both sheltered and imprisoned him for, about the same date, Jacopo had purchased the house he was never to leave. The stricken man would live in semi-quarantine in the midst of this little leper colony, surrounded by family, loving them all the more as the Others who hated him grew more numerous. When we come upon him *at home*, in his work, in his relations with his wife and children, he reveals quite another face to us—that of an austere moralist. Wasn't there even something of the Calvinist in him? All the characteristics were there: pessimism and the passion for work, profit motive and family devotion. Human nature is tainted by original sin, men divided by self-interest. The Christian will only be saved through his works. He must struggle against all men, as harsh to himself as to others, he must labor ceaselessly to beautify the earth which God has entrusted to him, for he will only obtain the sign of divine favor with the material success of his endeavors. As for the stirrings of his heart, they must be reserved for the flesh of his flesh, for his sons. Could Venice have been subject to the influence of the Reformation? This is indisputable. For in the second half of the century we encounter a curious figure, Fra Paolo Sarpi, highly influential in patrician circles, friend of Galileo, enemy of Rome, and who, in full view of the authorities, maintained close ties with Protestant groups abroad. But even if, within certain intellectual circles, we can discern currents vaguely favorable to the Reformation, it is more than probable that the *petite bourgeoisie* remained entirely unaware of their existence. It would be more accurate to say that the Republic was in the process of reforming itself, and that this had been going on for some time. These merchants depended on credit for their livelihood. They couldn't accept the sentence which the Church passed upon those whom she persisted in calling usurers. These men approved of science when it furthered their ends, and they scorned the obscurantism of Rome. The Venetian State had always affirmed the precedence of Civil Law, and it never changed this basic doctrine. In practice, it was always the State which had the upper hand over the clergy, and when Pius V attempted to withdraw ecclesiastics from the jurisdiction of lay tribunals, the Venetian State flatly refused to comply with this edict. For many reasons, moreover, the government considered the Vatican a temporal and military power far more than a spiritual one. Not that this prevented Venice from allying itself with the

Pope when her own interests were at stake, or from exiling
heretics to please a Very Christian Monarch, or from organizing a lavish celebration in honor of St. Bartholomew's
Day. But Tintoretto's pseudo-Calvinism derived from the
city itself. He unconsciously absorbed the larvae of Protestantism which, at that time, was to be found in all the
great capitalist cities.* Throughout this period, the status of
artists was highly equivocal, especially in Venice. But
chances are that this very ambiguity will help us to understand Jacopo's somber puritanical passion.

It has been said that "The Renaissance [had] attributed
those characteristics to artists which antiquity had reserved
to the man of action, and which the Middle Ages had bestowed upon her saints."† And this is not untrue, but to me,
the contrary observation seems no less true: "In the sixteenth century, painting and sculpture were still considered
manual arts; all the honors were reserved for poetry. This
explains the efforts of the figurative arts to rival literature."†† And we know for a fact that Aretino, the poor
man's Petronius and the rich man's Malaparte, was the
arbiter of elegance and taste for the snobbish patricians of
Venice, and that Titian himself felt honored to be his
friend. With all his fame, this artist never felt himself the
equal of Aretino. And Michaelangelo? He had a weakness
for imagining himself a *born* aristocrat, and this illusion
ruined his life. As a very young man, he had wanted to

* The same one which was to vaccinate the Italian cities against the
Lutheran plague, and which led Italy to start its own religious revolu-
tion under the name of the Counter-Reformation.
† Vuillemin.
†† Eugenio Battista, in an excellent article on Michaelangelo, pub-
lished in *Epoca*, August 25, 1957.

cultivate the Humanities and to write, believing that a nobleman deprived of the sword could take up the pen without demeaning himself. But necessity forced him to take up the brush instead, and he never got over it. Contemplating sculpture and painting from the pinnacle of his shame, Michaelangelo had the empty and shriveled joy of feeling superior to what he did. Forced into silence, he tried to make the dumb arts speak; he multiplied allegories, symbols, finally writing a whole book on the Sistine ceiling and torturing marble, forcing it to speech.

What should we conclude? Were these Renaissance painters demi-Gods or manual laborers? The only thing to conclude is that it all depended. It depended upon the clientele and the mode of remuneration. Or rather, they were manual laborers *first*, and afterwards, they might become employees of the court, or remain local masters. It was for them to choose—or be chosen. Raphael and Michaelangelo were employees, living in magnificent dependence. But one disgrace—and there they were out in the street. To compensate for this insecurity, the sovereign took charge of their publicity. This sacred personage accorded a portion of his supernatural powers to his elect. The royal glory shone upon them like a ray of sunlight, reflecting it to the populace. The divine right of kings created painters by divine right. Thus we see daubers transformed into supermen. For what were they, after all, these *petits bourgeois* whom a gigantic hand had plucked from the crowd, suspending them between heaven and earth, these satellites which shone with borrowed splendor, if not men raised above the level of humanity? Heroes yes, but in the sense of intercessors and intermediaries. Even today, in the name of genius, nostalgic republics continue to worship the light of that dead star, Monarchy.

Tintoretto was of another sort. He worked for merchants and bureaucrats, or for parish churches. Not that he was uneducated. He was sent to school at seven, and must have remained until he was twelve, when he had learned how to read and write. Moreover, how could the name of culture be denied to that patient education of the senses, the hand and the imagination, that conservative empiricism which still, in 1530, defined studio painting? But he would never have the cultural accoutrements of the court painters. Michaelangelo wrote sonnets, and it is claimed today that Raphael knew Latin. Intellectual associations ended by giving even Titian a certain veneer. Compared to these worldly painters, Tintoretto seems an ignoramus, for he always lacked the leisure and taste to devote any time to the play of ideas and words. Furthermore, he had nothing but ridicule for the *literati*. Venice had few poets and fewer philosophers, but for him, these few were already too many. Not that he avoided them, he simply had no contact with any of them. He was willing to admit their social superiority and Aretino had every right to congratulate him with patronizing benevolence. For this exalted personage was *received* in the best houses, and considered an indispensable part of the *Tout-Venice*. He was invited to dine by patricians who would not have even nodded to a painter in the street. But why should Tintoretto have envied him? Was he to be envied merely because he wrote? In Jacopo's mind, the works of the imagination had a strongly immoral air of the gratuitous. God placed us on earth to earn our bread by the sweat of our brow, and writers don't sweat. Do they really even work? With the exception of his missal, Jacopo never opened a book. He would have been the last painter to have the outlandish idea of extending his talents to rival literature. His paintings contain everything, but *mean* nothing. They are as mute as the world. At heart, this artisan's son had respect only for physical effort, manual creation. What enchanted him about the craft of painting was its aspect of professional skill pushed to the point of prestidigitation, and the frailty of merchandise reduced to quintessence. The artist was the supreme laborer, depleting and exhausting matter, in order to produce and sell his visions. This wouldn't have prevented him from working for princes had he liked them. But he didn't like them, and that was the heart of the matter. They terrified him without inspiring him. He never tried to approach them or make them aware of his existence. It was as though he forced himself into confining his fame within the walls of Venice. Do most people even know that he only left the city once, when he was sixty? And that was to go next door to Mantua. Even then, he had to be implored to go. His clients wanted him to hang his paintings himself, but he flatly declared that he wouldn't come unless he could bring his wife. This stipulation would seem to indicate deep conjugal devotion, but actually says more about his horror of traveling. And do not think that this phobia was shared by his Venetian colleagues, for they had long since traveled every road. A hundred years earlier, Gentile Bellini was sailing the seas. What adventurers they were! But Jacopo was a mole, at home only in the narrow galleries of his underground dwelling. When he imagined the world outside, agoraphobia paralyzed him. Still, if he had to choose, he preferred to save his pictures rather than his skin. So he accepted commissions from abroad—and abroad for him began at Padua—but he never solicited them. What a contrast between his frenzied eagerness at the Doges' Palace, for the *Crociferi,* and this indifference! He even left the execution of foreign commissions to his assistants, only supervising these ready-made products from afar, taking care not to put his own hand to them, as though he feared to venture even the smallest part of his talent outside the boundaries of his native city. Europe would only have the right to his "B pictures." At the Uffizi, the Prado, the National Gallery, the Louvre, Munich, Vienna, there are Raphaels, Titians, and a hundred others. All the great painters, or almost all, are represented, except for Tintoretto. That painter ferociously saved himself for his fellow-citizens. And you will never learn anything about him without seeking him in his native city, for the simple reason that he never *wanted* to leave it.

But to be more precise, he had, even within Venice itself, two very distinct clienteles. He besieged public officials, and if the Senate gave him a commission, his entire studio, the head of the family included, was put to work on it. There may still be seen in the Doges' Palace, lit in such a way as to show them to best advantage, works by a strong collective personality which bore the name of Tintoretto. But if you seek Jacopo Robusti, then leave the Piazzetta, cross the Piazza San Marco, cross the sloping bridges of the canal, thread your way through a maze of dark alleys, enter still darker churches, and there he is. At the Scuola di San Rocco, you will find him in person, without Marietta, or Domenico, or Sebastian Casser. There he worked alone. A murky haze has darkened these canvases, or else they are

corroded by artificial light. But be patient, until your eyes
have become accustomed to the light. Finally, you will see a
rose emerge through the shadows, a genius through the
mist. And who paid for these paintings? Sometimes it was
the parishioners; at other times, the members of the
Confraternity—bourgeois great and small; this was his real
public, and the only one he liked.

This shopkeeper-painter had nothing of the demi-God
about him. With a little luck he would be notorious, even
famous, perhaps, but exalted, never! His profane clientele
was not adept at consecrating him. Naturally, the renown
of his august colleagues did honor to the whole profession,
so that he also shone just a little. Did he covet their fame?
Perhaps. But he did none of the things necessary to obtain
it. To hell with the favor of princes! It was only slavery.
Jacopo Robusti took pride in remaining a small businessman, a peddler of Fine Arts, payed by the order, master
of his own shop. He made no distinction between the economic independence of the producer and the freedom of
the artist. His activities prove that he had a secret desire to
reverse the conditions of marketing, creating the demand
through the supply. Hadn't he slowly, patiently, through
his work for the Confraternity di San Rocco, created a need
for art—and a certain kind of art—which he alone could
satisfy? His autonomy was all the better preserved because
he worked for collectivities—*consorterie*, parishes—which
had to take their decisions from the majority.

Michaelangelo, the counterfeit noble, and Titian, the son
of peasants, were strongly attracted to the monarchy. But
Tintoretto sprang from a milieu of self-employed workers.
The artisan was amphibious. As a manual laborer, he was

proud of his hands, and as a *petit bourgeois*, he was attracted to the *grande bourgeoisie*, for by encouraging open competition, they assure a certain degree of ventilation in the midst of suffocating protectionism. And in those days, there was *a bourgeois hope* in Venice, although a slim one, to be sure, since the aristocracy had long since taken precautions against its realization. In that stratified universe, men might *become* rich, but they had to be born patrician. Even wealth, moreover, was restricted. Not only was the small businessman, as well as the industrialist, confined to his class, but the most lucrative forms of trade were prohibited to them. For example, the State restricted *l'appalto*—or shipping franchise—to the aristocracy. Sad and wistful bourgeoisie! Everywhere else in Europe their class was hastening to deny its origins, buying titles and castles as soon as they were able to afford them. But in Venice, everything was denied them, even the humble joy of betrayal. Thus, the Venetian bourgeoisie was obliged to betray through its dreams. Giovita Fontana came to Venice from Piacenza, started in business, and after amassing a vast fortune, spent it all to build a palace on the Grand Canal. A whole life is revealed in these few words. Bitter yearning, once satisfied, becomes wistful snobbery. A dead merchant revived in the form of an imaginary patrician. Rich commoners danced round in circles to hide their nocturnal fantasies. Forming confraternities, they threw themselves into good works, their melancholy austerity contrasting sharply with the melancholy orgies of the jaded patricians.

For the Republic had lost her sovereignty of the seas. Little by little, the aristocracy fell into decay. Bankruptcies multiplied and the number of ruined gentlemen increased, while others lost their spirit of initiative. Sons of ship-builders bought land and became gentlemen-farmers. Already, mere "citizens" began to replace them in certain functions. Finally, the galleys themselves came under the control of the bourgeoisie, who were still far from considering themselves a rising class, and never thinking that after the fall of the nobility, their turn would come. Still, let us say that the bourgeois were seized by a mysterious restlessness, which only made its condition less bearable and resignation more difficult.

But Tintoretto never dreamed. If other people's ambitions were governed by their future social possibilities, then the most ambitious commoners in Venice were the *petits bourgeois*, for they, at least, had a chance of rising above their class. But the painter felt deep affinities for his clients. He understood their passion for work, their moralism and practical common sense. He liked their nostalgia and, above all, he shared their deepest aspiration. For all of them needed freedom, if only to produce, to buy and sell. This was the key to his opportunism—a cry for the air of the summits. Heavenly strife, a far off, invisible ascent opened a vertical future to him. Borne aloft like a balloon, he was permeated by the new spirit. But the contradictions of his class of origin limited his ambitions. A peddler can hope to cross class lines, but a laborer works with his hands, and that suffices to keep him in his place. In the Venice of that time, there were approximately 7,600 patricians, 13,600 citizens, 127,000 artisans, workers and small tradesmen, 1,500 Jews, 12,900 servants and 550 beggars. Leaving aside the Jews, nobles, beggars and servants, Tintoretto had eyes only for that imaginary line of demarcation which separated the commoners into two groups; 13,600 on one side, and 127,-000 on the other. He wanted to be the first in the former group and last in the latter, that is, the most humble of the rich and the most distinguished of their tradesmen. In the heart of a restless Venice, such a desire made this artisan into a false bourgeois, more real than the real ones. The members of the Confraternity of San Rocco loved in him and in his paintings, the embellished image of a bourgeoisie who would never betray.

Michaelangelo felt that he was demeaning himself even when working for the Supreme Pontiff. His disdain gave him a certain sense of distance. This gentleman took a dim view of art. But with Tintoretto it was just the reverse. He had risen above himself. What would he have been without art? A dyer. Art was the force which wrenched him from the circumstances of his birth, and from the environment which had produced him. It was his claim to dignity. He had to work or fall back to the bottom of the well. Perspective? Distance? Where would he have found such ideas? He had no time to question himself about painting. Who knows whether he even saw it? Michaelangelo thought too much. He was an intellectual giving himself the airs of a marquis. Tintoretto didn't know what he was doing. He was too busy painting. So much for his opportunism. This artist's fate was to be the incarnation of bourgeois puritanism in an aristocratic Republic during its decline. In other times and places, this somber humanism would have been inevitable. In Venice it disappeared without ever becoming aware of its own existence, but not before it had aroused the distrust of an ever-wary aristocracy. The ill-will shown towards

Tintoretto by official and bureaucratic Venice was the same kind which the patricians bore towards the Venetian bourgeoisie. These rebellious merchants and their painter posed a threat to the Order of the Most Serene Republic; they would both have to be carefully watched.

A MAN AT BAY   *T*here is something splendid in the stubborn refusal to compete. "I am without rival and acknowledge no judge." This is what Michaelangelo might have said. Unfortunately, Tintoretto did not. Quite the contrary. When invited to submit a sketch, he hastened to accept. But afterwards, he launched his thunderbolts, rather the way a squid spurts its ink. Blinded by his lightning, Tintoretto's spectators couldn't really see the painting, moreover, everything was carefully arranged that they need never examine, or above all, evaluate it. When the blinding haze lifted, the canvas was already in place, the gift accepted; they had only seen an explosion. I may be altogether mistaken, but I think this was a form of evasion—he was afraid to confront his adversaries. Would he have bothered to be so ingenious, had he felt assured of being accepted on the strength of his talent? Would he have demeaned himself to astound his contemporaries by the quantity of his output, if they had unreservedly admired the quality? Insulted by the slightest comparison of his work with that of others, their proximity worried him. Competition emphasized his raging need for assertion through disappearance. This was his style and his trademark. In 1559, the Church of San Rocco commissioned him to paint *The Healing of the Paralytic,* as pendant to a Pordenone. No one asked him to imitate his predecessor's style. Nor could there have been a question of a contest between the two painters*—Antonio di Sacchis had been dead for twenty years. Had he once been able to influence the younger painter, the time of influence was long passed, for Jacopo possessed the consummate mastery of his art. But this sense of competition was stronger than he; he couldn't help "painting a Pordenone." Others have already shown how he "exaggerated the baroque violence of the gestures . . . by the clash between the monumentality of the figures and the architecture into which they are closely squeezed" and that he "achieved this effect by lowering the ceiling of the hall . . . utilizing even the columns to arrest and freeze the violence of their gestures."† In short, Tintoretto trembled at the thought of being caught forever in frozen confrontation. "Compare, if you like, my Pordenone with the other. I, Jacopo Robusti, am now leaving." Naturally, he took care that the false di Sacchis should obliterate the real one. His departure was not a flight, for he left shouting a challenge. "I shall take on the old masters and the new, all of them, and beat them on their own ground!" But this attitude is just what arouses our suspicion. Why did he feel compelled to play their game, submitting himself to their rules, when he could have crushed them by being himself? There is so much resentment in his insolence. This Cain had

* Ridolfi, taken in by the resemblance of style, says that this work was painted *in concorrenza con il Pordenone.*
† Vuillemin.

to assassinate every Abel favored over him. "So you prefer Veronese? Well, I can surpass him, when I deign to imitate him. You think he is a man when he is only a technique." But what humility as well. From time to time, this outcast slipped into another's skin, just to savor the joy of being loved. And then, at other times, he seemed to lack the courage to manifest his outrageous genius. Weary of war, he left his genius half in shadow, and tried to prove it through *the absurd.* "Since I can make better Veroneses and better Pordenones, just imagine *what I am capable of doing* when I allow myself to be me!" But in fact, he hardly ever gave himself such permission, unless confidence had been shown in him beforehand, and he had been left alone in an empty room. The origin of all this is, of course, the hostility with which he had been treated. But the painter's inhibitions and the prejudices of his Venetian fellow-citizens had their roots in the same uneasiness: in 1548, under Tintoretto's brush, before patricians, art lovers and aesthetes, *painting was seized with dread.*

A long evolution had begun, in which the profane was everywhere substituted for the sacred. Frozen, sparkling with icicles, the diverse branches of human activity surged forth, one after another, from their lulling and divine promiscuity. Art's turn had come, and as the fog lifted, the sumptuous disenchantment of painting emerged. It still recalled the era when Duccio and Giotto had showed Creation to God, just as He had made it, and when He recognized His works in theirs, painting began. For Eternity, the world would be enclosed in a frame. Sometimes the transparent persons of monks and prelates came and stood between the painting, the fief of the Sun, and the Divine Eye.

They tiptoed past, to see what God saw, and then, bowing, they left. Then it all ended. The Eyes were closed, the Heavens blind. What had happened? First, the clientele had changed. As long as painters still worked for the Church, all was well. But on that day when the richest Florentine banker had the outrageous idea of decorating his house with frescoes, the Almighty, in disgust, buried himself in his role of *Amateur* of souls. This was followed by the other Florentine adventure, the conquest of perspective. Perspective is profane, sometimes even a profanation. Look at Mantegna's outstretched *Christ*,* seen feet-first, his head in the distant background. Do you imagine that God the Father was pleased with a foreshortened Son? God is absolute proximity, the universal envelopment of Love. Can he be shown from afar His universe, which He has made and which, at every moment, he saves from annihilation? Is Being to conceive and engender Non-Being, the Absolute to engender the Relative, Light to contemplate Shadow, Reality to take itself for Appearance? No, the eternal story was simply beginning anew: Innocence, the Tree of Knowledge, Original Sin, and Expulsion from Eden. This time, the apple was called "perspective." But the Florentine sons of Adam nibbled at it, rather than eating it, which prevented them from discovering their fall immediately. In the middle of the fourteenth century, Ucello still believed in Paradise, and poor Alberti, the theoretician of the "perspectivists," was still trying to present his Geometrical Optics as an Ontology of Visibility. Nonetheless, he was still ingenuous enough to ask the Divine Gaze to vouch for the convergent lines. But Heaven never replied to this absurd re-

* In the Brera Gallery in Milan. (*Trans.*)

quest and man was swiftly dispatched to that nothingness where he really belonged and which he once again discovered; distance, exile, alienation. These negations mark our boundaries. Only man has a horizon. Alberti's window opened up on a measurable universe, but this precise miniature depended entirely upon that point which defined both our anchorage and our dispersal, that is, upon our eye. In his *Annunciation** Piero placed a flight of columns between the Angel and the Virgin. This is an illusion. In themselves, and to their Creator, these inert blocks of whiteness still slumber, identical and incomparable. Perspective was the violence which human weakness inflicted upon God's little world. A hundred years later in the Lowlands, being will be rediscovered in the depth of appearance, and appearance will once more assume the dignity of apparition. Painting will have new goals and will find new meaning. But before Vermeer can give us the sky, the stars, day and night, the moon and the earth—all in the form of a patch of brick wall, the bourgeois of the North must still achieve their greatest victory, the forging of their humanism.

In sixteenth-century Italy, faith still enflamed the artist's heart, vanquishing the atheism of eye and hand. In trying to clutch the Absolute, painters perfected techniques leading to a relativism they themselves detested. These bewildered dogmatists could go neither backward nor forward. If God no longer saw their paintings, who would be their witness? For man, they only reflected his own impotence. Where would he find the power to vouch for his picture? And further, if painting's sole objective was to measure our myopia, then it wasn't worth a single hour of labor. To

---

* In the Galleria Nazionale, Perugia. (*Trans.*)

reveal man to the Almighty who had deigned to raise him from the primordial ooze was an act of thanksgiving, of sacrifice. But why reveal man to man? Why show him to be *as he is not?* The artists born around 1480—Titian, Giorgione, Raphael—will make their compromise with Heaven. We shall return to this point. Moreover, the wealth and efficiency of the means still dissimulated the fearful irresolution of the ends. And we may further suppose that Raphael had some presentiment of these ends. He thumbed his nose at everyone and everything, caroused with whores, sold "chromos," and through *Schadenfreude*, incited his collaborators to make obscene engravings. His was a suicide through facility. But in any case, the joy of painting disappeared with these sacred monsters. In the second quarter of the century, painting went out of control, destroyed by its own perfection. In the barbarism of their contemporaries, as evidenced by their taste for *realisations*, we can discern a certain uneasiness. The public demanded that all the splendors of realism be used to mask its subjectivity. The painter must efface himself, and in the presence of life, cause his existence to be forgotten. Ideally, one should come upon paintings by surprise in the midst of a wood, and the persons depicted should burst through the canvas in a shower of splintering frame, seizing the passers-by by the throat. The object should re-absorb its visibility, and containing it from within, distract our attention by the continuous appeal to all the senses, and particularly, to the sense of touch. Everything in the work of art should aim to replace *representation*, forcing the spectator into mute participation in the spectacle. Through horror and pity men should be brought face to face with their simulacra, and if possible, thrown in their midst. Desire, consuming the fires of perspective, should discover this *ersatz* for divine ubiquity, the urgent presence of flesh. The logic of the eye should be respected, but at the same time, vanquished, by the logic of the heart. It was *the thing itself* they wanted, shattering, larger than life, more immediate and more beautiful. And this was Terror. But Terror is a disease of Rhetoric. Art, humiliated, would hide its face, once having lost its letters of credit. Fettered, under surveillance, subject to all the restrictions of the State, the Church and popular taste, yet more surrounded by admiration, more honored, perhaps, than ever before, the artist, for the first time in History, became conscious of his solitude. By whom was he invested? Where had he received this right which he arrogated to himself? God had extinguished himself, darkness reigned. How could he paint in the dark? For *whom?* And for *what?* And *why?* The object of art remained the *world*, that absolute. But reality slipped away, and the relationship of the finite to the infinite was reversed. Once, an immense plenitude had supported the torments and fragility of the body. Now fragility was the only plenitude, the only security. Infinity was emptiness and darkness, inside and outside the human creature. The Absolute was absence, it was God taking refuge in human souls. It was the desert. Too late to *portray*, too soon to *create*, the painter was in hell. But something was being born, a new damnation—genius, that uncertainty, that wild desire to traverse the world's darkness and contemplate it from without, and then to crush it against walls and canvases, sifting from it unknown splendors. We are confronted by a new word in Europe—genius—the conflict of the relative and the absolute, of bounded presence and infinite absence. For the painter knew full well that he would not escape the world, and more, that even should he escape, he would carry with him everywhere this nothingness which impales him. Perspective could not be transcended as long as he was denied the right to create other plastic spaces.

Michaelangelo died haunted by this, resuming his despair and disdain in two words: original sin. Tintoretto said nothing. He cheated. Had he admitted his solitude, he could never have endured it. But for this very reason, we can surmise that he suffered from it more than anyone else. This fake bourgeois working for bourgeois lacked even the alibi of fame. There was the viper's nest. This fidgety little dyer, victim of a typical neurosis which Henri Jeanson has so well described as "the horrifying moral wholesomeness of the ambitious" had set himself modest objectives; to rise above his father's station by the judicious exploitation of his talents, and to create a demand for his works by flattering the public's taste. Nimble opportunism, resourcefulness, alacrity, talent—nothing was missing, but everything was corroded by an overwhelming void, by Art without God. This Art was ugly, wicked, nocturnal, the imbecilic passion of the part for the whole, an icy darkening wind, hissing through lacerated hearts. Inflated by emptiness, Jacopo was swept along on a motionless journey from which there was no return.

Genius does not exist: it is the shameful audacity of nothingness. It was the little dyer who existed and who knew his limitations. This sensible boy tried to mend the tear. All he asked was modest fulfillment. What would he do with the infinite? And how could he know that the merest stroke of his brush sufficed to challenge his judges? His sullen, stubborn ambition unraveled in the Night of Ignorance. After all, it was not his fault if painting was a lost dog without a collar. Later on, he would have found madmen who rejoiced in their abandon, but in mid-sixteenth-century Italy the first victim of one-point perspective tried to conceal his. To work alone and for nothing is to die of fear. He needed arbiters at any cost, an honorific jury. God was silent, but Venice remained—Venice which would fill gaps, seal cavities, plug outlets, and stop hemorrhages and leaks. In the Doges' Republic, loyal subjects were expected to justify their activities to the State. And if they happened to be painters, they were to beautify the city. Jacopo placed himself at the disposal of his fellow-citizens, hastily adopting their strongly academic concept of Art, and all the more fervently, as it had always been his own. From his earliest childhood, he had been told and had always believed that the worth of a craftsman was measured by the number and importance of the commissions given him, and of the honors accorded him. He would hide his genius under his opportunism and consider social success as the only outward sign of mystical victory. His bad faith was blinding. Cheating at poker, he then rolled his dice towards heaven without cheating. Winning on earth, with all the aces he had up his sleeve, Jacopo had the nerve to claim that he would win in heaven. If he sold his paintings, it was only because he fooled everyone. But who can reproach him for his cunning? The nineteenth century proclaimed the divorce of the artist from his public. In the sixteenth century *it is true* that painting merely went mad. It had ceased to be a religious sacrifice, but *equally true* is the fact that it had rationalized itself into becoming a social service. Who, in Venice, would have dared say "I only paint for myself, and serve as my own witness"? And can we be sure that those who say this today aren't lying? Everyone and no one is a judge. Try and find your way out of that! Tintoretto appears more miserable than guilty. His art rent the age with slashes of fire, but he could only view it with the eyes of his own day. The fact remains that he chose his hell. With a single stroke the finite closes down upon the infinite, ambition upon genius and Venice upon its painter who would never escape. But even imprisoned, infinity gnaws away at everything. Jacopo's reasonable opportunism became a frenzy. The problem was no longer one of succeeding; now he had *to prove*. A voluntary defendant, the wretched man put himself endlessly on trial, a trial where he alone was the defense. Each painting a witness in his behalf, he pleaded his case without respite. For he had a whole city to convince, with all its magistrates and bourgeois, whose verdict, to be rendered by them alone and not subject to appeal, would decide his mortal future and his immortality. But he and he alone had brought about this strange amalgam. He was the one who had to choose; whether to be his own last resort, or transform the Most Serene Republic into an absolute tribunal. This being said, he made the only choice possible for him. To his everlasting grief. How well I can understand his indifference towards the rest of the universe! German or Florentine approval meant nothing to him. Venice was the richest and most beautiful city. She had the best painters, the best critics, the most enlightened connoisseurs. The game had to be played *there*, and not a single round could be re-played. *Here*, in this corridor of brick, between a thin strip of sky and stagnant water, under a flaming absence of sun, Eternity would be lost or won, in one lifetime, and forever.

Well and good, we shall say. But why did he have to cheat? Why trick himself out in Veronese's plumage. If he wanted to overwhelm them with his genius, why did he smother it so frequently? And why choose judges, only to bribe and deceive them?

Why? Because the court was biased, his case already lost, the sentence passed, and because he knew all this. In 1548, he asked Venice to guarantee the infinite. She grew frightened and refused. What a fate! Abandoned by God, he had to cheat in order to find judges. Then, finding them, he had to cheat again to obtain a recess of his trial. His whole life was spent keeping them in suspense, sometimes by fleeing them, at other times, by turning on them to blind them. It is all there. Pain and ill humor, arrogance and compromise, ferocious effort, rancor, implacable pride and the humble yearning to be loved. First and foremost, Tintoretto's painting is the passionate love affair between a man and a city.

A MOLE IN THE SUN   In this tale of madmen, the city seems still madder than the man. She had showered honors upon all her painters. Why did she persist in inflicting upon this one, the greatest of them all, this narrow-minded distrust, this morose ill will? The answer is very simple. She loved another.

The Most Serene Republic was starved for prestige. Her vessels had long since been her glory. Weary and tottering, she swelled with pride in one artist. Titian alone was worth a fleet of galleys. From crowns and coronets, he had snatched sparks of fire to fashion himself a halo. But his country of adoption primarily admired him for the respect he inspired in the Emperor. In the sacred light which shone around his head, awesome but perfectly harmless, Venice could pretend to see her only glory. Only the painter of Kings could be the king of painters, and by adopting him as her son, the Queen of the seas reclaimed something of her lost majesty. She had once given him a profession and fame; but now, when he worked, divine light radiated through the shutters of his studio, its beams reaching the Piazza di San Marco, and then Venice knew that he rendered a hundred-fold what she had given him. He was a National Treasure. What was more, this man was going to live as long as the trees. He endured for a century, imperceptibly transformed into an institution. But the presence of this one-man Academy, born before their time and bent upon outliving them, demoralized the younger painters. It exasperated them into losing their ambition. Believing their city had the power to immortalize the living, they concluded that she had reserved this privilege for Titian alone. A victim of this misunderstanding, Tintoretto, using the excuse—"I deserve it"—demanded that he be made the equal of his illustrious predecessor. But merit was not the issue here. One cannot ask of Republics something which belongs by right to hereditary monarchies. Jacopo was wrong to reproach the City of the Doges for having focused her entire spotlight on the monkey tree of the Rialto. It was just the reverse. A luminous shaft, whose source was Rome or Madrid, but in any case, outside the city walls—struck this old tree trunk, and, in a manner of speaking, reflected upon Venice, illuminating its shadows by indirect light. And I was wrong, as well, when I first thought of calling this chapter "In Titian's Shadow." *For Titian had no shadow.* Now ponder this for a while. When Jacopo was born, the Old Man was forty-one; and he was seventy-two when the younger painter first tried to assert himself. This would have been a graceful moment for him to die, and cede his place to the other. But he did nothing of the kind. This invincible monarch reigned for another twenty-seven years. When he finally did die, the centenarian had the supreme joy of leaving an unfinished *Pieta* behind him, as though he were an aspiring painter cut off in his prime. For more than half a century, Tintoretto-the-Mole burrowed in a labyrinth whose walls were spattered by another's glory. Until the age of fifty-eight, this nocturnal creature was dazzled by sunlight, blinded by another's pitiless fame. When that brilliance was finally dimmed, Jacopo Robusti was old enough to be a corpse himself. He determined to survive the tyrant, but won nothing by his persistence. Titian's skill had consisted in accumulating two contradictory positions, becoming both a court employee while retaining, at the same time, the independence of a modest employer. This happy conjunction is not often found in History. And Tintoretto, who put all his eggs in one basket, was far from providing another example. Visit both their tombs, and you will know the price he pays, even today, for having prepared his country for everything that was to come. The radioactive corpse of the Grand Old Man lies buried in Santa Maria dei Frari, under a mountain of sculptured lard, in this Church which is a veritable Doges' cemetery. Tintoretto's body lies under a slab in the dim shadows of a parish church. For my part, I find this perfectly appropriate. Lard, sugar and caramel are poetic justice for Titian; I would have preferred it still more had he been buried in Rome under the monument to Victor Emmanuel, the most hideous structure in Italy, after the Milan Railroad Station. For Jacopo, it was the obsequies of naked stone; his name suffices.

But this is a strictly personal opinion, I can understand how an indignant traveler might well demand an explanation of Venice. "Is this the best you could do, ungrateful city, for the best of your sons? Why, spiteful town, do you flank that Titianesque opera, the *Assumption*,* with a ramp of floodlights, and stint on electricity for Tintoretto's paintings?" I know what Venice's answer would be. It is found as early as 1549 in Aretino's letters. "If Jacopo Robusti wants to be honored, why doesn't he paint like Vecellio?" And Jacopo had to listen to this refrain every day of his life; they repeated it in front of every painting, after as well as before his death; and they are still saying it today. "Why did he go astray? Why did he leave the Royal Road when he was so fortunate as to have it marked out for him in advance. Our great Vecellio carried painting to such heights of perfection that no one could dare touch it again. Either newcomers must follow in the Master's steps, or Art will fall into barbarism." Perverse Venetians! Fickle bourgeois! Tintoretto was *their* painter. He portrayed what they saw, what they felt, but they couldn't bear him. Titian cared nothing for them, and they worshipped him. He spent the

* In Santa Maria dei Frari. (*Trans.*)

better part of his time soothing princes, reassuring them through his paintings that all was for the best in the best of all possible worlds. Discord was only an illusion, mortal enemies were secretly reconciled by the colors of their cloaks. Violence was a ballet, danced without conviction by fake toughs with soft woolly beards. There was war vindicated! The art of the painter approached that of the apologist, becoming Theodicy. Suffering, injustice, evil didn't exist, and neither did mortal sin. Adam and Eve sinned only in order to know, and make it known to us, that they were naked. In an expansive quadruple gesture, noble and yielding, God reaches forth from the heights of Heaven, while man, lying supine, stretches out his arms to Him. Order reigns; perspective, subdued and enslaved, respects the hierarchies. Discreet reservations assure kings and saints of the best seats. If, in the distance, someone has gone astray, in an unknown land shrouded in mist, or under the smoky lamps of some place of ill fame, it is never by chance. This murky light corresponds to the obscurity of his condition. But more, it is essential to bring alive the brilliance of the foreground. The brush pretends to recount an event and portrays a ceremony, sacrificing movement to order and relief to unity, it caresses bodies more than it models them. Of all the bearded observers glorifying the ascension, not one of them exists as an individual. They first emerge as a group with several legs and outstretched arms; a flaming bush. Afterwards this substance assumes diversity, revealing fleeting figures scarcely distinguishable from the collective background momentarily threatening to re-absorb them. To Titian, this was the natural condition of the common people. Individuality was reserved for Great

Men. But even there, he took pains to soften their outline.
The group in relief detaches itself and slips away, the per-
sonification of pessimism, while the courtier, an optimist by
the nature of things, leads a chorus of colors in chanting the
glory of God whom he both embodies and outshines. After
this, Titian applied himself to finishing the painting, scrap-
ing and polishing with lacquers and varnishes, sparing no
effort to conceal his work; and he ended by destroying it.
We enter a deserted painting, strolling among flowers under
a judicious sun. The proprietor is dead, and the stroller so
alone that he forgets himself and disappears. All that remains is the greatest treason of all, the betrayal of Beauty.

But for once, the traitor has the excuse of believing in his
treason. No city dweller he, but a parvenu peasant. When
he arrived in Venice, he emerged from a rustic childhood,
from the far reaches of the Middle Ages. This yokel had long
nurtured the commoner's reverential love for nobility. He
moved through the ranks of the bourgeoisie without even
seeing them, to join his real masters in heaven, all the more
assured of pleasing them as he truly respected them. People
like to say that he secretly considered himself their equal,
but I don't believe it. Where would he have acquired this
illuminating thought? He was a born vassal, ennobled by the
glory which only kings can confer. He owed everything
to his masters, even his pride. Why would he want to turn
it against them? His insolent self-satisfaction, the hierarchy of
power and the beauty of the world were all, in his eyes,
complementary reflections. With the best faith in the
world, he placed the bourgeois techniques of the Renaissance in the service of feudalism. But he had stolen the tools.

Nonetheless, he was admired by bourgeois and patricians

alike, for he provided an alibi for the technocrats of Venice. He spoke of happiness, glory, pre-established harmony, at just that moment when all their efforts went into masking their bankruptcy. All the merchants—whether noble or commoners—were enchanted by these smiling canvases which reflected the serenity of kings. If everything was for the best, if evil was only a glittering apparition, if everyone remained forever in his hereditary position within the social and divine scheme of things, then it meant that nothing had happened for a hundred years. The Turks hadn't taken Constantinople, Columbus hadn't discovered America, the Portuguese hadn't even dreamed of "dumping" their spices, nor the continental powers of forming alliances against the Republic. They had believed that Barbary pirates roamed the seas, that the African mines had been exhausted, that the scarcity of currency during the first half of the century had brought business transactions to a standstill, and that the Peruvian gold which suddenly poured from the Spanish reservoirs had reversed this movement, bringing about inflation and swamping the market. But all these were only bad dreams. Venice still reigned supreme over the Mediterranean, at the height of her power, wealth and grandeur. In other words, these anxious men craved beauty to reassure them. And I sympathize with them. I have traveled by plane at least two hundred times now, without getting used to it. I am too old and earth-bound ever to find flying a normal means of locomotion. Every now and then my fear revives —especially when my fellow-passengers are as ugly as I am. But as soon as I see a beautiful young woman, a handsome young man, or a charming couple in love, my fear evaporates. Ugliness is a prophecy, containing within it some sort of extremism which tries to carry negation to the point of horror. The beautiful seems indestructible, its sacred image protects us. As long as it resides in our midst, no catastrophe can happen. And so it was with Venice. She feared being swallowed up in the mire of the Lagoon, and imagining that Beauty, the supreme lightness, would save her, made buoys and floats of her palaces and paintings. Those who assured Titian's success were the same men who had abandoned the sea, who sought escape from their disenchantment in orgies, who preferred the security of an income derived from property to the profits of commerce.

Tintoretto was born in a turbulent city. He breathed Venetian anxiety deep in his lungs, and it gnawed away at him, until he could paint nothing else. In his place, his severest critics would have done the same. But the fact is, they were not in his place. They could not help feeling this anxiety, but they didn't want to see it, and they condemned paintings which *portrayed* it. Fate had decreed that Jacopo should unknowingly bear witness to an age which refused to know itself. This time, all at once, we discover the meaning of this destiny and the secret of the Venetians' grievances. Tintoretto was offensive to everyone: to the patricians because he revealed the puritanism and restless dreams of the bourgeoisie, to the craftsmen because he destroyed the corporate system, unmasking the rumblings of hatred and rivalry behind the illusion of professional solidarity, to patriots because his brush conveyed the confusion of painting and the absence of God in an absurd and perilous world where anything could happen, *even* the death of Venice. At least, we shall say, this painter-become-bourgeois must have pleased his adopted class. But no, not even the bourgeoisie could accept him unreservedly. He always fascinated them, but more often terrified them. Because they lacked any class consciousness. His Lordship Zigninoni dreamed of nothing but betrayal, furtively groping for ways to become a patrician, seeking, in short, to escape that bourgeois reality which, in spite of himself, he had helped create. What was most repugnant to him in Robusti's paintings was their radicalism and their "de-mystifying" virtues. He had to disavow their testimony at any price, and proclaim Tintoretto's efforts a failure, denying their originality—anything, *to get rid of him.*

What exactly were the charges brought against him? First of all, that he worked too fast, and left too much evidence of himself in his work. They wanted "licked," finished paintings, *impersonal*, above all. If the painter revealed himself, it was a challenge. And if he challenged, it was the public whom he called into question. Venice imposed the maxim of the puritans upon her painters: *no personal remarks.* She took care to confuse Jacopo's lyricism with the haste of an overworked contractor whose work is sloppy. And added to this was Ridolfi's slanderous story, which claimed that Tintoretto had written on the wall of his studio: "Titian's color and Michaelangelo's drawing." This is imbecilic, and the proof is that this formula was first found in the writings of Venetian art critics, with no reference to Robusti. Moreover, Tintoretto could only have known Michaelangelo's work through copies by Daniele da Volterra, which means, only in 1557, at the very *earliest.* What did they take him for? Could anyone have *really* believed that he *seriously* tried to follow this absurd formula? The truth was that this simply reflected wishful thinking prevalent at the time. Confronted by the Spanish menace, the cities of northern and central Italy had contemplated an alliance, but too late. However, this flickering of national consciousness, even though evanescent, would not have been without fleeting influence on art. "Michaelangelo and Titian" meant Florence and Venice. Painting united—how splendid that would be!

Nothing wrong with that: this dream was perfectly innocuous, as long as it remained everyone's dream. But those who claimed to see it as Robusti's obsession alone, must have really wanted to destroy this artist by planting an explosive nightmare in the heart of his painting. Color is Jake laughing, drawing is Jake crying. One is unity, the other the permanent threat of disorder. On the one hand, the harmony of the spheres, and on the other, disintegration. The two titans of the century hurled themselves upon one another, locked in each other's strangling grip, with Jacopo as the battleground. Titian wins some rounds easily, while others are narrowly carried by Michaelangelo. In any case, the vanquished retains just enough strength to mitigate the triumph of the victor. And the result was a pyrrhic victory, and a bad painting. Spoiled by excess, Tintoretto appeared to his contemporaries as a Titian gone mad, a Titian devoured by the somber passion of a Buonarroti, and jerking with St. Vitus' Dance. Obviously, this weird split-personality must mean that he was possessed by demons. In one sense, Jacopo didn't exist, or if he did, it was only as a battlefield; and in another sense, he was a monster, an evil spirit. Thus, Vasari's fable takes on new meaning: Adam Robusti wanted to taste the fruits of the Tree of Knowledge, but the Archangel Titian, with pointing finger and flapping wings, chased him from Paradise. Being a victim or a carrier of bad luck is still one and the same thing in Italy, even today. If you have had financial troubles recently, an automobile accident, a broken leg, or if your wife has just left you, don't expect to be asked to dinner. No hostess would willingly expose her other guests to premature baldness, a head cold, or in extreme cases, to a broken neck caused by falling down her stairs. I know one Milanese who has the evil eye. This was discovered only last year, and now he hasn't a friend left and dines alone at home. So it was with Jacopo. He was a sorcerer because a spell had been cast upon him, or perhaps upon his mother when she was carrying him. In fact, the *jettatura* is Venetian in origin. Anxious and cursed, Venice produced a man riddled with *angst*, and cursed in him her own anxiety. The wretched creature desperately loved this despairing city which wanted no part of him. His love only inspired horror in the beloved. People drew aside when Tintoretto passed. He smelled of death. And it was perfectly true. He did. But of what did they smell, with their patrician carnivals, and bourgeois charity, or their pink houses with flooded cellars, whose walls were crisscrossed by the horizontal scamperings of rats? Of what did they smell, the stagnant canals with their urinous watercress, the gray mussels, stuck with vile glue to the stone bellies of the bridges? In the depths of a canal, a bubble clings to the clay; loosened by the movement of the gondolas, it rises through the murky water to the surface, spins, shimmers, bursts with a noiseless fart, and everything bursts with it: bourgeois nostalgia and the grandeur of the Republic, God and Venetian painting.

Tintoretto was the chief mourner for Venice and its

world. But when he died unlamented, silence fell and hands of pious hypocrisy hung veils of crepe over his pictures. But if we tear away this black veil, we find one portrait, painted a hundred times. Was it a portrait of Jacopo or the Queen of the seas? Whichever you prefer; the city and her painter have but one and the same face.

The Living Gide

*T*hey thought him sacred and embalmed. He dies, and they discover how much he remains alive. Embarrassment and resentment appear through the funeral wreaths which they grudgingly braid for him, to show that he displeases and will continue to displease for a long time to come.

He managed to array against him the union of reactionaries of the Left and the Right, and we can well imagine the joy of a few august mummies as they cried: "Thank you, Lord: Since I live on, it is thus he who was wrong." It suffices to read in *L'Humanité*—"A corpse has just died" —to realize how heavily this man of eighty-four, who scarcely wrote any more, weighed upon today's writing.

Thought has its own geography. Just as a Frenchman, wherever he goes, cannot take a step without *also* drawing nearer or farther from France, so also every movement of the mind either carries us nearer or farther from Gide. His clarity, his lucidity, his rationalism, his rejection of pathos, allowed others to hazard thinking in more obscure and uncertain areas. They knew, while on their voyage of discovery, that a luminous intelligence upheld the rights of analysis, of purity, of a certain tradition; should they be shipwrecked, the mind would not founder with them. All of French thought in these past thirty years, willing or not, whatever its coordinates may have been elsewhere—Marx, Hegel, Kierkegaard—must also be defined in relation to Gide.

For my part, I was too infuriated by the mental reservations, the hypocrisy, and not to mince words, the revolting

Originally published in Les Temps Modernes, *March, 1951.*

stench of the obituaries devoted to him, for me to dream of emphasizing here the things which separated us from him. It is much better to recall the priceless gifts he bestowed upon us.

I have read from the pen of his contemporaries—whose gall has never surprised me—that "he lived dangerously swathed in three layers of flannel vests." What imbecilic scorn! These timorous creatures have invented a strange defense against the audacity of others. They do not deign to acknowledge it unless manifested in every domain. They would have forgiven Gide for having risked his ideas and reputation if he had also risked his life, or to be specific, if he had braved pneumonia. They affect not to know that there are varieties of courage and that they differ according to people.

Well, yes, Gide was careful, he weighed his words, hesitated before signing his name, and if he was interested in a movement of ideas or opinions, he arranged it so that his adherence was only conditional, so that he could remain on the margin, always prepared to retreat. But the same man dared to publish the profession of faith of a *Corydon*, the indictment of the *Journey to the Congo*. He had the courage to ally himself with the Soviet Union when it was dangerous to do so, and greater still, he had the courage to recant publically, when he felt, rightly or wrongly, that he had been mistaken. Perhaps it is this mixture of prudence and daring which make him exemplary. Generosity is only estimable in those who know the cost of things, and similarly, nothing is more prone to move us than a deliberate temerity. Written by a heedless fool, *Corydon* would have been reduced to a matter of morals. But when its author is this sly Chinese who weighs everything, the book becomes a manifesto, a *testimony* whose import goes far beyond the scandal which it provoked. This wary audacity should be a "Guide rule for the mind": withhold judgment until the evidence is presented, and when conviction is acquired, consent to pay for it with your last penny.

Courage and prudence. This well-measured mixture explains the inner tension of his work. Gide's art aims to establish a compromise between risk and rule, in him are balanced Protestant law and the nonconformity of the homosexual, the arrogant individualism of the rich bourgeois, and the puritan taste for social restraint, a certain dryness, a difficulty in communicating, and a humanism which is Christian in origin, a strong sensuality which would like to be innocent; observance of the rule is united in him with the quest for spontaneity. This play of counterbalances is at the roots of the inestimable service which Gide has rendered contemporary literature. It is he who raised it from the worn groove of symbolism. The second generation of symbolists were convinced that the writer could only treat, without loss of dignity, a very small number of subjects, all very lofty, but that within these well-defined subjects, he could express himself any way he liked. Gide liberated us from this naïve *chosisme**: he taught or retaught us that *everything* could be said—this is his audacity—but that it must be said according to specific rules of good expression—that is his prudence.

From this prudent audacity stems his perpetual turnings, his vacillation from one extreme to the other, his passion for

---

* *chosisme:* Sartre's own word, designating the rule of the thing (*chose*) or the tyranny of subject-matter. (*Trans.*)

objectivity—one should even say his "objectivism," very bourgeois, I admit—which made him even look for Right in the enemy's camp, and caused his excessive fascination with the opinion of others. I do not maintain that these characteristic attitudes can be profitable for us today, but they allowed him to make of his life a rigorously conducted experiment, and one which we can assimilate without any preparation. In a word, he *lived* his ideas, and one, above all—the death of God. I can not believe that a single devout person today was led to Christianity by the arguments of St. Bonaventura or St. Anselm. But neither do I think that a single unbeliever was turned away from faith by arguments to the contrary. The problem of God is a human problem which concerns the rapport between men. It is a total problem to which each man brings a solution by his entire life, and the solution which one brings to it reflects the attitude one has chosen towards other men and towards oneself. What Gide gives us that is most precious is his decision to live to the finish the agony and death of God. He could well have done what others did and gamble on his concepts, decide for faith or atheism at the age of twenty and hold to this for his entire life. Instead, he wanted to put his relationship with religion to the test and the living dialectic which led him to his final atheism is a journey which can be repeated after him, but not settled by concepts and notions. His interminable discussions with Catholics, his religious effusions, his returns to irony, his flirtations, his sudden raptures, his progress, his standstills, his backsliding, the ambiguity of the word "God" in his works, his refusal to abandon Him even when he believed only in man, all this rigorous experiment, has done more ultimately to enlighten us than could a hundred proofs. He lived *for us* a life which we have only to relive by reading. He allows us to avoid the traps into which he has fallen or to climb out of them as he did. The adversaries whom he has discredited in our eyes, if only through publishing his correspondence with them, can no longer seduce us. Every truth, says Hegel, has become so. We forget this too often, we see the final destination, not the itinerary, we take the idea as a finished product, without realizing that it is only its slow maturation, a necessary sequence of errors correcting themselves, of partial views which are completed and enlarged. Gide is an irreplaceable example because he chose, on the contrary, *to become his truth*. Chosen in the abstract, at twenty, his atheism would have been false. Slowly earned, crowning the quest of half a century, this atheism becomes his concrete truth and our own. Starting from there, men of today are capable of becoming new truths.

Reply to
Albert Camus

*M*y Dear Camus:

Our friendship was not easy, but I will miss it. If you end it today, that doubtless means that it had to end. Many things drew us together, few divided us. But these few were still too many. Friendship, too, tends to become totalitarian. It insists upon either total agreement or total discord. And even the partyless behave like militants in an imaginary party. I shall not go through all this again: it is in the order of things. But precisely for this reason, I would have so much preferred that our present quarrel went straight to the heart of the matter, without getting confused with the nasty smell of wounded vanity. Who would have said, much less thought, that everything would finish between us in a petty author's quarrel, in which you would play Trissotin to my Vadius?* I did not want to reply. Who would I be convincing? Your enemies certainly, perhaps my friends. And you, whom do you hope to convince? Your friends and my enemies.

What is certain is that both of us have given our common enemies—who are legion—a good laugh. Unfortunately, you have so deliberately put me on trial, and in such an ugly tone of voice, that I can no longer remain silent without losing face. Thus, I shall answer you, without anger, but

---

Originally published in Les Temps Modernes, *August, 1952, in reply to a "Letter to the Editor of* Les Temps Modernes" *of Albert Camus, which appeared in the same issue. The occasion of both texts was a review by Francis Jeanson of Camus's* L'Homme Révolté *which had appeared in* Les Temps Modernes *for June, 1952.*

* Trissotin and Vadius: characters in *Les Femmes Savantes* by Molière. Trissotin is an overly refined and pretentious poet, and Vadius a pedant, embraced only "for love of Greek." (*Trans.*)

unsparingly (for the first time since I have known you). Your combination of dreary conceit and vulnerability always discouraged people from telling you unvarnished truths. The result is that you have become the victim of a dismal self-importance, which hides your inner problems, and which you, I think, would call Mediterranean moderation. Sooner or later, someone would have told you this. It might just as well be me. But have no fear. I am not trying to paint your portrait, as I do not want to incur the reproach which you so gratuitously made to Jeanson. I shall speak of your letter, and of that only, with a few references to your works, when necessary.

Your letter amply suffices to show—if one must speak of you the way an anti-Communist speaks of the Soviet Union, the way, alas, that *you* speak of it—that you have made your Thermidor. Where is Meursault,* Camus? Where is Sisyphus? Where, today, are those Trotskyites at heart who preached permanent revolution? Without doubt, assassinated or exiled. A formal and violent dictatorship has established itself in you, dependent upon an abstract bureaucracy, and which claims to bring about the reign of moral law. You wrote that Jeanson "wants a revolt against everything except the Communist Party and the Communist State." But, in turn, I fear that you are not so much revolting against the Communist state as against yourself. The concern of your letter seemed to be to place yourself, *as quickly as possible,* outside the debate. From the first lines, you warn us that it is not your intention to discuss the criticism addressed to you, nor to argue, man to man, with your opponent. Your object is *to teach.* And in the didactic

* Meursault: the hero of Camus's novel, *L'Etranger.* (*Trans.*)

and praiseworthy aim of edifying the readers of *Les Temps Modernes*, you take Jeanson's article, which you see as symptomatic of the evil corroding us, and make it the subject of a master lesson in pathology. I feel as though I am looking at Rembrandt's painting: you are the doctor, Jeanson is the corpse, and you point out his wounds to an astonished audience. Because it is totally immaterial to you, is it not, that the incriminated article does or does not discuss your book? The latter is not on trial. A god has vouchsafed its value. Your book will serve only as a touchstone to reveal the bad faith of the guilty party. While doing us the honor of joining this issue of *Les Temps Modernes*, you bring a portable altar with you. It is true that you change methods in the middle of the road, abandoning your professorial demonstration and your "exasperated serenity" to attack me with vehemence. But you took care to say that you were not defending your own cause. To what purpose? It is just that Jeanson's criticisms—so biased, of course, that they could not possibly apply to you—could be injurious to intangible principles and venerable personalities. It is these persons and principles which you are defending: "It is not to me . . . that he was unjust, but to our reasons for living and fighting, and to our legitimate hope of transcending our contradictions." From that point on, silence was no longer possible.

But tell me, Camus, for what mysterious reasons may your works not be discussed without taking away humanity's reasons for living? By what miracle are the objections made to you transformed within the hour, into sacrilege? When M. Mauriac's *Passage du Malin* had its "great success," I read no article by him in *Le Figaro* saying that the critic had endangered the Catholic faith. You are another's mandate. You are speaking, so you say, "in the name of that poverty which finds hundreds of advocates but never a single brother." After this blow, we surrender our weapons. If it is true that poverty sought you out and said to you: "Go and speak in my name," we can only be silent and listen to its voice. Only I admit that I find it difficult to grasp your thoughts. You who speak in its name, are you its advocate, its brother, its brother advocate? And if you are the brother of the impoverished, how did you become so? Since it is not through ties of blood, it must be through those of the heart? But no, for you *select* your objects of pity, and I do not believe that you are the brother of the unemployed Communist worker in Bologna, or of the wretched field laborer fighting against Bao-Dai and the Colonialists in Indo-China. Is it through the bond of circumstances? You may have been poor, but you are poor no longer. You are a bourgeois, like Jeanson and me. Through devotion, then? But this is intermittent, and there we are closer to Madame Boucicault and her charitable works, and if we dare to call ourselves the brothers of those in misery, we must devote every instant of our life to them, and in that case, you are not their brother. Whatever may be your solicitude, it is not your only incentive, and you are far from being a St. Vincent de Paul, or a "sister" of Charity. Their brother? No! You are an advocate who says, "These are my brothers," because these are the words which stand the best chance of making the jury weep. You see, I have heard too many paternalistic speeches. Bear with me if I distrust that kind of fraternalism. And poverty has not charged you to speak on its behalf. Believe me, I would not dream of denying you the right to speak of it, but if you do so, let it be, as it is with us,* at your own risk, accepting in advance the possibility of being disavowed. What difference should it make to you, moreover? If your impoverished fellow men are taken from you, plenty of other allies remain. Former members of the Resistance, for example. Jeanson had no intention of insulting them, the poor fellow. He simply meant that in 1940, political choice confronted our fellow Frenchmen (because then we were fellow Frenchmen, with the same culture, principles and even interests). He did not claim that the Resistance could have been easy, and, although he had not yet had the benefit of your lectures, he had just happened to have heard about the tortures, firing squads and deportations, about the reprisals which followed attacks, and the excruciating decisions they involved for the individual conscience. Imagine, he really had been informed of all this. But these problems arose from the action itself, and to understand them, one had to be already engaged in it. If he remains convinced that the decision to resist wasn't difficult *to make*, neither does he doubt that it required a great deal of physical and moral courage *to keep*. Nevertheless, he suddenly saw you calling to the men of the Resistance for help and—here I blush for you—invoking the dead. "He is not obliged to understand that the Resistance . . . never seemed to me to be a happy or easy form of history, anymore than it was for those who really suffered for it, who were killed or who died for it."

No, he was not, in fact, obliged to understand it. He was not in France at the time, but in a Spanish concentration

---

* Because you must have acquired the habit of projecting your own faults of thinking onto others. Otherwise you wouldn't think that Jeanson claimed to speak *in the name* of the proletariat.

camp, for having tried to join the French Army in Africa. Let us leave these claims of glory out of it. If Jeanson had left an arm in the camp where he almost died, his article would be neither better nor worse. *L'Homme Révolté* would be neither better nor worse if you had not joined the Resistance or if you had been deported.

But here is another objector. Jeanson—rightly or wrongly, and I am not taking sides—reproaches you for a certain ineffectiveness of thinking. No sooner summoned, than the old soldier appears on stage. He is the insulted one. You, however, limit yourself to pointing at him and to informing us that you are tired. Tired, certainly, of receiving lectures in efficiency, but *above all*, of seeing them given by idlers or solid family men. To this, of course, it could be answered that Jeanson was not speaking of militants, young or old, but that he hazarded, as is his right, a judgment of this henceforth historical fact which is called revolutionary trade-unionism—because, one can, you see, judge a movement to be inefficient, while at the same time, admiring its courage, spirit of enterprise, self-sacrifice, and even the efficiency of those who took part in it—and above all, that he was speaking of *you*, who was not a militant at all. And suppose I were to summon as witness an old militant Communist, having taken care first to burden him with years and troubles sure to stir the heart, suppose I make him appear on stage and make this speech to you: "I am sick of seeing bourgeois like you furiously going about destroying the Party, which is my sole hope, when you are incapable of putting anything in its place. I am not saying that the Party should be above all criticism. I am saying that one has to earn the right to criticize it. I have had my fill of your moderation, Mediterranean or otherwise, and still more of your Scandinavian Republics. Our hopes are not yours. And for all that you may be my brother—brotherhood is cheap —you certainly aren't my comrade." What emotion, eh? There would be a militant, a militant and a half! And we two shall lean against the wings, both of us overcome by a wholesome fatigue, to the applause of the audience. But you know perfectly well that I do not play that kind of game. I have never spoken, save in my own name. And even then, if I were tired, it seems to me that I would feel some shame in saying so. There are so many who are wearier. If we are tired, Camus, then let us rest, since we have the means to do so. But let us not hope to shake the world by having it examine our fatigue.

What are we to call these methods? Intimidation? Blackmail? In any case, their object is to terrorize. The poor critic, suddenly surrounded by this crowd of heros and martyrs, ends by standing at attention like a frightened civilian among the military. And what a betrayal of confidence. These militants, prisoners, Resistants, these wretched poor—do you really expect us to believe that they stand ranked behind you? Come off it. It is you who are standing behind them. Have you changed so much? You used to denounce the use of violence everywhere, and now you subject us, in the name of morality, to virtuous acts of violence. You were the first servant of your moralism, and now you help yourself to it.

What is disconcerting about your letter is that it is too *written*. I do not reproach you its formality, which comes naturally to you, but the facility with which you manipulate your indignation. I realize that our times have some very unpleasant aspects, and that on occasion it must be a relief for sanguine natures to pound the table, shouting. But I am sorry to see you base a rhetorical order upon this disorder of the intelligence, even when there are excuses for it. The indulgence we may extend to involuntary violence will be refused when the violence is managed. With what double-dealing you play at being calm, so that your thunderbolts will take us more by surprise. With what art you reveal your wrath, only to dissimulate it immediately under a smile which is intended to be falsely reassuring. Is it my fault if these procedures remind me of criminal court? Only the Attorney General, in fact, is so skilled in becoming expediently enraged, in retaining mastery of his wrath until its final transports, and then changing it if need be, into an air for cello. The Republic of Hearts and Flowers would have named you Chief Prosecutor.

They discourage me, they beg me not to attach too much importance to these stylistic devices. I am agreed. Only it is difficult in your letter to distinguish a device from a nasty device. You call me *Monsieur le Directeur,* when everyone knows that we have been friends for ten years. I agree, it is only a device. You speak to me when your apparent subject is to refute Jeanson. That is a dirty device. Is it not your real aim to transform your critic into an *object,* a dead man? You speak *of him* as though he were a soup tureen or a mandolin, never *to him.* This means that he has been made extra-human. In your person, Resistants, prisoners, militants and the poor turn him into a stone. There are moments when you manage to obliterate him entirely, and you calmly write "your article," as though I were its author. This is not the first time you have used this trick. Hervé attacked you in a Communist review and someone in *L'Ob-servateur* mentioned his article, describing it as "remark-able," but without any other commentary. You answered *L'Observateur*, asking the publisher of this newspaper how he could justify the adjective used by his colleague. You explained at length *exactly* why Hervé's article was not remarkable. In short, you replied to Hervé, but without addressing a word to him.

But I ask you, Camus, just *who* are you, to stand off at such a distance? And what gives you the right to assume, apropos of Jeanson, a superiority which nobody accords you? Your literary merits are not on trial. It makes no difference that you write better and that he thinks better, or the inverse. The superiority which you accord yourself, and which gives you the right not to treat Jeanson as a human being must be a *racial* superiority. Would Jeanson, by his criticism, have emphasized that he differed from you as the ant differs from man? Are we dealing here with a racism of moral beauty? You have a beautiful soul, his is ugly: communication is not possible between you. And it is here that the method becomes intolerable. Because to justify your attitude, you will have to discover the blackness of his soul. And the simplest way of discovering this is to put it there, is it not? Because, finally, what is at stake here? Jean-son did not like your book. He said so and that did not please you. So far, nothing but the normal. You wrote to criticize his criticism. No one can blame you. M. de Mon-therlant does this every day. You could have gone much further, said that he did not understand a thing in it, that I am an idiot, place in question the intelligence of all the editors of *Les Temps Modernes*. That would have been a fair way. But when you write, "Your colleague would like us to revolt against everything except the Communist Party and the Communist State," I confess that I feel very uneasy. I thought I was dealing with a writer, and I find I am involved with a judge who is condemning our case on biased police evidence. Yes, again you are content to treat him as marine life. But you have to make him into a liar and a traitor in order to do it: "The author pretended to be mistaken about what he had read . . . I found (in the article) neither generosity nor loyalty, but only the *futile will to betray* a stand which he could not explain without immediately putting himself into the position of really wriggling out of it." You set about to reveal "the purpose" (apparently hidden) which leads him to "practice omission and (to) travesty the thesis of the book . . . to make you say that the sky is black when you said blue etc." to avoid the real problems, to hide from all France the existence of Russian concentration camps, which your book exposed. And why? Well, let's see—perhaps to show that all thinking which is not Marxist is reactionary. And why, in the last analysis, should he do that? There you are somewhat less clear, but as I interpreted it, this shamed Marxist was afraid of the light. He tried, with clumsy hands, to block the openings of your thinking, to halt the blinding shafts of evidence. Because, if he had thoroughly understood you, he *could no longer* call himself a Marxist. The wretched creature thought he was allowed to be bourgeois and Marxist at the same time: he was playing both sides. You point out to him that he must choose: join the Party or become, like you, bourgeois.*

---

* For you *are* bourgeois, Camus, like me. What else could you be?

But, this is exactly what he refuses to see. Here then, is the result of the investigation: premeditated guilt, deliberate travesty of others' thinking, bad faith, reiterated lies. You can well imagine the mixture of incredulity and laughter with which those who know Jeanson, his sincerity, his rectitude, his scruple, his love of truth, will greet this lawsuit. But what will delight them above all, I can guess, is the passage in your letter where you invite us to come and confess: "I would find it normal, and almost courageous if, attacking the problem frankly, you were to justify the existence of these camps. What is abnormal and betrays your embarrassment, is the fact that you don't mention them." We are now on the Quai des Orfèvres, the cop walks by and his shoes creak, just like the movies. "I tell you, we know everything. It is your silence which makes you suspect. Go on, say it, you are an accomplice. You know about these camps. Well, admit it, and the jury will take your confession into account." My God, Camus! How *serious* you are, and, to use one of your own words, how frivolous! And suppose you are wrong? Suppose your book simply attested to your philosophic ignorance? Suppose it were to consist of hastily assembled and second-hand knowledge? Suppose it only served to give a clear conscience to the privileged? As witnessed by the critic who wrote, only the other day: "With M. Camus, revolt changes camps." And suppose your reasoning was false? And suppose your thinking is muddled and banal? And suppose, very simply, that Jeanson was struck by its poverty? Suppose that, far from hiding your luminous proofs, he was obliged to hold up lanterns in order to distinguish the outlines of weak and confused ideas? I am not saying that this is so, but can you not really envisage *a single moment* where this might be true? Are you so afraid of being challenged? Must you hastily devalue all those who look straight at you and only accept those who look at you with bowed heads? Is it impossible for you to defend your thesis, to persevere in finding it correct, while understanding that another could find it wrong? You who defend *risk* in history, why do you reject it in literature? Why must you be protected by a whole universe of intangible values, instead of fighting against us—or with us—without divine intervention? You once wrote: "We are stifling among those who believe that they are absolutely right, whether in their machines or their ideas." And it was true. But I am deeply afraid that you have moved into the camp of the stiflers, and that you are abandoning forever your former friends, the stifled.

But what passes all measure, is that you succumb to this practice, only recently denounced under the name, I believe, of *amalgam*—in the course of a meeting in which you participated. In certain political trials, if there are several accused, the judges confuse the counts of indictment in order to confuse the penalties. Of course, this only happens in totalitarian states. But that is the procedure which you have chosen: From one end of your indictment to the other, you pretend to confuse me with Jeanson. The means is a simple one, but you had to think of it. You bewilder the reader by an artifice of language, to the point where he no longer knows which of us you are talking about. First instance: I direct *Les Temps Modernes,* thus it is to me that you address yourself: a blameless procedure. Second instance: you invite me to acknowledge that I am responsible for the articles published there. I agree to that. Third instance: it *thus* follows that I approve of Jeanson's attitude, and to speed things up, that this attitude is my own. From then on, it makes no difference which one of us held the pen. The article, in any case, is by me. An expert use of the personal pronoun completes the amalgam: "Your article . . . *You* should have . . . *you* had the right . . . *you* had no right . . . From the moment *you* were speaking," Jeanson only filled in the canvas which I had outlined. The advantage is twofold: you introduce him as my *valet de plume* and the henchman who does my dirty work, there you are avenged. Besides which, there I am, a criminal in turn. It is I who insult militants, Resistants and the poor; I who cover my ears when Soviet concentration camps are mentioned; I who seek to hide your light under a bushel. One example suffices to denounce the method: we shall see that the "misde-meanor" which loses all consistency if imputed to its real author, changes into a crime when attributed to one who did not commit it.

When you write: "No critic of my book can ignore the fact (of the Russian camps) you are addressing Jeanson alone. You reproach the critic for not having spoken of the camps *in his article*. Perhaps you are right. Perhaps Jeanson could have replied by saying that it is ludicrous to see the author deciding what the critic should say; and that you yourself, moreover, do not say much about the camps in your book. Hence there seems no reason for you to suddenly demand that the subject be raised, unless for the precise reason that poorly informed sources should have led you to believe that this would embarrass us. In any case, this is a question for legitimate debate between you and Jeanson. But when you write next: "*You* keep the relative right to ignore the fact of the concentration camps in the Soviet Union, as long as you do not raise the questions posed by revolutionary ideology in general, and Marxism in particular. *You* lose this right when you raise these questions and you raise them *in speaking of my book*." Or else: "I would find it normal . . . that you justify the existence of these camps": *it is to me* that you are speaking. Very well, I am replying to you that these interpolations are misleading, because you are taking advantage of the undeniable fact that Jeanson, *as is his right*, did not speak of the Soviet camps while on the subject of your book, to insinuate that I, as editor of a review which considers itself committed, never broached the subject, which would be, in fact, a serious breach of honesty. It just so happens to be untrue.

Several days after Rousset's declaration, we devoted an editorial to the camps, as well as several articles, which committed me entirely, and if you compare the dates, you will see that this issue was set up *before* Rousset intervened. But it makes little difference. I only wanted to show you that we brought up the subject of the camps and took a stand, at the same moment when French opinion discovered them. We returned to the same subject several months later *in another editorial* where we clarified our point of view in articles and notes. The existence of these camps might enrage us, horrify us, we might be obsessed by them, but why *should it embarrass us?* Have I ever retreated when it was a matter of saying what I thought of the Communist attitude? And if I am a submarine, a crypto, a shamefaced sympathizer, why is it that they hate me and not you?

But let's not boast about the hatreds we inspire: I can tell you frankly that I regret this hostility deeply—sometimes I go so far as to envy the profound indifference the Communists manifest towards you. But what can I do about it, except to stop speaking what I believe is the truth? What exactly do you mean when you write: "You keep the relative right to ignore . . ."? Either you are insinuating that Jeanson doesn't exist and that this is one of my pseudonyms, which is absurd; or you are claiming that I never breathed a word about the camps, which is calumny. Yes, Camus, like you, I find these camps inadmissible, but equally inadmissible is the use which the so-called bourgeois press makes of them every day. I am not saying, "The Malagasy before the Turkestani." I am saying that you cannot utilize the sufferings inflicted upon the Turkestani to justify those to which *we* subject the Malagasy. I have seen these anti-Communists rejoice in the existence of these prisons. I have seen them exploited to give themselves a clear conscience. And I did not get the impression that they were bringing aid to the Turkestani, but that they were exploiting his sufferings as the USSR exploits his labor. That is what I call the *full-employment* of Turkestan. Be serious, Camus, and please tell me what emotion the "revelations" of Rousset could have evoked in the heart of an anti-Communist. Despair? Affliction? The shame of being a man? Go on, go on! It is difficult for a Frenchman to put himself in the place of a Turkestani, to feel sympathy for this abstract being which is a Turkestani seen from here. At most, I will allow that the memory of the German camps aroused, in the feelings of better sorts, a very spontaneous kind of horror. And then, of course, fear as well. But don't you see, in the absence of any relation with the Turkestani, what must provoke indignation and perhaps despair is the idea that a socialist government, supported by an army of bureaucrats, could systematically have reduced men to slavery. But *that,* Camus, could not affect an anti-Communist *who already believed that the Soviet Union is capable of anything.* The only emotion which these facts aroused in him—and it pains me to say it—is *joy.* Joy because he finally had his *proof,* and now we shall really see something! It was not the workers he had to play upon—the anti-Communist isn't as mad as that—but upon all the solid people who remained *on the Left.* He had to intimidate them, strike terror into their hearts. If we opened our mouths to protest against some extortion, they would close it for us on the hour with: "And what about the camps?" They *summoned* people to denounce the camps under pain of being accomplices to them. Excellent method: either the poor wretch turned his back upon the Communists, or he became an accomplice to "the greatest crime on earth." It was then that I began to find them despicable, these blackmailers. For, to my way of thinking, the shame of the camps puts us all on trial—you as well as me, and all the others. The Iron Curtain is only a mirror, where each half of the world reflects the other. Each turn of the screw *here* corresponds to a twist *there,* and both here and there, to finish, we are all both the screwers and the screwed. An American freeze, which is translated by an outburst of witch-hunting, provokes a Russian freeze, which perhaps will be translated by intensifying arms production and increasing the number of slave laborers. The inverse, certainly, could also be true. He who condemns today, should know that our situation tomorrow will force him to do worse than what he is condemning, and when I see this joke on the walls of Paris, "Go spend your vacation in the USSR, land of freedom," with gray specters behind bars, it is not the Russians whom I find ignoble. Believe me, Camus, I know that you have a hundred times denounced and fought, in the measure of your power, the tyranny of Franco, or the Colonial policy of our government. You have acquired the *relative* right to speak of the Soviet concentration camps. But I have two reproaches to make you. To mention the camps in a serious work, and one which proposed to provide us with an explanation of our times was your strict right and obligation. What strikes me as inadmissible is that you make use of them today as the excuse of a street-corner rally, and that you too, exploit the Turkestani and the Kurd to demolish a critic who did not happen to praise you. I am also sorry that you produce your clinching argument to justify a quietism which refuses to make a distinction between the masters. Because it is all the same thing—you say so yourself—to confuse the masters and the slaves. And if you refuse to make a distinction between the two, you condemn yourself to give them only a sympathy of principle, since, as it often happens, the "slave" is the ally of one of those whom you call "masters." This is the explanation of why the war in Indo-China plunged you into such embarrassment. If we are to apply your principles, the Vietnamese are the colonized, and thus slaves, but they are also Communists, and thus tyrants. You blame the European proletariat because he has not publically declared his disapproval of the Soviets, but you also blame the European governments because they are about to admit Spain into UNESCO. In this case, I see only one solution for you, the Galapagos Islands. On the contrary, I feel that the only way of helping the enslaved out there is to take sides with those who are here.

I was going to end here, but in re-reading you, I find that your indictment seems to include our ideas* as well. Everything indicates, in fact, that with the words "liberty without restraint" you are taking aim at our concept of human liberty. Would I insult you if I believed these words to be yours? No, you could not have made such a mistake; you found them in the study by Father Troisfontaines—I have at least this in common with Hegel. You have not read either of us. You have such a mania for not going to the source. But nevertheless, you know perfectly well that a brake can only be applied to real forces in the world, and that the physical action of an object is restrained by acting upon one of the factors which condition it. But liberty is not a force. It is not me who wills this to be so, it is inherent in its definition. It either is or it is not; but if it is, it escapes the chain of causes and effects, being of another order. Wouldn't you laugh if they spoke of the *clinamen* without restraint of Epicurus? Since this philosopher, the concepts of determinism and, consequently, of liberty, have become somewhat more complicated. But there remains the idea of a rupture, of an unleashing, of a solution of continuity. But I don't dare advise you to consult *Being and Nothingness*. Reading it would seem needlessly arduous to you: you detest difficulties of thought, and hastily decree that there is nothing in them to understand, in order to

---

* I am not called upon to defend those of Marx, but allow me to tell you that the dilemma in which you pretend to enclose them (either Marx's "prophecies" are true, or Marxism is only a method) reveals the whole truth of Marxist philosophy, and everything which for me (who am not a Marxist) constitutes its profound truth.

avoid the reproach in advance of not having understood them. The fact remains that there I explained precisely the conditions of this rupture. And if you had devoted a few minutes to reflecting upon someone else's ideas, you would have seen that a brake cannot be applied to liberty. It has no wheels. Neither has it hoofs or jaws in which to put a bit, and as it is determined by its undertakings, it finds its limits in the positive but necessarily *completed* character of the former. We have embarked and we must choose. The *project* lights our way and gives its meaning to the situation, but reciprocally, it is nothing but a certain way of understanding it. Our project is ourself, through its light our relation to the world becomes specified; the ends and the means appear which reflect to us, at the same time, the hostility of things and our own objective. Having said this, you have permission, Camus, to call liberty "without restraint" only that liberty which can establish *your own exigencies*. (For if man is not *free*, "how can he require a meaning"? You just prefer not to think of that.) But then it will have no more significance than if you said: liberty without esophagus or liberty without hydrochloric acid; and you would simply have revealed that you, like so many people, confuse politics and philosophy. Without restraint, of course, without police or magistrature. If they accorded the liberty of consuming alcoholic beverages, without setting any limits, what would become of the drunkard's virtuous wife? But the thought of 1789 is much clearer than your own. The limits of a right (which is to say, a liberty) is another right (that is to say, still another liberty) and not some "human nature" or other, since nature, whether "human" or not, can crush man, but cannot reduce him to the state of an object. If man is an object, it is for another man's use. And it is these two ideas—difficult ones, I concede; man is free, man is the being through whom man becomes an object—which define our present status and allow us to understand *oppression*. You had believed (on whose word, I wonder) that I first endowed my fellow men with celestial liberty in order next to throw them in chains. I am so far gone that I see around me only liberties *already enslaved* and which are trying to tear themselves from their *congenital* slavery. Our liberty today is nothing except the *free choice to fight in order to become free*. And the paradoxical aspect of this formula simply expresses the paradox of our *historical* condition. Do you see, it is not a matter of caging my contemporaries: they are already in a cage. On the contrary, it is a question of uniting with them to break the bars. Because we too, Camus, are in a cage, and if you really hope to prevent any movement of the people from degenerating into tyranny, don't begin by condemning it without appeal, and by threatening to retreat to a desert. To merit the right to influence men who are struggling, one must first participate in their struggle, and this first means accepting many things, if you hope to change a few of them. "History" presents few situations as desperate as ours —it is what excuses prophecies. But when a man can only see in present struggles the idiotic duel of two equally abject monsters, I hold that this man has already abandoned us. He has gone into a corner all by himself to sulk. Far from dominating, as arbiter, an era upon which he deliberately turns his back, I see him as wholly conditioned by this era, and blocked by the refusal which a very historical resentment provokes in him. You complain that I have a guilty conscience (which isn't true), but even were I thoroughly poisoned by shame, I would feel less alienated and more open than you, because, in order to keep a clear conscience, you need to condemn. You need a guilty party; if it isn't you, then it must be the universe. You pronounce your sentence, and the world doesn't say a word. But your condemnations cancel each other out when they touch it. You always have to start again, for if you stopped, you might see yourself; you have condemned yourself to condemn, Sisyphus.

You had been for us—you could again be tomorrow—the admirable conjunction of a person, an action, and a work. This was in 1945. We discovered Camus, the Resistant, as we discovered Camus, the author of *L'Etranger*. And when the editor of the clandestine *Combat* was joined with Meursault, who carried honesty to the point of refusing to say that he loved his mother and his mistress, and whom our society condemned; when we knew, above all, that you had ceased neither to be one nor the other, when this apparent contradiction made us progress in the knowledge of ourselves and of the world, then you were not far from being exemplary. For in you were resumed the conflicts of our times, and you transcended them through your ardor to live them. You were a *person*, the most complex and the most rich, the last and most welcome heir of Chateaubriand, and the conscientious defender of a social cause. You had every opportunity and every reward, because you united the sense of grandeur to the passionate love of beauty, the joy of life to the sense of death. Even before the war you chose to defend yourself against the bitter experience of what you called *the absurd* by disdain, but you were of the opinion that "all negation contains within it a flowering of *yes*," and you wanted to find consent in the heart of refusal, "to consecrate the accord of love and revolt." According to you, "man is not wholly himself except when he is happy." And "what is happiness, if not the simple accord between a being and the existence he leads. And what more legitimate accord can bind man to life, if not the double consciousness of his desire to endure and his destiny of death?" Happiness was neither quite a state nor an act, but this tension between the powers of life and the powers of death, between acceptance and refusal, by which man defines the present—that is, the instant and the eternal at the same time —and changes it into himself. Thus, when you described one of these privileged moments which realize a provisory accord between man and nature, and which from Rousseau to Breton have provided our literature with one of its major themes, you were able to inject it with an altogether new shade of meaning, that of *morality*. To be happy, was to do the job of being a man: you revealed to us "the duty to be happy." And this duty was mingled with the affirmation that man is the sole being on earth who has a meaning "because he is the sole being who demands to have one." Similar to the *Supplice* of Bataille, but richer and more complex, you erected the experience of happiness in the face of an absent God as a reproach, but also as a challenge. "Man must affirm justice to struggle against eternal injustice, create happiness to protest against the universe of unhappiness." The universe of unhappiness is not *social* or at least, not at first: it is indifferent and empty nature where man is alien and condemned to die: in a word, it is "the eternal silence of the Divinity." Your experience thus closely linked the ephemeral and the permanent. Conscious of being perishable, you only wanted to be concerned with truths "which must rot." Your body was one of those. You rejected the fraudulence of the Soul and of the Idea. But since, in your own terms, injustice is *eternal*—that is, since the absence of God is a constant throughout the changes of history—the immediate relation and one which is always begun anew, of man who demands *to have* a meaning (which is to say, who demands that one be given him) to this God who maintains eternal silence, is itself transcendent to History. The tension by which man realizes himself— and which is, at the same time, intuitive joy in living—is thus a veritable conversion which wrenches him from his daily "agitation" and from "historicity," in order finally to make him coincide with his condition. We can go no further: there is no place for progress in this instantaneous tragedy. An *absurdist* before the letter, Mallarmé already wrote: "(The Drama) is immediately resolved, in the time needed to show the defeat which unfolds there like lightning"; and he seems to me to have given the key in advance to your plays, when he wrote: "The Hero unfolds the hymn (maternal) which creates him and restores himself within the theater, that it was part of the Mystery where this hymn had been buried."

In short, you remain within our great classical tradition which, since Descartes, and with the exception of Pascal, has been completely hostile to History. But you, at last, made the synthesis between aesthetic pleasure, desire, happiness and heroism, between rewarded contemplation and duty, between Gidean plenitude and Baudelairean "insatisfaction." You achieved the immoralism of Menalque through an austere moralism. The content was unchanged: "There is only one love in the world. To embrace a woman's body is also to hold against oneself this strange joy which descends from the sky towards the sea. Soon, when I drown myself in absinthe to make its fragrance penetrate my body, I shall have the unprecedented awareness of fulfilling a truth which is that of the sun, and which will also be that of my death." But as this truth belongs to everyone, as its extreme singularity is precisely what makes it universal, as you tore away the bark from the pure present where Nathanial seeks God and opened it to the "profundity of the world," that is, to death, you discovered, in terms of this somber and solitary joy, the universality of an ethic and human solidarity. Nathanial is no longer alone: he is "conscious and proud of sharing this love of life, stronger than death, with an entire race." Naturally, all ends badly: the world swallows up this unreconciled libertine. And you liked to quote this passage from Obermann: "But let us perish while resisting, and if nothingness awaits us, let us not live in such a way that it becomes an act of justice."

So don't deny it: you didn't reject History through having suffered from it and because you discovered its face with horror. You rejected it, previous to all experience, because our culture rejects it, and because you once placed human values in the struggle of man "against heaven." You chose and created yourself, such as you are, by meditating upon the griefs and anxieties which were your lot, and upon the solution which you gave them. It is a bitter wisdom which strives to deny time.

War came, however, and you gave yourself unreservedly to the Resistance. You lived through a fight which was austere, without glory or fanfare. Its dangers were hardly exalting; and worse, you took the risk of being degraded and vilified. This effort, often painful and always solitary, *necessarily* presented itself as a *duty*. And so for you, your first contact with History took on the aspect of a *sacrifice*. You wrote this yourself, moreover, and you said that you were fighting for "this nuance which separates the sacrifice from the *Mystique*." Understand me: If I say "your first contact with History," it is not to infer that I had another kind and that it was better. All of us, we other intellectuals, we only had that same one then, and if I call it *yours*, it is because you *lived* more deeply and fully than many of us (myself included). Notwithstanding the circumstances, this struggle fixed you in the idea that we must occasionally pay tribute to history, if only to earn the right of returning to our real duties afterwards. You accused the Germans of taking you away from your struggle against heaven, of forcing you to take part in the temporal combats of men. "For so many years now, you tried *to make me enter into History*," and further on, "You did what you had to do, *we entered History*. And for five years, it was no longer possible to enjoy the birds' singing."* History was the war, and this, for you, was *the madness of others*. It did not create, it destroyed. It prevented the grass from growing, the birds from singing, and man from making love. It happened, in fact, that exterior circumstances seemed to confirm your point of view; *in peacetime*, you waged an intemporal battle against the injustice of our destiny, and in your eyes, the Nazis took sides with this injustice. Accomplices of the blind forces of the universe, they sought to destroy man.

---

* *Letter to a German Friend*. The italic is mine.

You fought, as you wrote, "to save the *idea* of man."*
Briefly, you didn't think of "making history" as Marx said,
but of preventing it from making itself. The proof: after
the war, you envisaged only the return to the *status quo*.
"Our condition (has not) ceased to be desperate." The
meaning of the Allied victory seemed to you to be "the
acquisition of two or three nuances which will perhaps have
no other use than that of helping a few among us to die
better."

After you served your five years with history, you
thought you could return (and all men with you) to the
despair from which man must derive his happiness and
"give proof" that we do not deserve such injustice (in
whose eyes?) by taking up the desperate fight which man
wages against his intolerable destiny. How we loved you
then. We too, were neophytes of History and we endured
it with repugnance without understanding that the war of
1940 was neither more nor less so than the years which
preceded it. We applied to you these words of Malraux:
"Let victory be theirs who made war without loving it."
And we became rather maudlin about ourselves while repeating it. During this time, we were being threatened, as
you were, without realizing it.

It often happens that cultures produce their richest works
when they are about to disappear, and these works are the
result of the mortal marriage of old values with new ones,
which kill them, while seeming to fertilize them. In the
synthesis which you were attempting, happiness and assent
came from our old humanism, but revolt and despair were
the intruders, coming from outside: from outside where

* *Ibid.*

strangers stared at our spiritual banquets with eyes full of hate. From them, you borrowed this look to weigh our cultural heritage. It was their simple naked existence which questioned our tranquil pleasures. The challenge to destiny, the revolt against absurdity, all that came from you or passed through you; but thirty or forty years earlier they would have seen to it that you had gotten over these bad manners, and you would have rejoined the aesthetes or the Church. Your revolt only assumed such importance because you had been prompted by this mysterious crowd. You had scarcely the time to divert it against heaven, when it vanished. And the moral exigencies which you revealed were only the idealizations of the very real needs, which sprang into being around you, and which you seized. The equilibrium which you achieved could only occur a single time, for a single moment, in a single man. You were fortunate in that the common fight against the Germans symbolized, in your eyes and ours, the union of all men against inhuman fatalities. By choosing injustice, the German, of his own accord, allied himself with the blind forces of nature, and in *La Peste* you were able to have his role played by microbes, without anyone getting the joke. In short, for a period of several years, you were what could be called the symbol and the proof of class solidarity. This is also what the Resistance appeared to be and what you proclaimed in your first works: "Men will discover their solidarity in order to join the struggle against their intolerable destiny."

Thus, a concurrence of circumstances, one of those rare accords which make, for a brief time, life the image of truth, allowed you to conceal from yourself the fact that man's struggle against Nature is, at the same time the cause and effect of another struggle, equally old and pitiless, man's struggle against man. You revolted against death, but in the iron belts which surround cities, other men revolted again social conditions which raised the toll of mortality. Should a child die, you accused the absurdity of the world and this deaf and blind God which you had created in order to spit in his face. But the child's father, if he were a laid-off worker or unskilled laborer, accused men. He knew very well that the absurdity of our condition is not the same in Passy as in Billancourt. And, finally, for him, the microbes were almost hidden by men. In the worst slums, children die in twice the numbers as in wealthy sections, and since a different division of wealth could save them,* in the minds of the poor, half of these deaths appear as death sentences, where the microbe is only the executioner. You wanted to realize within yourself, by yourself, the happiness of all through a moral *tension:* the somber crowd whose existence we began to discover asked that we renounce being happy in order that they might become a little less unhappy. Suddenly, the Germans no longer counted. One almost might have said that they had never counted. We had believed that there was only one way of resisting; we discovered that there were two ways of *seeing* Resistance. And even when, for us, you still incarnated the man of the immediate past, perhaps even the man of the near future, you had already become, for ten million Frenchmen, one of the privileged. They didn't recognize their only too real anger in your ideal revolt. This death, this life, this earth, this revolt, this God, this no and yes, this love, were, they said to you, the

* This is not entirely exact. A certain number of them are condemned in any case.

games of a Prince. Others went as far as to call them circus acts. You had written (in *Noces*): "One thing alone is more tragic than suffering, and that is the life of a happy man." And again, "A certain continuity within despair can bring forth joy." And also, "I wasn't sure that this splendor of the world might not be (the justification) of all men who know that an extreme point of poverty always rejoins the luxury and riches of the world."* And certainly, I, who like you, am one of the privileged, understand what you meant, and I think you have paid for saying it. I imagine that you have been closer to certain death and to certain privation than many men, and I think you must have known real poverty, if not destitution. Coming from your pen, these phrases *do not have* the meaning they would assume in a book by M. Mauriac or M. de Montherlant. And more, when you wrote them, they seemed natural. But the essential point is that today they seem natural no longer. We *know* that if not wealth, then at least culture, that priceless and inequitable treasure, is needed in order to find luxury in the midst of poverty. People think that the circumstances of your life, even the most painful of them, elected you to bear witness that personal salvation was accessible to all: and that the thoughts which predominated in everyone's heart, thoughts of menace and hate, were only possible for a few. What can we do about these thoughts of hate? They gnaw at everything; even you. You didn't even want to hate the Germans, but there is a hatred of God which emerges in your books, to the point where one could call you "anti-theist" still more than "atheist." All the value that an oppressed man can still have in his own eyes, he puts into the hatred that he bears

* These three quotations are from *Noces*.

other men. And his affection for his comrades is surpassed by the hatred he bears his enemies. Neither your books, nor your example, can do anything for this man. You teach an art of living, a "science of life," you teach us how to redis-cover our body, but when this man discovers his body at night, after it has been stolen from him all day, it is nothing more than a huge ache which weighs upon and humiliates him. This man is *made* by other men. His enemy No. 1 is man, and if this strange nature he discovers at the factory or on the work site still speaks to him of man, it tells him that he has been transformed by men into a convict for their use. What could you have done? Modify yourself in part, in order to keep some of your beliefs, while, at the same time, answering the needs of these oppressed masses? Perhaps you might have done this, if their representatives hadn't insulted you, as is their habit. Cutting short the gradual transition which was taking place within you, you determined, with new defiance, to proclaim to everyone the union of all men faced by death and class solidarity, when the classes had already taken up their fight under your very eyes. Thus, what a short time before, had been an *exemplary reality*, became the totally empty affirmation of an *ideal*, the more so since this false solidarity had given way to combat within your own heart. You decided against history, and rather than interpret its course, you preferred to see it as one more absurdity. In essence, you merely resumed your first atti-tude. From Malraux, from Carrouges, from twenty others, you borrowed some idea or other of the "deification of man," and while condemning mankind, you stood next to it, but outside its ranks, like "the last of the Mohicans."

Your personality, alive and authentic as long as it was nourished by the event, became a mirage. In 1944, it was the future. In 1952, it is the past, and what seems to you the most intolerable injustice, is that all this is inflicted upon you from the outside, and without your having changed. You feel that the world offers the same riches as before, and that it is men who no longer want to see them. Well, just reach out your hand, and you will see whether everything doesn't melt away. Even Nature has changed meaning, because men's rapport with her has changed. Only memories are left for you, and a language which grows more and more abstract. Only half of you lives among us, and you are tempted to withdraw from us altogether, to retreat into some solitude where you can again find the drama which should have been that of man, and which is not even your own any more, that is, simply, into a society retarded at a lower stage of technical civilization. What is happening to you is, in a sense, completely unjust. But in another sense, it is pure justice. You should have changed had you hoped to remain yourself, and you were afraid to change. If you find me cruel, have no fear. Presently, I shall speak of myself and in the same tone. You will try in vain to strike back at me, but have faith, I shall take care to pay for all this. For you are completely insufferable, but you are still my "brother creature" by the force of circumstances.

Committed to History, like you, I don't see it in your way. I don't doubt that for those contemplating it from Hell, it has this absurd and fearful face, because they have nothing left in common with those who are making it. And if this were a history of ants or bees, I'm sure we would view it as a hilarious and macabre succession of penalties, lampoons and murders. But if we were ants, perhaps we would judge ourselves differently. I didn't understand your dilemma: "Whether History has a meaning or whether it doesn't . . ." etc. before re-reading your *Letters to a German Friend*. But everything became clear to me when I found there that sentence which you addressed to a Nazi soldier: "For years now, you have tried to make me enter History."

"So that's it," I said to myself, "since he believes himself *outside*, it's only normal that he makes conditions before entering." Just like the little girl who tries the water with her toe, while asking, "Is it hot?" you view history with distrust, you dabble a toe which you pull out very quickly, and you ask, "Has it a meaning?" You didn't hesitate in 1941, but there you were asked to make a sacrifice. There it was simply a question of preventing the Hitlerian madness from destroying a world where solitary exaltation was still possible for a few, and you were agreeing to pay the price for your future exaltations. Today, it is different. It is no longer a matter of defending the *status quo*, but of changing it. This is what you will not accept, unless accompanied by the most formal guarantees. And I suppose that if I believed, with you, that History is a pool of filth and blood, I would do as you, and look twice before diving in. But suppose that I am in it already, suppose that, from my point of view, even your sulking is the proof of your historicity. Suppose one were to reply to you, like Marx: "History does nothing . . . It is man, real and living man who does everything. History is only the activity of man pursuing his own ends." If this is true, he who believes himself to be moving away from history will cease to share the ends of his contemporaries and will only be sensitive to the absurdity of human agitations. But if he declaims against them, he will nevertheless return, and against his will, into the historical cycle, because he will unwillingly provide those of both camps who remain on the ideological defensive (that is, those whom the culture abuses) with the necessary arguments to discourage the other. On the contrary, it will be incumbent upon whoever pursues the concrete ends of men to choose his friends, since, in a society torn by civil war, it is not possible to assume the ends of all, nor is it possible to reject them all at the same time. But from the moment he makes a choice, all things take on meaning. He knows why the enemies resist, and why he is fighting. Because it is within historical action that the understanding of history is given. Does History have a meaning, you ask? Has it an objective? For me, these are questions which have no meaning. Because History, apart from the man who makes it, is only an abstract and static concept, of which it can neither be said that it has an objective, nor that it has not. And the problem is not to *know* its objective, but to *give* it one. For the rest, no one acts in view of History *alone*. In fact, men are engaged in short-term projects illuminated by far-off hopes. And these projects have nothing of the absurd. Here it is the Tunisians revolting against the Colonialists. Elsewhere it is miners striking for their demands or for reasons of solidarity. We won't argue whether there are or are not transcendent values to History. We shall simply observe that, if there are any, they are manifested through human actions which are, by definition, historical. And this contradiction is essential to man: he makes himself historical in order to undertake the eternal, and discovers universal values in the concrete action that he undertakes in view of a specific result. If you say that this world is unjust, you have already lost the game. You are already outside, in the act of comparing a world without justice to a Justice without content. But you will discover Justice in each effort that you make to order your undertakings, in each effort to reapportion the burdens of your comrades, in each effort to subject yourself to discipline or to apply it. And Marx never said that History would have an objective. How could he? One might as well say that one day man would be without goals. He spoke only of an objective to prehistory, that is, of an objective which would be reached in the womb of History itself, and then surpassed, like all objectives. It is not a question of knowing whether History has a meaning and whether we should deign to participate in it, but to try, from the moment we are in it up to the eyebrows, to give History that meaning which seems best to us, by not refusing our participation, however weak, to any concrete action which may require it.

Terror is an abstract violence. You became violent and terrorist when History—which you rejected—rejected you in turn. You are no longer anything but an abstraction of revolt. Your distrust of men made you presume that every defendant was, before the fact, a guilty man. From this stemmed your police tactics with Jeanson. Your morality first changed into moralism. Today it is only literature. Tomorrow perhaps it will be immorality. I do not know what will happen to us. Perhaps we shall meet again in the same camp, perhaps not. The times are difficult and confused. In any case, it was good that I should tell you what I thought. The review is open to you if you want to reply, but I shall not reply further. I have said what you were for me, and what you are now. But whatever you may say or do in return, I refuse to fight you. I hope that our silence will cause this polemic to be forgotten.

Albert Camus

Six months ago, only yesterday, we asked: "What is he going to do?" Torn by conflicts which must be respected, he had provisorily chosen silence. But he was one of those rare men who are worth waiting for because they choose slowly and remain faithful to their choice. One day he would speak. We would not have even dared hazard a conjecture as to what he would say. But we thought that he was changing with the world like each of us: this sufficed for his presence to remain alive.

We had quarreled, he and I. A quarrel is nothing—even should you never see each other again—only another way of living together and not losing sight of each other in the narrow little world which is given us. That did not prevent me from thinking of him, from feeling his gaze upon the page of the book, upon the paper that he was reading, and from asking myself: "What is he saying about it? What is he saying about it *at this moment?*"

His silence, which, according to the events and my own mood, I sometimes found to be too prudent and sometimes painful, had about it a quality of everydayness—like light or heat, but *human*. One lived with or against his thought, such as he revealed to us in his books—*La Chute*, above all, perhaps the most beautiful and the least understood—but always through it. It was a singular adventure of our culture, a movement whose phases and final term one tried to guess.

He represented in this century, and against History, the present heir of that long line of moralists whose works per-

Originally published in France-Observateur, *January 7, 1960, after Camus's death.*

haps constitute what is most original in French letters. His stubborn humanism, narrow and pure, austere and sensual, waged a dubious battle against events of these times. But inversely, through the obstinacy of his refusals, he re-affirmed the existence of moral fact within the heart of our era and against the Machiavellians, against the golden calf of realism.

He *was*, so to speak, this unshakable affirmation. For, as little as people may read or reflect, they collide against the human values which he held in his closed fist. He put the political act in question. He had to be avoided or fought: in-dispensable, in a word, to this tension which makes the life of the mind. Even his silence, these last years, had a positive aspect: this Cartesian of the absurd refused to leave the sure ground of morality, and to engage upon the uncertain paths of the *practical*. We guessed this, and we also guessed the conflicts which he silenced: because morality, in order to take it up alone, demands revolt and condemns it at the same time.

We were waiting, we had to wait, we had to know: what-ever he might do or decide afterwards, Camus could never cease to be one of the principal forces in our cultural domain, nor to represent, in his own way, the history of France and of this century. But we should have known, perhaps, and understood his itinerary. He had achieved everything—a whole life's work—and, as always, every-thing remained to be done. He said it: "My works are before me." It is finished. The particular shame of this death is the abolition of the order of men by the inhuman.

Human order is still only a disorder. It is unjust, precari-ous, in it we kill, we die of hunger. But at least it is established, maintained and fought for by men. With that order, Camus had to live. This man on the march placed us all in question, was himself a question which sought its answer; he was living, *in the middle of a long life;* for us, for him, for those men who make order reign, and for those who refuse it, it was important that he emerge from silence, that he decide, that he conclude. Some die old, others, always deferred, can die at any instant, without the meaning of their life, of life, being changed thereby. But for us, uncertain, disoriented, it was imperative that our best men arrive at the end of the tunnel. Rarely have the qualities of a work and the conditions of the historical moment so clearly required that a writer live.

I call the accident that killed Camus shameful, because it revealed the absurdity of our most profound demands within the midst of the human world. Camus, at the age of twenty, suddenly struck down by a disease which upset his life, discovered the absurd, the idiotic negation of man. He made himself by it, he *thought* his insufferable condition, he got over it. And we would nevertheless believe that only his early works spoke the truth about his life, since this cured invalid was snuffed out by an unforeseeable death which came from elsewhere. The absurd would be this question which no one will any longer ask him, which he will no longer ask anyone, this silence which isn't even silence, which is absolutely *nothing* anymore.

I do not believe it. As soon as it manifests itself, the inhuman becomes part of the human. Every interrupted life—even that of so young a man—is, at the same time, *a record that is broken* and a complete life. For all those who loved him, there was an unbearable absurdity in this death. But we shall have to learn to see this mutilated life-work as a whole life-work. In the same measure that the humanism of Camus contained a humane attitude towards the death that was to take him by surprise, in the measure that his proud quest for human happiness implied and re-claimed the inhuman necessity of dying, we shall recognize in this work and in the life which is inseparable from it, the pure and victorious endeavor of a man to recover each instant of his existence from his future death.

Paul Nizan

Paul Nizan

1   One day when Valéry was bored, he went to the
        window, and staring fixedly into the transparence of
a pane, asked "How to hide a man?"

Gide was present. Disconcerted by this studiedly laconic
remark, he remained silent. However, answers were not
lacking: all ways are good, from poverty and hunger to
dinners by formal invitation at the Académie Française. But
these two notorious bourgeois had a high opinion of themselves: every day they bedecked their twin souls in public,
and thought they were revealing themselves in their naked
truth. When they died, a long time later, one morose, the
other satisfied, and both in ignorance, they hadn't even
heard the young voice crying for all of us, their grand-
nephews, "Where is man hidden? We are stifling. From
childhood on, they mutilate us. They are all monsters!"

It does not even suffice to say that the one who thus
denounced our real situation suffered in the flesh. While he
was alive, there was not a single hour when he was not in
danger of losing his way. Dead, he risked a still worse danger: to make him pay for his clairvoyance, a conspiracy of
cripples tried to do away with his body.

He was a member of the Communist Party for twelve
years, after which time, in September, 1939, he announced
that he was leaving. This was the unatonable sin, this sin of
despair which the Christian God punishes with damnation.
But Communists do not believe in Hell, they believe in
nothingness. They planned the obliteration of Comrade
Nizan. An exploding shell had struck him, among other

Originally published as the foreword to Aden Arabie, *by Paul Nizan
(Éditions Maspero, Paris, 1960).*

places, on the nape of the neck, but this liquidation satisfied no one. It was not enough that he ceased to live; he must never have existed. They persuaded the witnesses of his life that they never really knew him: he was a traitor, he had sold out. He was in the pay of the Ministry of the Interior, and receipts were found there which bore his signature. Another comrade made a benevolent exegesis of the works he had left behind him, discovering in them the obsession to betray. How could an author who put stool pigeons into his novels know their habits unless he himself were one of them? A profound argument, as you can see, but a dangerous one. In fact, his commentator himself became a traitor, and has just been dropped from the Party. Should one reproach him for projecting his own obsessions into his victims? In any case, the maneuver succeeded. The suspect books disappeared. They intimidated the publisher who let them rot in basements, readers no longer dared ask for them. This germ of silence was to bear fruit: in ten years it would produce the most radical negation. This dead man would leave History; his name fall into dust; they would tear the page of his birth from our common past.

They quit when they were ahead: a grave snatching, in the dead of night, in a poorly guarded cemetery is just a little repair work. If they lost the first round, it was only because they were too contemptuous of us. Blinded by mourning and fame, the Party intellectuals began to take themselves for a chivalric order, among friends referring to themselves as "the permanent heroes of our time." Just about then, one of my former students said to me with suave irony, "We others, we Communist intellectuals, we suffer, you see, from a superiority complex!" Sub-humans, in a word, unconscious of their sub-humanity. Thus, they carried their arrogance so far as to try out their calumnies on Nizan's best friends, as a kind of test. The result was decisive. Challenged to produce their proofs in public, they disbanded, reproaching us for being so suspicious, and for not being at all nice.

The second round was one which we lost. Confusing people is nothing. We should have convinced them, pressed our advantage, and cut off the enemies' retreat. Our victory frightened us. We really liked them at heart, these unjust soldiers of Justice. Someone said: "Let's not make an issue of it, or they will really get angry." We heard nothing more about the affair, but it was whispered around the C.P., nevertheless, and new recruits, like Bergerac and Mazamet, learned dispassionately, but without any shadow of a doubt, of the former penalties of an unknown named Nizan.

When I think about it, our negligence appears suspect. I will admit, if need be, that we may have believed in good faith that the man would be reinstated in all his innocence. But what of his works? Is it forgivable that we in no way attempted to save them from obscurity? His books wanted to displease: that is their great merit, and now I am sure that then they displeased even us. In fact I remember that we had just acquired beautiful new souls, souls so beautiful that I still blush for them. Not wanting to lose anything, the Nation decided to entrust us with those insatiable and empty gaps for which it had done nothing—the stifled pains, the unsatisfied demands of the deceased, in short, everything which was unrecuperable. They would transfer the wreaths of these martyrs to our heads; alive, we were to be decorated posthumously: honorific dead men, in sum.

Everyone whispered that we were the Just. Smiling, light-hearted, funereal, we took this noble vacuity for plenitude, and hid our unrivaled rank beneath the simplicity of our manners. Virtue, along with whiskey, was our principal diversion. Everybody's friend! The enemy had invented classes to make us lose: beaten, it carried them away with it. Workers, bourgeois and peasants all communed in the sacred love of Country. In official circles, they thought they had discovered that self-sacrifice pays *cash*, that crime doesn't pay, that the worst is never certain, that moral progress advances technical progress. We proved by our very existence, and by our infatuation, that the wicked are always punished and the good always rewarded. Illustrious and appeased, the Left had just begun this rigid death agony which, thirteen years later, would bury it to the tune of military fanfares, while we, poor fools, found its complexion blooming. Soldiers and politicians from England and Algeria crushed the Resistance under our very eyes, taking the Revolution with them, and we wrote in the newspapers and in our books that all was going well. Our souls had transferred the distilled essence of these abolished movements to their own account.

Nizan was a spoilsport. His was a call to arms, to hatred: class against class, against a patient and mortal enemy with whom there is not accommodation. Kill or be killed, there is no middle course. And never sleep. All his life, he had repeated, with his graceful insolence, staring at his fingernails: "Don't believe in Santa Claus." He was dead, the war had just ended. Shoes and boots were set out in all French chimneys and Santa Claus filled them with American canned goods. At that time, I'm sure that those who leafed through *Aden*, or *Antoine Bloyé*, quickly interrupted their reading, with lofty pity: "pre-war literature, simple-minded and decidedly out of date." What need have we of a Cassandra? Had he lived, we thought he would have shared our new subtleties, or, might as well say it—our compromises.

What had preserved his violent purity? A stray bullet, nothing else. Nothing in that to brag about. This nasty dead man was quietly laughing. In his books he had written that a French bourgeois, after the age of forty, was nothing but a carcass. And then, at thirty-five, he slipped away. Now we, his friends and fellow workers, puffed up by this flatulence we called our souls, waltzed around the city squares, distributing our *baisers Lamourette** to one and all. And we were forty years old. Protecting innocence was our business. As just men, we were dispensing Justice. But we left *Aden* in the hands of the Communists because we abominated those who challenged our merits. This attitude is punishable under law: refusing to come to the aid of someone in danger. If we didn't morally liquidate our friend, it was only because we lacked the means to do so. Rehabilitation was a farce. "You talk, you talk, that's all you know how to do."† And we talked on: our beautiful soul was the death of others, our virtues were our basic impotence. In truth, it should have been the young men who revived Nizan the writer. But the young men of that time—today, forty-year-old carcasses—didn't dream of it. Having barely recovered

---

* Adrien Lamourette (1742-1794), a French prelate and legislator, who gave a moving speech in the Assembly hoping to reconcile the Left and Right. Overcome, his enemies embraced each other. But their accord was forgotten the same night. His achievement has been immortalized by the ironic expression: "Lamourette's kisses." (*Trans.*)

† The unique and oft-repeated comment of the parrot, in Raymond Queneau's *Zazie dans le Métro*. (*Trans.*)

from an epidemic, why should they concern themselves with this endemic evil, bourgeois death? Nizan was asking them to return to themselves just when they thought they were finally going to escape. Oh, of course, they would die. Socrates is mortal; Madame is dying, Madame is dead; at school they had been made to memorize a few celebrated pages, *Le Lac*, a sermon of Bossuet. But there is a time for everything, and now was the time to live, since, for five years, they had thought they would die.

As adolescents, they had been stunned by the defeat, in despair at having no one to respect, neither their fathers, nor the best army in the world, which had fled without a battle. The most generous among them had given themselves to the Party, which had restored them everything: a family, monastic rule, a tranquil chauvinism, respectability. The day after the war, this youth went mad with pride and humility. It found its pleasure in an orgy of obedience: I have already said how disdainful they were of us, through compensation. They pinched tomorrow until it bled, forcing it to sing. One can well imagine that the horrible screech of these fowl drowned out Nizan's thin and frozen voice, the voice without tomorrow, of death and eternity. Other adolescents found sweet release in cellar nightclubs. They danced, they made love, they visited one another, and in great floating potlatches, they threw their parents' furniture out of the window. In a word, they did everything that a young man could. A few of them even read. In sheer despair, of course. Everyone was in despair. It was the thing to be, the fashion, to despair of everything, except the vigorous pleasure of despairing, except of life. After five years, their future was beginning to thaw. They had plans, the

ingenuous hope of renewing literature with despair, of experiencing the distaste of long trips around the world, of
the unbearable boredom of earning money or seducing
women, or, very simply, of becoming a desperate pharma-
cist or dentist, and remaining for a long time, for a very
long time, with no other worry but that of the human
condition in its generality. How gay they were! Nizan had
nothing to say to them. He spoke little about man's condition, a great deal about social matters and about our alienation. He was an intimate of terror and anger as opposed to
the languors of despair. He hated his reflection in the young
bourgeois with whom he associated, and whether or not
they were desperate, he despaired of them. They put his
books away for the lean years, and they did well to do so.

Finally came the Marshall Plan. The Cold War went
straight to the heart of this generation of dancers and vassals. The rest of us, the old ones, merely lost a few feathers
and all our virtues. "Crime pays, and is paid for." With the
return of these fine homilies, our beautiful souls burst with
corruption. Good riddance! But our younger contemporaries paid for all of us. These cellar rats became elderly,
stupefied young men. Some grew gray, others bald, still
others grew a pot belly. Frozen, their decompression was
nothing more than an inert cavity. They modestly did what
was expected of them, earned their bread, owned a *Quatre-
chevaux*, a country house, a wife and children. But in one
flap of the wing, hope and despair both abandoned them.
These boys were just getting ready to live, they "set off,"
but their train stopped in the middle of a field. They would
go nowhere and do nothing. Occasionally, a confused memory of their splendid turbulence would come back to them.

Then they asked themselves, "But what did we want?" But they couldn't remember. These, the "well-adjusted," suffered from a chronic maladjustment; they would die of it. Derelicts without poverty, they were gorged and they refused to help themselves. I still see them at twenty, so vital and gay, determined to relieve us at the next shift. Today I see their eyes eaten away by a cancerous astonishment, and I think to myself, they didn't deserve this. As for the faithful vassals, some of them didn't renew their vows of fealty, others fell out of favor. All of them are wretched. The first plunged to earth without finding a place to land. These appalled mosquitoes lost everything, their sense of gravity being the first to go. The second, sacrificing their organs of locomotion, dug themselves into the sand, but the slightest gust of wind could transform these vegetables back into a swarm of insects. Just where had their lives gone? Nizan can answer for the desperate as well as for the faithful. Only I doubt whether they are willing or able to read him: for a lost and confounded generation, this vigorous dead man tolls the bell.

But they had sons who are now twenty, our grandsons, who bear witness to their defeat and ours. Until recent times, precocious children said "Shit" to their fathers, and joined the Left with their luggage and weapons. The rebel became a militant, this was classic. But what happens when the fathers are left wing? What do the sons do then? A young man came to see me. He loved his parents. "But," said he severely, "They're such reactionaries!" I have grown old and words have aged along with me. In my mind, they are my own age. I became confused, thinking I was dealing with the black sheep of a rich, slightly bigoted, perhaps even liberal family, who voted for Pinay. He disabused me: "My father has been a Communist since the Congress of Tours." Another boy, the son of a socialist, condemned at the same time, the *S.F.I.O.* [*Section Française de l'Internationale Ouvière*] and the Communist Party. "Some betray, others grow moldy." And what would happen when the fathers are conservative, when they support Bidault? Could the sons then be attracted by the Left, that corpse, lying on its back and full of worms? This cadaver stinks. The power of the military, dictatorship and fascism are rising or will rise from its decomposition. One would have had to be very devoted to it, not to turn away in revulsion. It had made us, the grandfathers; we lived on it. It is in it, and by it, that we shall die. But we have nothing left to say to these young men. Fifty years of living in the backward province which has become France are very degrading. We shouted, protested, signed and countersigned. We declared, according to our habits of thinking, "It is not permissible . . . ," or, "The proletariat will not tolerate . . ." And now at last, here we are. So we have accepted everything. Shall we communicate our wisdom and the glorious fruits of our experience to these unknown young men? Sunk lower and lower, we have learned only one thing—our basic impotence. This is the beginning of Reason, I agree, of the fight for life. But our bones are old, and at the age when most people think about writing their will, we are discovering that we have done nothing. Shall we say to them, "Be Cubans, be Russians, be Chinese, or, if you prefer, be Africans?" They will reply that it is a little late to change one's birth. Briefly, accountants or brawlers, *blousons noirs* or graduates of *Polytechnique*, they struggle

alone and without hope, against strangulation. Don't believe
that those who chose family and profession are resigned.
They have only directed their violence inwards and are
destroying themselves. Reduced by their fathers to impotence, they make themselves into cripples in revenge.
Others destroy everything else, strike out at anyone with
anything handy, a knife, a bicycle chain. To escape their
predicament, they will blow up everything. But nothing
explodes, and they find themselves at the police station
covered with blood. It was a fine Sunday, next Sunday
they'll do better. Giving the blows or taking them is all the
same thing, as long as blood flows. In the stupor which
follows these brawls, it is only their wounds which hurt.
They have the grim pleasure of thinking of nothing.

Who will speak to these *angry young men*. Who can
enlighten their violence? Nizan is their man. Year by year,
his hibernation has made him younger. Yesterday he was
our contemporary, today he is theirs. When he was alive,
we shared his rages, but none of us, finally, was capable of
"the most simple surrealist act"; and now, here we are, old,
having betrayed our youth so many times that it is only
decent to ignore it in silence. Our old memories have lost
their claws and teeth. Twenty years old, yes, I must have
been twenty once, but now I am fifty-five, and I wouldn't
even dare write "I was once twenty. I will let no one say
that it is life's most wonderful age." So much passion—and
so lofty—from my pen would be demagoguery. Moreover,
I would be lying. The pain of our younger brothers is all-
encompassing. I know it, perhaps I even felt it once. But it
is still human, since it comes to them through their fathers
or older brothers. Ours comes from our arteries. Strange

objects, half eaten away by nature, covered with ants, we look like those tepid offerings, those idiotic paintings which amused Rimbaud. Young and full of rage, struck down by sudden death, Nizan can break ranks, speak to the young people about Youth. "I will let no one say . . ." They will recognize their own voice. He can say to some of them: "You are dying of modesty. Dare to desire. Be insatiable. Release those fearful powers which clash and whirl around beneath your skin. Don't be ashamed to crave the moon. You should have it." And to others: "Direct your rage to those who cause it. Don't try to run away from your pain. Find its causes and smash them." He can say everything to them, because he is a young monster, a handsome young monster like them, who shares their terror of dying and their hatred of living in the world which we have created for them. He was alone, he became a Communist, ceased to be one, and died alone, near a window, on a staircase. This life is explained by its intransigence. Through revolt, he made himself a revolutionary, and when the revolution had to give way to war, he found his violent youth once more, and ended as a rebel.

Both of us wanted to write. He published his first book before I had written a word of mine. If we had then prized those solemn presentations, he would have written the preface to *La Nausée* when it was published. Death has reversed the roles. Death and systematic defamation. He will find readers without my help, and I have already said who his real public will be. But I thought he needed this foreward for two principal reasons: to hold up to all eyes the scientific abjection of his slanderers, and to warn our young men to allow his words all their weight. These words were young and tough—it is we who caused them to age. If I want to restore to them the luster which they had before the war, I must recall the wonderful era of our refusals, and make it live again with Nizan, the man who said no to the end. His death was the end of a world: after him the Revolution was established, the Left was so characterized by assent that one day in the autumn of 1958 it expired, murmuring a final yes. Let us try to go back to the time of hatred, of unquenched desire, of destruction, that time when André Breton, scarcely older than we were, expected to see the Cossacks watering their horses in the fountain of the Place de la Concorde.

II   *I* myself made the mistake which I hope my readers will avoid, making it during Nizan's lifetime, and even though we were such close friends as to be taken for one another. In June, 1939, Leon Brunschvicg met both of us in the offices of Gallimard, and congratulated me for having written *Les Chiens de Garde*, "although," as he said to me without rancour, "you certainly didn't spare me." I smiled at him in silence. Next to me, Nizan was smiling at him: the great idealist left none the wiser. For the eighteen years during which it lasted, this confusion contributed to our social status, and we ended by accepting it. From 1920 to 1930 especially, lycée and then university students, we were indistinguishable. Nevertheless, I never saw him as he really was. I could have done his portrait: medium height, black hair. Like me, his eyes were out of focus, but in the opposite direction, that is, agreeably so. This divergent squint made my face into a battlefield. His gave him an air of malicious absence even when he was paying close attention to us. He followed the fashions closely, but insolently. At seventeen, he had his trousers made to hug his ankles, so tightly, in fact, that he had trouble getting into them; a little later, they flared into bell-bottomed trousers, to the point of hiding his shoes; then with one blow, they rose to the knee, and puffing out like skirts, were metamorphosed into golf knickers. He carried a Malacca walking stick, wore a monocle, little round collars, then turned collars. He traded in his steel-rimmed glasses for enormous tortoise-shell ones; and succumbing to the Anglo-Saxon snobbery then ravaging youth, he called them "guggles."

I tried to follow his example, but my family put up effective resistance, going so far as to bribe the tailor. But then, I must have been under an evil spell: on me, these beautiful outfits merely became ugly clothes. I resigned myself to contemplating Nizan, with an astonishment filled with admiration. At the École Normale, no one payed the slightest attention to their dress, with the exception of a few provincials who wore their spats proudly, and tucked silk handkerchiefs into their jacket pockets. I don't recall, however, that anyone disapproved of Nizan's costumes. We were proud of having a dandy in our midst. He was attractive to women, moreover, but he kept them at a distance. To one of them, who followed him to his study in order to offer herself to him, he replied: "Madame, we would only defile each other." The truth was that he only liked young girls: he preferred them stupid and virginal, fascinated by the dizzying secret of stupidity, our only real depth, and by the shining glow of flesh without memories. In fact, throughout the only affair which I had known him to have, he was tormented ceaselessly by the most foolish jealousy. He couldn't bear the fact that his mistress had a past. I couldn't understand these attitudes, which were, nevertheless, perfectly clear. I insisted upon seeing them only as other character traits, such as his charming cynicism, his "black humor," his implacable and gentle aggressiveness. He never raised his voice, I never saw him frown, nor speak angrily. He merely folded his hands, and, as I have said, became absorbed in the contemplation of his fingernails, letting his fearful remarks drop with a sly and misleading serenity. Together we fell into all the traps.

At sixteen, he proposed that I should be a superman, and I accepted eagerly. We would be two supermen. He gave us Celtic names, and we covered whole blackboards with these strange words, R'ha and Bor'hou. He was R'ha. One of our friends wanted to partake of our new-found dignity. We had to put him to the test. He had to declare out loud, for example, that he would befoul the French army and the flag; these suggestions didn't have the boldness which we ascribed to them. They were current at the time, and reflected the internationalism and anti-militarism of former prewar attitudes. The candidate fled, nevertheless, and the two supermen remained alone, and ended by forgetting their superhumanity. We walked around Paris, for hours, for days. We discovered flora and fauna, stones, and we were moved to tears when the first neon advertisements were turned on. We thought the world was new because we were new in the world—Paris was our bond, we loved each other through the crowds of this gray city, under the light skies of its springtimes. We walked, we talked, we invented our own language, and intellectual slang, such as all students create. One night, these supermen-at-large climbed the hill of Sacré Coeur, and saw at their feet, a jeweler's shop in disarray. Nizan stuck his cigarette in the left corner of his mouth, twisted his face into a hideous grimace, and said simply, "Hey! Hey! Rastignac." I repeated. "Hey! Hey!" as I was meant to, and we climbed down, pleased to have revealed so discreetly the extent of our literary knowledge, and the measure of our ambitions. No one has captured these walks, this Paris, better than my friend. To re-read *La Conspiration* is to rediscover the charm, new and yet old-fashioned, of this world capital which didn't yet know that it would become a provincial seat. The ambition, the bursts of bad temper, the rages, both white hot and gentle, I took all these as they came. This is the way Nizan was, calm and perfidious, charming, the way I loved him.

He describes himself in *Antoine Bloyé* as "a taciturn adolescent, already enmeshed in the adventures of youth, and who abandoned childhood with a sort of avid exaltation." And so I see him. I experienced his taciturnity painfully. In *hypokhagne,** we remained estranged for six months, and I suffered deeply because of this. At the École Normale, where we shared the same study, he didn't speak to me for days. In the second year, he grew even more somber, undergoing a crisis whose end he couldn't foresee; he disappeared and was found three days later, drunk, with

* *hypokhagne:* course of preparation for the École Normale. (*Trans.*)

some strangers. When my friends questioned me about his "pranks," I found that I had nothing to tell them, only that he had a "bitch of a temperament." He had told me, however, that he was afraid of dying, but being mad enough to believe myself immortal, I blamed him for this, and simply decided that he was wrong. Death didn't deserve a thought; Nizan's terrors were like his retroactive jealousy, they were eccentricities that a healthy morale should overcome. But, unable to stand any more, he took off. He became a tutor to an English family in Aden. We regulars of the École Normale were shocked by this departure, but, as Nizan intimidated us, we found a harmless explanation for it: love of travel. When he returned the following year, in the middle of the night, no one expected him. I was alone in my study. The misbehavior of a girl from the provinces had plunged me, since the day before, into pained indignation. He came in without knocking. He was pale, grim, a little out of breath. He said to me, "You don't look very cheerful." To which I replied, "Neither do you." With which we went off drinking, and put the world on trial, delighted that our friendship had resumed.

But it was only a misunderstanding. My anger was only a bar of soap, his was real. He gagged on the horror of returning to his cage, and entered it undone. He was looking for help that no one could give him. His words of hate were pure gold, mine were counterfeit. And the very next day, he fled. He lived with his fiancée's family, joined the Communist Party, married, had a daughter, almost died of appendicitis; then taught philosophy in Bourges, and ran for the legislature there. I saw less of him. I was a professor in Le Havre, and then too, he had a family, his wife having given birth to a second child, a son. But above all, it was the Party which separated us. I was a sympathizer, but not an initiate. I remained his childhood friend, a *petit bourgeois*, of whom he was still fond. Why didn't I understand him? Clues weren't lacking. Why did I refuse to see them? I think it was through jealousy. I denied feelings which I couldn't share. I immediately guessed that he had incommunicable passions, a destiny which would separate us: I was afraid and I blinded myself. At fifteen, this son of a pious mother had wanted to take Orders. I only discovered this a long time afterwards. But I still recall my shocked amazement when he said to me, as we strolled around the lycée yard, "I had lunch with the minister." Then, seeing my stupor, he explained, with a detached air, "I may convert to Protestantism." "You," I said indignantly, "but you don't believe in God." "Well, no, I don't," he replied, "but their morality appeals to me." Madame Nizan threatened to cut off his allowance, and the project was abandoned. But this instance sufficed to let me see through the "childishness," the restlessness of a sick man who tosses back and forth to escape his pain. I didn't want him to harbor this inaccessible wound. We had superficial melancholies in common, that was enough. For the rest, I tried to impose my optimism upon him. I repeated to him that we were free. He didn't answer, but the slight smile at the corner of his mouth said a great deal about this idea.

Other times, he called himself a materialist—we were barely seventeen—and then it was my turn to smile scornfully. Materialist, determinist, he felt the physical weight of his chains. I refused to feel the weight of mine. I hated the fact that he entered politics, because I didn't feel the need to. Communist, then monarchist, then Communist again, it was easy to make fun of him, and I didn't hesitate to do so. But in fact, these ample oscillations proved his opinionated nature: to hesitate between two extremes—nothing is more excusable at eighteen. It was his extremism which didn't vary. In any case, he had to shatter the established order. For my part, I wanted this order to exist in order to be able to throw bombs at it—my words. In his real need to unite with all men, to lift together the stones which crushed them, I only wanted to see the extravagance of a dandy. He was a Communist just as he wore a monocle, from a slight fondness for shocking people. He suffered at the École Normale, and I reproached him for his suffering: we were going to write, we would create wonderful books which would justify our existence. Since I wasn't complaining, what did he have to complain about? In the middle of our second year he abruptly announced that literature bored him, and that he wanted to be a cameraman. A friend was going to give him some lessons. Angry with him, I explained to myself that he had developed a horror of words from having read too much, written too much, and that now he wanted to act upon things, transform them silently with his hands, and that this would only aggravate his case. This quitter of the word couldn't condemn writing without bringing judgment against me. The idea never struck me at the time that Nizan was, as we used to say, searching for his salvation and that "written cries" do not save.

He never became a cameraman and I triumphed. But it was a brief victory. His departure for Aden upset me: for him it was a matter of life or death. Guessing this, I made it into just another eccentricity, in order to reassure myself. I was forced to admit to myself that I hardly counted at all for him, but I ask myself today: "Whose fault was that?" Where could you find a more stubborn refusal to understand, and consequently to help? When he returned from these forays, these flights of panic, turning around in circles, I greeted him without a word, tight-lipped, with the dignity of an old wife who resigns herself to such outrages on condition that she makes it very plain that she is well aware of what is going on. It is true that he hardly encouraged me to do otherwise. He sat down at his table, somber, bearded, his eyes bloodshot, and if I happened to say a word to him, he gazed at me with a stupor that was full of hate. No matter: I reproach myself for having only these words in my mind: "What a filthy temper," and for never having attempted, even from curiosity, to explain to myself his escapades. I completely misunderstood his marriage. I was fond of his wife, but I had made of bachelorhood a moral precept, a rule of life—thus it couldn't be otherwise for Nizan. I decided that he had married Rirette because he couldn't have her any other way. To tell the truth, I didn't know that a young man in the prey of a fearful family can only deliver himself from them by starting a family of his own. I was a born bachelor, but I didn't understand that bachelorhood weighed heavily upon this celibate who lived alongside me, that he hated casual affairs—because they leave an aftertaste of death—just as he hated traveling, and that when he said "men are sedentary" or "give me my field, my needs, my men," he was simply claiming his share of happiness: a house, a wife, children.

When *Aden, Arabie* was published, I found the book very good and I was delighted with it. But I only saw it as a nimble pamphlet, a whirlwind of airy words—many of my friends made the same mistake: we had already taken sides. From the first day, the École Normale was, for many of us, for me, the beginning of independence. Many can say, as I do, that they found four years of happiness there. But here was a man who leaped at our throats in rage. "The École Normale, a laughable and more often odious entity, presided over by a little old patriot, powerful and hypocritical, who admires the military . . ." We were "adolescents who were worn out by years of lycée, corrupted by the humanities, morality and bourgeois cooking." We decided to take this as a joke. "Now, really, he didn't spit on the École when he was there. Then, he really had a good time, with all those worn-out adolescents." And remembering all our clever pranks, we recalled that he had participated in them wholeheartedly. Forgetting his moods, his scorn, the great uprooting which carried him to Arabia, we saw in his anger only exaggerated rhetoric. For my part, though, I was foolishly hurt; he had tarnished my memories. Since Nizan had shared my life at the École, he had to have been happy there, or else our friendship must have already been dead at the time. I preferred to salvage the past. I said to myself, "He is exaggerating." Today I think that this friendship was already dead then, without it being either of our faults, and that Nizan, gnawed by loneliness, felt the need to struggle in the midst of men, instead of chattering with his own unfaithful and all-too-familiar mirror image. It is I who preserved and embalmed our friendship, with lies and premeditated ignorance. Our paths never ceased to diverge from one another, and the real truth is that I needed many years, and the final understanding of my own way, to be able to speak today of his.

The more disastrous life is, the more absurd death. I do not maintain that a young man who is in the midst of his work, of his hopes, might not be overwhelmed by the shattering evidence of death. I do say that a young man is afraid of dying when he is dissatisfied with his fate. Before he is led by the hand to the lecture-hall seat which is assigned him, a student is the infinite, the indefinite, moving easily from one doctrine to another. None of them hold him, he feels the equivocal nature of all thought. And it is true that what we call the "humanities" in the curriculum, is only the teaching of the great errors of the past. Formed by our Republics in the image of Valéry's *Monsieur Teste*—that ideal citizen who says nothing, does nothing, but who nonetheless thinks—these young men will need twenty years to understand that ideas are stones which have an inflexible order, and that we must use them to build. As long as burnt-out men, discreet to the point of transparency, push bourgeois objectivity as far as to require students to penetrate the points of view of Nero, Loyola and M. Thiers, each of these apprentices is going to take himself for pure Spirit, a colorless and flavorless gas which sometimes reaches to the galaxies, and other times is condensed into formulas. The young elite is at once everything and nothing. This means that it is supported by the state, by families—under this vaporous confusion its life wastes away. Suddenly, pure mind runs into this obstacle: death. In vain does the mind try to envelop death in order to dissolve it; death cannot be thought. An accident strikes down a body, a brute fact puts an end to the brilliant indetermination of ideas. The horror of this awakens more than one terrified adolescent in the middle of the night. Universal culture is no recourse against capital punishment and its incomprehensible singularity.

Later on, when the individuality of his body is reflected in that of his undertaking, a young man will integrate his death with his life, seeing in the former only one danger among all those which threaten his life and his family. For those men who have the rare fortune to love what they do, the final shipwreck will take the form of small worries, and therefore appear less frightening as it approaches.

I have described the average fate. This is nothing. But when anguish survives adolescence, when it becomes the deepest secret of the adult, and the mainspring of his decisions, the invalid knows his wounds. His terror of soon being no longer alive simply reflects his horror in still having to live. Death is the irremediable sentence. It condemns for eternity those wretched at having been nothing but that: shameful calamities. Nizan feared this fate. This monster, stalking by chance among monsters, was afraid of exploding one day, and that there would then be nothing left. For a long time he had known that death was the illumination of life. He knew it when he gave these words to one of his characters: "If I think of death, I do well to do so. Because my life is hollow, and only deserves death." In the same book, Bloyé begins to fear "the uniform face of his life . . . and (this fear) comes from a still deeper region than those bleeding parts of the body where the warning of illnesses appears."

From what did he suffer, in sum? Why did I, more than any of the others, seem ridiculous when I spoke of our liberty? If he believed, from the age of sixteen, in the inflexible chain reaction of causes, this is because he felt constrained and manipulated. "We are composed of divisions, alienations, wars and palaverings . . . ," he said. "Each man is divided among the men he could have been." A lonely child, he knew his singularity too well to throw himself, as I did, into universal ideas. A slave, he came to philosophy to be freed, and Spinoza furnished him with his model. In the first two kinds of knowledge, man remains enslaved because he is incomplete. Knowledge of the third kind breaks the bars, or negative determinants: in this mode, it is all one whether we return to the infinite substance or realize the affirmative totality of its particular essence. Nizan wanted to do away with all the walls: he would unify his life through the proclamation of his desires and by quenching them.

The easiest desire to name stems from sex and from its overflowing lusts. In a society which reserves its women for the old and rich, this is the first pain of a poor young man with a premonition of his future enemies. Nizan spoke bitterly of the old men who embraced our women, and who dared to chastise us. But to be fair, we were living in an era of Great Desire. The Surrealists were trying to awaken this infinite concupiscence whose object was no less than Everything. Nizan was looking for medicine and took what he could find. Through his works he discovered Freud and placed him in his Pantheon. Revised and corrected by Breton, and by a young man in danger, Freud bore a resemblance to Spinoza: he tore away the spider's web and with it the veils, imposed peace upon the enemies who slaughtered each other in our tunnels, dissolved our furious abortions in the light, and reduced all of us to the unity of powerful appetites. My friend tried him for a time, not without some happiness. We find traces of his influence in *Antoine Bloyé*, where it is the source of this beautiful sentence. "As long as

men are not free and complete, they will dream at night."
Antoine dreams of the women he hasn't possessed, hasn't
even dared desire, but when he wakes, he refuses to listen to
"this wise voice." For the waker and the sleeper rarely make
a happy couple. Antoine is an old man, but here Nizan speaks
from his own experience: I know this. He dreamed, he
dreamed until the day of his death. His letters from the
front are filled with his dreams.

However, these were merely working hypotheses, a
provisory means of unifying himself. He adored the women
walking by, pale apparitions effaced by the light and smoke
of Paris, fugitive hints of love; but he loved, above all, the
fact that they were inaccessible. This well-behaved and
literary young man was intoxicated by privations: these are
useful for books. But let us not believe that he bore his
chastity uneasily: one or two affairs, brief unhappiness—and
the rest of the time proper and slippery young girls whom
he scarcely touched. He would have been only too happy
had he discovered within himself the conflict of the flesh
and the law. Then he could have decided and condemned
the law. *"Morale, c'est trou de balle!"* ["Morality is a hole in
the head!"], he used to say at twenty. But, in fact, taboos are
much more insidious, even our bodies become their accomplices. Morality wasn't apparent, but confronted by any
women except virgins, his awkwardness was accompanied
by strong disgust. Later on, when he had his land and his
men, he vaunted the beauty of *every* female body, with an
astonished but precise sense of wonder. Even at that moment,
I wondered what had prevented him from making this wide-
spread discovery at the time of his painful love affairs. Now
I know. It was distaste, an infantile revulsion towards bodies

which he felt were worn out by old caresses. As adolescents, when we looked at women, I wanted all of them, he only wanted one, but one who would be his. He couldn't imagine making love unless it was from dawn to dusk, nor that possession could exist when the whole woman is not possessed, when she doesn't possess you entirely. He believed that man is sedentary, that casual affairs are like voyages: mere abstractions. One thousand and three women are a thousand and three times the same one. He wanted only one who would be another a thousand and three times. Within her he would love, as a promise against death, the secret signs of her fecundity.

In other words, the dissatisfaction of the senses was an effect, not a cause. When he was married, it disappeared. Great desire took its place, becoming a need among so many other needs that are satisfied poorly, too quickly, or not at all. And actually, Nizan only suffered from present contradictions in order to decipher them in the light of the future. If, at one point, he wanted to kill himself, it was to stop immediately what he believed was only starting over again. From childhood on, he had been marked by Breton bigotry—either too much so or too little for his own happiness: contradiction established itself under his own roof. He was the child of old parents: these two adversaries had conceived him in the course of a truce. When he was born, they resumed their quarrel. His father, first a worker, then an engineer for the railroad, gave him the example of a technical, nonbelieving and adult mind, and his statements bore the evidence of a sad fidelity to the class he had left behind. From his earliest childhood, Nizan interiorized this mute conflict of an elderly, childish and middle-class mother with a renegade member of the working class, and he made of this conflict the jury of his future self. However small he may be, the child of a housekeeper participates in the future of his family: the father makes plans. The Nizans had no future. This head of a railroad yard found himself at the farthest point of his career; what had he to look forward to? The promotion due him, a few honors, retirement and death. At the same time, Madame Nizan lived in that moment where "the onions are starting to cook" and "the chop goes into the frying pan next," and in that fixed moment called Eternity. The child wasn't far from his point of departure, nor the family from its point of decline. Carried along by this undertow, he wanted to learn, to build, and everything disintegrated under his gaze, even the conjugal quarrel. On the exterior, it was transformed into indifference; it existed nowhere, except within himself. The child heard their dialogue where there was silence: the futile and ceremonious babbling of Faith was occasionally interrupted by the harsh voice which taught him the names of plants, stones and tools. These two voices devoured each other: at first he felt carried away by the pious discourse. It spoke of Charity, Paradise, Supreme End, a whole terminology which challenged the technician's concrete activity. What good was it to make locomotives? There were no trains in heaven. As soon as he could, the engineer left his house in the morning. Between the age of five and ten, his son followed him into the fields, held his hand, ran at his side. At twenty-five, he tenderly recalled these walks of two men by themselves, so obviously directed against the wife and the mother. I should point out, nevertheless, that he preferred the tired courtesy of the Word, to the Sciences. A worker becomes an engineer; he suffers from his lack of culture; his son is headed for *Polytechnique*. This is standard. But Nizan showed a suspicious repugnance for mathematics. He studied Greek and Latin. Stepson of a Polytechnician, I share the same distaste, but for different reasons. We both loved vague, ritualistic words and myths. But his father had his revenge. Under the influence of his positivism, his son tried to break the shackles of religion. I have showed the steps of this deliverance; from the mystic transport to the last leap, which made him consider taking Orders, his flirtation with Calvin, the metamorphosis of his devout Catharism into political Manicheism, royalism, and finally, Marxism. For a long time, we both retained a Christian vocabulary. Atheists, we had no doubt that we had been put on this earth to find our salvation, and with a little luck, we would find it for others as well. One big difference: I was certain of being one of the elect. He often wondered whether he wasn't among the damned. From his mother and from Catholicism, he had retained a basic contempt for the works of this world, the fear of losing his way in this century, and the tendency—which never left him—to pursue an absolute End. We persuaded him that hidden within him, beneath the undergrowth of daily cares, was a white, flawless totality: he had only to hack it out, pull up the weeds, set fire to the brush, and this boundless Eternity would manifest itself in all its purity. Thus, it was at this time that he judged his father's profession to be an obsessive and meaningless agitation. It sacrificed the order of primary ends to that of means, man was sacrificed to the machine. He had quickly stopped believing in those little white pills of life called Souls, but he still secretly believed that his father had lost his.

These old supersititions don't prevent one from living, *on the condition that one has the Faith*. But even once disqualified, technique takes its revenge by strangling religion. Nizan kept his dissatisfactions, only they were deprived of roots, up in the air. Secular activities are ludicrous, but if nothing else exists but earth and the human creatures scratching away there, then the sons of men have to take up the next shift and begin to scratch. For there is no other occupation, unless we travesty the old Christian words. When he made me the curious proposal of becoming a superman, he was not goaded by pride, so much as the mysterious need to escape our condition. Alas, it was only a question of changing names. After this, and until his departure for Aden, he never stopped dragging his chains, or forging symbols of escape.

But we shall never understand his anguish, if we do not recall what I have said earlier: he was engaged in deciphering this laborious, disenchanted present, a present illuminated by short-lived exaltations, by the livid light of a future which was nothing else than his father's past. "I was afraid. My departure was the child of my fear." Afraid of what? He says it even here: "Mutilations await us. After all, we know how our parents live." He developed this sentence in a long and very beautiful novel, *Antoine Bloyé*. There he tells of the life and death of his father. And although he is scarcely visible in it, he speaks of himself constantly. At first he is the witness of this decrepitude. But then, M. Nizan never confided in anyone. All the thoughts and feelings which are attributed to him, we know that the author tears them from within himself, to project them into this deranged old heart. This constant double presence is the evidence of what psychoanalysts call father-identification.

I have already said that Nizan, in his early years, admired his father, envying him this sterile but visible power, those hands which had labored. M. Nizan spoke of his former comrades: fascinated by these men who knew the truth of life and who seemed to love each other, the little boy saw his father as a worker, and wanted to be like him in every way. He would have his father's pedestrian patience, needing nothing less than the mysterious inner density of things, this matter which would save the future monk from his mother, from the parish priest, from his own chatter. "Antoine," the author says with admiration, "was a corporal man, his conscience wasn't clear enough to be disinterested in the body which nourished it, and which, for so many years, had furnished it with the admirable proof of existence."

But this admirable man faltered, and suddenly the child saw him disintegrate. Nizan had given himself to his father unreservedly. "I will be like him." He was then obliged to watch the endless decomposition of his own future: "This will be me." He saw Matter run aground, and the maternal baby talk triumph. But what of the Spirit, the foam which tells of the shipwreck—what became of it? He speaks of this in *Antoine Bloyé,* for reasons which I don't quite know; for, although Nizan follows the truth quite closely in his book, he surely must have changed the circumstances of the man who served as the real model for Antoine. I think that from the age of forty, he wanted to settle his accounts. And everything had begun with this fake victory, with this crossing of the lines, at the time when the bourgeoisie promised everyone "the glorious future of equal opportunities," when every worker's son had in his satchel . . . "a diploma in bourgeois white." From the age of fifteen, his life already was like those rapids which he had to navigate later and "which carry with them a power full of certainty and suffocation." And then in 1883, he graduated from the École des Arts et des Métiers, eighteenth in a class of seventy-seven. A little later, at the age of twenty-seven, he married Anne Guyader, the daughter of his boss in the railway yard. From that point on, "everything is settled and established. There is no further appeal." He feels this even at the moment when the priest marries them, and then he forgets about his anxiety. The years pass, the household goes from one city to another, constantly moving in and moving out, never settling down anywhere. Time wears on, and life remains provisory, but, nevertheless, each day is like all the others in its abstraction. Yet Antoine dreams, without too much conviction, that "something will happen." But nothing happens. He consoles himself. He will reveal his true worth in the great struggles. But while he waits for these lofty circumstances, the little ones imperceptibly toss him and wilt him, like a salad. "True courage consists in overcoming small enemies." Nevertheless, he rises in the world, irresistibly. He first experiences "the most insidious peace of all," he listens to the bourgeois sirens. Performing the false duties which they give him—towards the Company, towards Society, *even* towards his former comrades—he learns how to extract from them what we would call a vital minimum of good conscience. However, "the pile of years mounts." The desires, hopes, memories of youth are all buried "within this darkness of condemned thoughts where human forces founder." The Company devours its agents: for fifteen years there has been no man less conscious of himself than Antoine Bloyé. "He is carried along by the demands, the ideas, the judgments of work." He hardly glances at the newspapers: "the events described there are taking place on another planet and don't concern him." He passionately reads "descriptions of machines" in the technical journals. He lives, or rather his body imitates the attitudes of life. But the sources of his life, the inner spring of his actions are not found within him, in fact, "complicated powers prevented him from coming down to earth." What Nizan wrote of a rich Englishman of Aden could be applied to his father by only changing a few words, nothing, really. "Each being is divided among the men he might have been; he had allowed to triumph that one for whom life consisted in raising or lowering the price of Abyssinian leather . . . Struggling against creatures of reason like firms, unions, corporations of dealers—do you call these actions?" Certainly Bloyé hasn't much power, but what of it? Isn't everything in his profession abstract? Projects, bills, stacks of paper, isn't everything *already* decided elsewhere, by others, far away? This man is only a showroom for his company; his "full employment" leaves him at the same time vacant and at large. He sleeps very little, works himself to the bone, carries sacks and wooden beams on his back, is the last to leave the office, but as Nizan says: "all his work serves to hide his essential inactivity."

I know this. I spent ten years of my life under the thumb of a polytechnician. He killed himself at his job, or rather, somewhere in Paris, his job had doubtlessly decided that he should kill himself. He was the most futile of men. When he returned to himself on Sunday, he found a desert in which he lost his way; he managed to hold on, nevertheless, saved by his somnolence or by tantrums of vanity. When they pensioned him off, it was war-time. Happily, he had newspapers to read. He cut out articles and pasted them in the pages of a notebook. At least he declared his game for one and all to see. His flesh was an abstraction.

For the child Bloyé, the outrage stemmed from an unbearable contradiction: Antoine had a real body, tough and capable, once even avid, and now this body imitated life. Mobilized by far-off abstractions, scuttling his rich passions, he changed himself into a creature of reason: "Antoine was a man who had a profession and a temperament: that was all. That is all that a man is, in the world inhabited by Antoine Bloyé. There are nervous merchants, cheerful engineers, bilious workers, ill-tempered notaries. People say these things and think they have arrived at the definition of a man, just as they would say, a black dog, a tiger cat. A doctor had said to him: 'You have a nervous, sanguine disposition,' and he had said everything. Everything there was to say. Everyone could handle him now. Like a piece of money whose value is known, he circulated among other coins."

The child adored his father. I don't know whether he would have noticed this inner destitution by himself. Nizan's grief was that his father was a better man than many others. Neglecting many warnings, he finally realized, too late, what he was, contemplating his life with horror; this meant that he saw his death and loathed it. He had lied to himself for half a century, trying to persuade himself that he could still "become someone new, unknown, who would be the real him." Suddenly he realized the impossibility of change. This impossibility was death in the midst of life. Death draws the line under the column of figures, and makes the addition. But for Nizan's father, the line was already drawn, the addition had been made. This schematic, half-generalized being shared the bed of a woman who wasn't, any more than he, a singular person, but only a center of diffusion for pious thought, prefabricated in Rome, and who, like him, had doubtlessly suppressed simple and voracious needs. He denounced their failure to his terrified son. One night he got out of bed: "He carried his clothes over his arm and dressed at the foot of the staircase ... He went out ... 'I am superfluous,' he told himself, 'I am a surplus man. I serve no purpose, already, I no longer exist. If I let myself fall into the water, there would only be an invitation to the funeral, I'm a failure, I'm finished . . .' Shivering, he started back to the house. He passed his hand over his face and felt his beard which had grown during the night. Near the house, his wife and sons had awakened and were looking for him, calling him. He heard their sharp voices from afar but he refused to answer. He left them in their anxiety to the very last minute, to punish them. They were afraid he might have committed suicide. Approaching them, he said with suppressed rage: 'So I no longer have the right to do as I please?' Ignoring them, he went up to his room."

These nocturnal flights were no novelist's invention. Nizan talked to me about his father, and I know that all of this is true. Meditation upon death incites suicide, from vertigo, or impatience. But I ask you to imagine the feelings of an adolescent, awakened in the middle of the night by his mother, who says: "Your father isn't in his room. This time I'm sure he is going to kill himself." Death enters him, settles down at the crossroads of all his paths. It is the end and the beginning. Dead in advance, his father wants to enlist before he is called. This is the meaning and the conclusion of a stolen life. But it is this paternal life which occupied Nizan like a foreign power. His father infected him with death, which should be a terminus. When this disillusioned old man—the doctors called him neurotic—fled from his house, driven by fear, his son feared two deaths in one: the first, in its imminence, presaged the other, giving to it its face of horror. The father howled at death and each night, the child died of fright. In this return to nothingness of a life which had been nothingness, the child believed he saw his own destiny: "everything is decided, established, from now on, there is no appeal." He would be this superfluous young man, then this carcass, and then nothing. He had identified himself with another man's strong maturity, and when the other revealed his wounds, my friend alienated himself from this mortal despair. The unseemly wanderings of the engineer multiplied when Nizan was fifteen, and between the age of fifteen and sixteen, this adolescent took out insurance for eternal life: in a final effort, he asked the church to give him immortality. Too late: when faith has once been lost, all the disgust of the century isn't enough to bring it back. He lived out his alienation. Believing himself another, he deciphered every minute in the light of another's existence. Everywhere he came upon the traps which had been set for his father. Affable and deceitful people surrounded him with flattery and false victories:

academic prizes, small gifts, invitations. The engineer's son would become a member of the teaching body. And afterwards? Professors, like heads of railroad yards, settle down and move off again. Running through cities, they find a wife among the provincial bourgeoisie, and align themselves, from self-interest and weakness, with their masters. Are they any less divided men than technicians. And which is better? To make locomotives which serve a few overlords of the bourgeois state, or to give children a foretaste of death by teaching them dead languages, manipulated history, false morality? Do academics show any more indulgence towards "those vast aches, those lusts coiled up in the crevasses of their bodies"? All these *petits bourgeois* are the same: an inbecilic dignity is imposed upon them, they castrate themselves, the real object of their work escapes them, and they wake up at the age of fifty just in time to see themselves die.

I had believed, from the age of sixteen, that we were united by the same desire to write. I was wrong. A clumsy hunter, words dazzled me because I always missed them. Nizan, more precocious, had a game bag full. He found them everywhere, in dictionaries, in books, and even at liberty, on people's lips. I admired his vocabulary and the way he could use the terms he had just acquired on the very first try—words like "bi-metalism" and "percolator." But he was far from committing himself wholly to literature. As for me, I was inside it. The discovery of an adjective thrilled me. He wrote better than I did, and, with his father's mournful eyes, watched himself write. The words deflated or changed into dead leaves: can we justify ourselves with words? Under fire of death, literature became a parlor game, a variation of canasta. A professor writes: this is only natural. They encourage him; the same traps will serve for the engineer and the writer: flattery, temptations. At the age of forty, all these valets are carcasses. Honors concealed Valéry: he frequented princes, queens, powerful industralists, dining at their tables. He was working for them. The magnification of the Word becomes direct profit for the great of this world: men are taught to take the word for the thing. It is less onerous. Nizan understood that. He was afraid of losing his life by resembling these whisps of voices.

He began *repeating* the dismal follies of his father. He started his nocturnal races, his flights. He walked through streets and suddenly "he realized that he must die (and) with one blow, be separated from these passers-by . . . He knew this thing with a single movement of knowledge, with a particular and perfect knowledge." It was not an idea, "but totally naked anguish . . . scornful of all forms." He then believed he possessed a fundamental and material intuition, that he apprehended the undivided unity of his body through the unity of its radical negation. I don't think it was any of these things: we don't even have that, we can't even communicate with our nothingness without intermediaries. In fact, a shock had aroused his old acquired pain. His father's life was coursing through him, the eye of this *dead other* reopened, tainting his modest pleasures; the street became hell.

During these periods, he detested us, "friends encountered, women perceived, these were the accomplices of life, they were bills drawn against time." He never would have thought to ask our help: we were unconscious, we never would have understood. "Which of these madmen loved him skillfully enough to protect him from death?" He fled our rapacious faces, our sucking mouths, our greedy nostrils, and our eyes, always on the future. He disappeared. Three days of suicide, ended by a hangover: he was reproducing the nocturnal crises of his father; they were amplified, completed by drink and still more words. I actually think he was forcing the tragic, for lack of attaining the total and sinster sincerity of a fifty year old. No matter: his anguish wasn't a lie, and if you want the most profound and singular truth, I would say it was *this* and nothing else: the death agony of an old man gnawing the life of a very young man. He had fire, passion, and then, that implacable regard froze everything. In order to judge himself from day to day, he stood on the other side of his tomb. In fact, he was going around in a circle. In this, there was, to be sure, both haste and the dread of arriving at the end of this time which was running out, the "pile of years," these snares which he rightly avoided, this hunt for man whose meaning he didn't quite understand, but also present, in spite of everything, were his muscles and his blood. How can a well-fed young bourgeois be prevented from having confidence in the future? On occasion, he felt a grim enthusiasm, but his own exaltation frightened him and aroused his disgust. Suppose it was still another trap, one of those lies which one fabricates to stifle anguish and suffering? His revolt was the only thing in himself that he liked. It proved that he was still resisting, that he wasn't as yet engaged in those rail tracks which lead irresistibly to the garage. But he was afraid that his revolt would weaken when he thought about it: "they have thrown so many coverings over me, they almost had me, they will try again. Suppose I am only accustoming myself gradually to the condition which they are preparing for me." This was his insane dread from 1925–26: habit. "So many chains to break, secret fears to conquer, small struggles to wage . . . I dread being . . . someone of unbearable singularity, of no longer being just anybody . . . , false courage lies in wait for great occasions; real courage consists in conquering small enemies every day." Would he manage to conquer them, these gnawing termites, all these bonds—more numerous each day—would he, in five or ten years, still be capable of breaking them? He lived within enemy territory, surrounded by the familiar signs of universal alienation: "Just try and forget your filial and civic memories within your zones and prefectures." Everything tempts you to sleep, to abandon, to resignation: he went on to enumerate his abdications, "the old dreaded habits." He was also afraid of that alibi, so dear to men of culture: the empty rattle of precious and uprooted words inside his head. Moreover, meditation upon death has other more serious consequences than these intermittent conversations: it disenchants. I pursued these sparks which, for him, were only ashes. He wrote, "I am telling you that all great men are bored." But the greatest damage caused by this boredom, "this continuous warning of death," is giving birth to that byproduct of sensitive souls: the interior life. Nizan feared that his very real disgust would end by giving him an overly refined subjectivity, and would rock his griefs to the purring croon of "empty thoughts and ideas which aren't ideas." These aborted rejects of our impotence turn us away from the sight of our wounds and hemorrhages. We must never sleep. But Nizan, his eyes wide open, felt sleep coming on.

I consider this revolt an example to sons of the bourgeois, because its direct cause is not hunger or exploitation. Nizan saw all lives through the cold windowpane of death. In his eyes they became balance sheets; his perspicacity was his fundamental alienation, dislodging all other types. With what solemnity he questioned us in the presence of our death, like a devout Christian: "What have you done with your youth?" What a profound and sincere desire to gather up each of us, in our dispersal, to contain our disorders within the synthetic unity of a form: "Will man always be only a fragment of man, alienated, mutilated, estranged from himself? How many parts of him lie fallow . . . how many things in him aborted!"

These claims of a "sub-man" form the outline in the hollow of the man that he wanted to be. He cast aside his mystical *élans*, his taste for adventure, his word castles. The inaccessible image remains simple and familiar: man would be a free and harmonious body. Within him exists a corporal wisdom—since Adam, always stifled and always present. "Our most authentic needs are concealed in the most mysterious parts of our being." It is no longer a question of passionate love nor of undertakings beyond our powers: man is sedentary, he loves the earth because he can touch it; he likes to cultivate his life. Great Desire is only an empty phrase. Desires in the plural remain, modest and concrete, which balance one another. Nizan had a great affinity with Epicurus, of whom he would later write so well. The latter addressed himself to everyone, whores and slaves alike, and he never lied to them.

We shall, inevitably, think of Rousseau, and we will be right in doing so. Nizan, this man of cities, retained,

through fidelity to his childhood, a kind of rustic naturalism. We may well ask ourselves how this noble savage could
have adopted himself to the necessities of socialist production and to interplanetary nomadism. True, we shall not
find our lost liberty unless we invent it; it is forbidden to
turn back, if only to take the measure of our "authentic"
needs.

But let us leave Epicureanism and Rousseau aside: to discuss them would be pushing to their extreme point indica-
tions which are only rapid and fleeting. Nizan began with
individualism, as did all the *petits bourgeois* of his time. He
wanted to be *oneself* and the entire world separated him
from himself. He was defending his very life against men of
reason, and against the symbolic entities which they were
trying to insinuate into his heart and his muscles. He never
stopped feeling pain when describing the plenitude of
moments and passions: this plenitude which doesn't exist. It
is this which they steal from us. But he said that love was
real and that we were prevented from loving: that life
could be real, that it could bring forth a real death, but
instead, they make us die even before we are born. In this
world in reverse where the verity of a life is ultimate defeat,
he has showed that we often have "encounters with death,"
and that, each time, these confused signs awaken "our most
authentic needs." Antoine and Anne Bloyé have a little girl;
she is condemned and they know it. Pain unites these abstract personages, living together in solitude in the heart of
their promiscuity, but only for a short time. The singularity
of an accident can never save individuals.

From the age of fifteen, Nizan had understood the essential; this understanding came from the nature of his disease.

Some kinds of alienation, are, in fact, the more to be feared as they take cover under an abstract belief in our liberty. But Nizan never felt himself to be free: he had been *possessed* by someone, the "awkward unhappiness" of his father had occupied him like a foreign power, imposing itself, destroying his pleasures, his *élans*, governing him by *diktat;* and it couldn't even be said that the former worker had caused this destiny of despair; it came from every horizon, from all France, from Paris. Nizan had tried for a while, at the time of his mysticism, of R'ha and Bor'hou, to fight alone and with words, to surmount his digusts and his discords. But no, the tissues of social man crush us. Spinoza came to his aid: we must act upon the causes. But suppose the causes arc out of our hands? He deciphered his experience: "What man can triumph over his fragmentation? He will not triumph over them alone, for the causes of his division are not within him." This is the moment to bid a scornful farewell to spiritual exercises: "I was under the impression that human life was discovered by revelation. What *mystique!*" The evidence shows that we have to fight, and that we can do nothing by ourselves—since everything comes from elsewhere, even the inner contradictions which have produced the most sincere traits of our character, it is elsewhere and everywhere that the battle will be waged. Others will fight for him *out there: here,* Nizan will fight for others. The problem is just to see clearly, and to recognize his brother shadows.

With the second year of the École, he drew closer to the Communists; in short, he had come to a conclusion. But decisions are made at night, and for a long time afterwards, we fight against our own will, without recognizing it. He needed to knock on all doors, to try everything, to experiment with solutions which he had long since rejected. I think he wanted to know the goods of this world before making a vow of poverty. He set out to bury his boyhood. And then fear welled up in him, he had to break with that life. Aden was his final effort, his last attempt to find an individual way out, and his last flight as well. Arabia attracted him, just as on certain nights, the Seine had lured his father. Didn't he write, later, of Antoine Bloyé, that he "would have liked to abandon this existence . . . to become someone new, unknown, who would be truly him . . . lost, like a man who has left no forwarding address, and yet who does things, who breathes." He had to flee us and himself.

We lost him, but he couldn't lose himself. He was gnawed by a new abstraction; pursuing the world, pursuing women, all this is to grasp nothing. Aden was a condensation of Europe, only white-hot. One day Nizan did what his father—still alive—had never dared to do: he took an open car and set off down the road, without a hat, at high noon. He was found in a ditch, unconscious but alive. This suicide liquidated some of the old fears. Returning to life, he looked around him and saw "the most destitute state of all, the economic state." The Colonies denounced a regime which, in Metropolitan France, was surrounded by clouds. He returned. He had understood the causes of our slavery. The terror in him became an aggressive force; it was hatred. He no longer battled insidious and anonymous infiltrations. He had seen the nakedness of exploitation, of oppression. He had understood that his adversaries had names, faces, that they were men—men who were doubtlessly unhappy and alienated like his father and himself, but who were "defending and preserving their unhappiness and its causes, with deceit, with violence, with obstinacy and skill." On the night of his return, when he knocked at my door, he knew that he had tried everything, that his back was to the wall, that the exits are all false windows save one: war. He came back into the midst of his enemies in order to fight them: "I must no longer be afraid to hate, I must no longer blush to be a fanatic . . . I owe them evil: they all but lost me."

Finished: he found his community, and was received within it; it protected him against them. But as I am now presenting him to the young readers of today, I must answer the question which they will be sure to ask: did he finally discover what he was searching for? What could the Communist Party give this man who was skinned alive, who suffered to his marrow from the disease of dying? We have to ask ourselves this scrupulously. I am here narrating an exemplary existence, which is just the opposite of an edifying life. Nizan made himself a new skin and nevertheless, the old man—the old young man—lived on. From 1929 to 1939 I saw less of him, but I can give the meaning of these encounters—the more lively as they were so brief. I believe that today we choose family against politics. Nizan chose both, with one gesture. Aeneas had grown weary of carrying the sad old Anchises for so long. With one shrug, he let him fall on his back: suddenly he was a husband and father, in order to kill his own father. But paternity alone doesn't suffice to cure childhood. On the contrary, the authority of a new head of a family condemns him to repeat the age-old childishness which Adam has bequeathed us through our parents. My friend knew the tune: from father to murdered son, from father to son renewed. He wanted to give this the death blow: he would become *another* and would restrain himself from family caprices through public discipline. It remains to be seen whether he succeeded.

Doctrine overwhelmed him. He detested conciliations, and Leibniz, their Great Master, more than all the others. Forced by the program to study the *Discourse on Metaphysics*, he took his revenge by drawing—with great talent, moreover—this philosopher put to flight, wearing a Tyrolean hat, his right buttock stamped with Spinoza's footprint. From the *Ethics* to *Das Kapital*, the passage, on the contrary, was easy. Nizan made Marxism into his second nature, or, if you prefer, his Reason. His eyes were Marxist, and his ears, as well as his head. Marx finally explained his incomprehensible wretchedness, his want, his anguish. He saw the world and saw himself in it. But above all, at the same time that this doctrine legitimized his hatreds, it reconciled within him the opposing speeches of his parents. The rigor of techniques, the exactitude of the sciences, the patience of reason—all these were retained. But, with the same stroke, the shabbiness of positivism, its absurd refusal "to know through causes" was left behind. The engineers were left with the sad world of means, and the means of the means. Absolute Ends were proposed to the worried young man who wanted to save his soul: bringing History to light, bringing about the Revolution, preparing man and his reign. They didn't speak of salvation, nor of personal immortality, but they gave him the right to survive, anonymous or famous, in the womb of a common undertaking which would only end with mankind. He placed everything within Marxism: physical and metaphysical, the passion both to act and to reclaim his acts, his cynicism and his eschatological dreams. Man was his future. But now was the moment to cut the pattern, others would take it upon themselves to sew it. He experienced the giddy pleasure of pulling everything to pieces for the good of humanity. At first this didn't include words, which had suddenly ceased to have any ballast. He distrusted them because they served evil masters; but everything changed when he could turn them against the enemy. He used their ambiguity to confound, their vague charms to seduce. In the service of the Communist Party, literature was even allowed to become small talk. If it wished, it could turn three somersaults, like the ancient wise men: all words are good against the enemies of man. The Revolution gave permission to steal them, nothing more. But that was enough. For ten years, Nizan went about pilfering, and then produced, with one stroke, the sum of his larcenies: vocabulary. He understood his role of Communist writer, and for him, it came to the same thing whether he discredited the enemies of man or their language. Everything is allowed: the law of the jungle. The Word of the masters is a lie: we shall demonstrate its sophisms, while, at the same time, inventing sophisms to be used against them. We shall lie to them, even going so far as to play the clown. This is how we prove, while we speak, that the words of the Master are clowning. Today these games have become suspect. The East edifies. It has given our provines a new respect for the "knick-knacks of sonorous inanity." I have said that we were serious: now we are caught between two counterfeit currencies, one of which comes from the Orient, the other from the West. In 1930, there was only one for us to destroy: the intellectual had as his mission to twist words and to tangle the strands of bourgeois ideology. Snipers set fire to the brush, whole linguistic sectors crumbled into ashes. Nizan rarely played the clown, seldom lending himself to this sleight-of-hand. He lied, as did everyone in this golden age, when he was sure that he wouldn't be believed. Calumny had just been born. Nimble and gay, it approached poetry. But these practices reassured him. We know that he wanted to write against death and that death had changed the letters under his pen into dead leaves. He was afraid of being duped, of losing his life by playing with the wind. Now he was told that he had not been wrong, that literature is a weapon in the hands of our masters, but he was given a new mission: in a negative period, a book can be an act if the revolutionary writer sets about deconditioning language. Everything is allowed him—even creating a style for himself. For the wicked, this will be the sugar-coating of a bitter pill; for good men, a call to vigilance. When the sea is singing, don't jump in. Nizan studied negative form. His hatred was a maker of pearls: he took the pearls and threw them at us, rejoicing that he could serve common ends through a world which was so personal. His fight against the particular dangers threatening a young bourgeois became a duty, without being forced to change its immediate objective. He spoke of impotent fury and of hatred. He wrote of Revolution.

Thus it is the Party who made the writer. But what of the Man? Did he finally have his "field," his plenitude? Was he happy? I do not think so. The same factors which take happiness away from us render us forever incapable of enjoying it. Then the Doctrine was clear and rejoined his

personal experience. Linked to the present structures of society, his alienations would disappear with the bourgeois
class. But he didn't believe that he would see socialism in his
lifetime, nor, even had he seen it in the last days of his life,
would he have believed that this metamorphosis of the world
would leave enough time to change the old habits of a dying
man. Nevertheless, he had changed. He never again returned
to his former desolation, he never again feared that he would
let his life be lost. He had tonic rages and joys. Wholeheartedly he accepted being only the *negative man,* the writer of
demoralization and debunking. Was that enough to satisfy
the serious child he had never ceased to be? In one sense,
yes. Before joining the Party, he clung desperately to his
refusals. Since he could not be real, he would be empty. He
would derive his unique value from his dissatisfaction, from
his frustrated desires. But sensing his torpor spreading, he
was in terror of its taking hold, and of one day, foundering
in consent. As a Communist, he consolidated his resistances.
Up to that point, he had never ceased to fear this cancer,
the social man. The Party socialized him without tears. His
collective being was none other than his individual person;
this was enough to consecrate the undercurrents which disturbed him. Did he judge himself a monstrous abortion?
They hoisted him onto the rostrum, where he showed his
wounds, and said: "This is what the bourgeois have done to
their own children." He had turned his violence against
himself; now he made bombs with it which he tossed at the
palaces of industry. These structures were undamaged, but
Nizan was delivered. He controlled his damnable surliness,
but he didn't feel it, any more than a loud singer hears his

own voice. This poor subject made himself into a dreaded object.

He was not so easily delivered of death, or rather, of the shadow which it cast across his life. But this adolescent, gnawed by a strange anguish, won, when he became a man, the right to die for his own sake. Marxism revealed to him his father's secret. Antoine Bloyé's solitude came from his betrayal. This worker-become-bourgeois incessantly thought of "the comrades he had known on the work sites of the Loire and among the guards of the railyard, those who were on the side of the servants, on the side of a life without hope. He said . . . a word which he would force himself to forget, which would then disappear, only to reappear at the time of his disintegration, on the eve of his own death: 'I am really a traitor.' And he was." He had crossed the line and betrayed his class, only to find himself, a simple molecule, in the molecular world of the *petits bourgeois*. He felt his destitution a hundred times, and one day, especially, when, during a strike, he watched the marching line of the workers: "These men without importance bore far away from him the force, the friendship, the hope from which he was excluded. That evening Antoine thought of how lonely he was. A man without communion. The truth of life was on the side of those who had not 'succeeded.' These men there aren't alone, he thought. They know where they are going."

This turncoat had disintegrated, whirling around in the pulverized dust of the bourgeoisie. He was experiencing alienation, the unhappiness of the rich in having become the accomplices of those who exploit the poor. This communion of "men without importance" might have been a defense against death. With them, he might have experienced the plenitude of grief and friendship. Without them, he was without shelter, defunct in advance, the same wrong move had severed his human ties and his life. Was M. Nizan really this disconsolate deserter? I know nothing about him. In any case, his son saw him as such. Nizan discovered, or thought he had discovered, the reason for a thousand slight resistances with which he had opposed his father: he loved the man in him, he detested the betrayal. I ask of the well-intentioned Marxists who pored over my friend's case, who explained him by the obsession to betray, to re-read his works with their eyes open, if they still can, and not to retreat from the truth which glows there. It is true: this traitor's son speaks often of treason; he writes in *Aden:* "I might have been a traitor. I might have suffocated." And in *Les Chiens de Garde:* "If we betray the bourgeoisie for the sake of men, do not blush to admit that we are traitors." Antoine Bloyé is a traitor to men, and again in *La Conspiration,* the sad Pluvinage is another traitor, the son of a policeman and a policeman himself. But just what does this much-repeated word mean? That Nizan was selling himself to Daladier? When they are speaking of others, our left wing reactionaries start having ignoble shudders of fright. I know of nothing dirtier or more puerile, unless it is "virtuous" women when they are slandering a woman who is free. Nizan wanted to write, he wanted to live. What need had he for thirty miserable pieces of silver drawn on secret funds? But, as the son of a worker-turned-bourgeois, he wondered what he might very well be, bourgeois or worker? His principal worry was, without any doubt, this civil war within himself. Traitor or proletariat, M. Nizan had made his son into a bourgeois traitor: this bourgeois in spite of himself crossed the line in the reverse direction; but that isn't so easy. When intellectual Communists want to laugh, they call themselves proletariats: "We do manual work at home." Lace-makers, in a manner of speaking. More lucid and more demanding, Nizan saw in them, in himself, *petits bourgeois* who had taken sides with the people. Between a Marxist novelist and a skilled worker, the gap isn't filled; one side smiles sweetly at the other, but if the writer takes a single step, he falls into the ditch. All very well for a bourgeois who is the son of bourgeois. Fine feelings can't change the facts of birth. But Nizan was a blood relative of his new allies. He remembered his grandfather who had "remained on the side of the servants of life without hopes." He had grown up like the children of the railroad workers, in landscapes of smoke and iron. A diploma from *Quat'zarts*, however, had sufficed to plunge his own childhood into solitude, to impose an irreversible metamorphosis upon his entire family. He never re-crossed the line. He betrayed the bourgeoisie without rejoining the enemy camp and was obliged to remain like "the Pilgrim," with a foot on each side of the frontier. To the end, he was the friend of "those who had not succeeded," but he was never able to become their brother. This was no one's fault, except the bourgeoisie who had made his father one of them. This discreet absence, this vacuum always troubled him. He had listened to the bourgeois sirens: he waited, scrupulous but worried. Unable to participate in the "communion of servants, of those who live without hope," he never consider himself sufficiently protected against temptations, against death. He experienced the comradeship of militants, without escaping his solitude, the heritage of a betrayal.

His life was not to be stolen from him. Saved from an unknown death, he looked at his own death. It would not be that of the head of a railroad yard. But this negative man, deprived of the most meager fulfillment, knew that, ultimately, he would meet with an irreparable defeat, following which, nothing more would happen than the disappearance of a refusal. In sum, a very Hegelian death. It would be the negation of a negation. I doubt whether Nizan derived the slightest consolation from this philosophic view. He made a long trip to the Soviet Union. Before leaving, he confided his hope to me; there, perhaps, men were immortal. Perhaps there, the abolition of classes filled the breaches. United in a long-term undertaking, workers were changed by death into other workers; these workers into still others, and the generations succeeded each other, always others, and always the same.

He returned. His affection for me didn't altogether preclude some zealous propaganda. He informed me that reality exceeded all hopes, except on one point. Revolution delivers men from the fear of living, but not of dying. He had questioned the best people there. They had all replied that they thought of death and that their zeal for work couldn't save them from this mysterious personal disaster. Stripped of his illusions, Nizan renounced forever the old Spinozist dream. He would never know this affirmative fulfillment of the complete mode, which, by the same token, overflows its boundaries and returns to infinite substance. In the heart of collective commitment, he would retain the singularity of his anxiety. He didn't want to think about himself any more, and he succeeded. His only attention was spent on objective necessities. However, through this hollow, indissoluble nothingness, through this ball of emptiness, he remained the most fragile and "the most irreplaceable" of human beings. Individualized in spite of himself, a few scattered phrases show that he ended by choosing the most individual solution: "A man needs many powers and many creations to escape from nothingness. . . . Antoine finally understood that he would only have been saved by the creations he might have achieved, by the exercise of his powers." Nizan was not an engineer, nor a politician. He was a writer. The exercise of his power could only be stylistic exercise. He put his faith in his books. Through them he would survive. In the heart of this disciplined existence, each day more militant, death brought its cancer of anarchy. That lasted, in spite of everything, for ten years. He devoted himself to his Party, lived in discontent, and wrote passionately. A squall came from Moscow— the Trials—which shook him, but without uprooting him. He endured. No matter. This revolutionary lacked blinders. His virtue and his fault was to demand everything *at once*, as young men are apt to do. This man of negation didn't take part in the mass denials of assents once given. He kept silent about the trials. That was all.

I thought of him as the perfect Communist; it was convenient to do so. In my eyes, he became the mouthpiece of the Politburo. I took his periods of ill humor, his illusions, his frivolities for attitudes acquired from on high. In July, 1939, in Marseille, where I ran into him by chance, for the last time, he was in gay spirits, about to sail for Corsica. In his eyes I read the joviality of the Party. He talked about the war, believing that we would avoid it: Immediately, I translated to myself: "The Politburo is very optimistic, its mouthpiece declares that the negotiations with the USSR will bear results. Before autumn, it says, the Nazis will be on their knees."

September taught me that it was advisable to disassociate my friend's opinions from Stalin's decisions. I was surprised by this, even annoyed. Apolitical, stubbornly refusing any commitment, my heart, of course, was with the Left, as was everyone's. Nizan's rapid rise had flattered me, given me some importance or other in my own eyes. Our friendship had been so precious, and we were still taken for one another so easily, that I, too, was writing lead articles on foreign policy for *Le Soir*—and I could tell you a thing or two about that! If Nizan knew nothing, what a comedown for both of us. We would again become one-legged men, or sitting ducks, unless, of course, he had fooled me deliberately. This conjecture amused me for a few days. I really believed it. I was an idiot. But he retained his important functions, his total knowledge of what was then called "the diplomatic checkerboard" and basically, I preferred it that way. A few days later, I learned from the newspapers, when I was in Alsace, that the mouthpiece of the Politburo had just left the Party, and that his rupture was a violent one. So, I was wrong about everything and always had been. I don't know what prevented my falling into a stupor then and there: my futility, perhaps. This, and the fact that at the same moment I discovered the monumental error of a whole generation—our generation—which had fallen asleep on its feet. They were pushing us towards massacres, across a ferocious prewar period, and we thought we were strolling across the lawns of Peace. In Brumath, I lived our immense, anonymous awakening. It was there, finally and forever, that I lost my distinguishing characteristics—that absorbed me.

Today, I recall that apprenticeship without displeasure, and I tell myself that Nizan also was *unlearning* at the same time. How he must have suffered! It isn't easy to leave a Party. There are all its laws that must be wrenched from oneself before they can be broken. There are all these men whose beloved, familiar faces will become the dirty mugs of the enemy, this somber crowd which will continue to march along stubbornly, and which he will watch marching off to disappear. My friend became an interpreter. He found himself alone in the north, surrounded by English troops: alone among the English, just as he had been during the worst moments of his life in Arabia, fleeing from the horsefly's sting, separated from everyone, and saying no.

To be sure, he gave political explanations for all this. His old friends accused him of moralism, while he reproached them for not being Machiavellian. He would have approved, he said, the sovereign cynicism of the Soviet leaders. All means are good to save the country for socialism. But the French Communists had refused to imitate that cavalier manner, nor, had they understood that they should have appeared to break with the Soviet Union. Now they would lose any influence they might have had, because they hadn't assumed an indignant pose.

He wasn't the only one to give these reasons; and how shallow they seem today! In fact, this recourse to Machiavelli was nothing more than a retort. Nizan wanted to prove his realism. A tactician, he was condemning a tactic: noth-

ing more. Above all, let no one think that he had resigned in
fury, or from a nervous disorder. But his letters prove the
contrary, that he was overcome with rage. Today we know
the circumstances and the documents better. We understand the motives for the Russian policy. I am inclined to
think that he acted rashly, that he shouldn't have broken
with his friends, with his real life. Had he lived, I tell myself, the Resistance would have led him, as it did many
others, back into the fold. But this is none of my business. I
only want to show that he was cut to the quick, pierced
through the heart, and that this unexpected turnabout revealed to him his own nakedness, sending him back to his
desert, to himself.

He wrote to *Le Soir*, where he had been in charge of
foreign policy. A single theme: unite with the Soviet Union
against Germany. He had developed this theme so many
times that he had become convinced by it. When Molotov
and Ribbentrop put the final signature to their Pact, Nizan
shouted himself hoarse, urging, at his own behest, and with
threats, a Franco-Soviet *reapprochement*. In the course of
the summer of 1939, he went to see the Soviet leaders in
Corsica. They spoke to him warmly, praised his articles, and
then, when he went to bed at night, they held long secret
meetings. Did they know what was in the offing for us?
Nothing is less certain. September's revelations shattered a
Party which was still on vacation. In Paris we watched
journalists taking on the gravest responsibilities in blind
confusion. In any case, Nizan didn't doubt for a moment
that they had lied to him. He suffered deeply from this, not
in his vanity, nor even in his pride, but much more profoundly, in his humility. He had never crossed class lines,

and he knew it. But suspect in his own eyes, he saw in the leaders' silence the sign of the people's distrust. Ten years of obedience hadn't disarmed him. They would never forgive this dubious ally for the betrayal of his father.

This same father had worked for others, for gentlemen who stole from him his force and his life. Nizan had become a Communist as a protest against that. But now he learned that the Communists had used him as a tool, hiding the real objectives from him. They had prompted him with lies, which he had repeated in good faith; from far away, invisible men had stolen his force and life from him, too. He had put all his stubbornness into refusing the corrosive and saccharin words of the bourgeoisie, and, with one blow, he found what he had most feared in the midst of the Party of Revolution: the alienation of language. Communist words, so simple, almost crude—what were they after all? Leaking gas. He had written of his father: "(He had committed) lonely acts which had imposed an exterior and inhuman power upon him . . . acts which weren't part of an authentic human existence, which had no real results. They were simply acts filed away in dusty folders and tied with string . . ." Now, his own militant acts came back to him, and they were identical with those of the bourgeois engineer: no "real results"; scattered articles in dusty newspapers, hollow phrases dictated by an exterior power, the alienation of a man to the necessities of international politics, a shallow life, void of its substance, an "empty reflection of this decapitated being who walked through the ashes of time with hasty steps, without directions or signposts."

He returned to his eternal worry: he was fighting for his life and the Party had stolen it from him. He had fought against death, and death had come to him through the Party. He was wrong, I think. The massacre was engendered by the Earth and rose everywhere. But I am describing what he himself felt. Hitler, his hands freed, was going to hurl himself upon us. In his state of shock, Nizan imagined that our army of peasants and workers would be exterminated with the consent of the Soviet Union. He spoke to his wife of still another fear. He would return too late, worn out by an interminable war. He would survive only in order to mull over his regrets, his bitterness, haunted by the base currency of memories. Against these returning threats, only revolt remained, the old anarchistic and desperate revolt. Since everything betrayed men, he would preserve the little humanity which remained by saying no to everything.

I know: the angered soldier of 1940, with his prejudices, his principles, his experience, all these instruments of thought, looked far different from the young adventurer who set out for Aden. He wanted to reason, to see clearly, to weigh everything, to keep his ties with those "who had not succeeded." The bourgeoisie was waiting for him, affable and corrupting. He had to thwart them. Betrayed, as he believed he was by the Party, he discovered the compelling need not to betray in turn. He persisted in calling himself a Communist. He patiently reflected: how to correct deviations without falling into idealism? He kept notebooks and ledgers, writing a great deal. But did he really believe that he alone was going to change the inflexible movement of these millions of men? A lone Communist is lost. The truth of his last months was hatred. "I want," he had written, "to fight real men." He was thinking then of the bourgeois, but the bourgeois have no faces. The one whom we think we are hating disappears, to be seen again at Standard Oil or at the Stock Exchange. Until his death, Nizan harbored special grudges: one friend had not stood by him, through cowardice; another had encouraged him to break with the Party and had then condemned him. His rage was fed by vivid memories. He saw eyes, mouths, smiles, the color of a skin, a harsh or hypocritical expression—and he hated these too-human faces. If he ever experienced fulfillment, it was during those violent hours when, choosing the heads to roll, his fury changed into delight. When he was completely alone, "without directions or signposts" and reduced to the inflexibility of his refusals, death came and seized him. *His* death, idiotic and savage, just as he had always dreaded and predicted it would be. An English soldier took the time to bury with him his diaries and his last novel, *La Soirée à Somosierra*, which he had almost completed. The earth swallowed that testament. When, in 1945, his wife tried, with precise directions, to find his papers again, among them the last lines which he had written for the Party, nothing was left. Around this time, the defamation started to take itself seriously. They condemned the dead man for high treason. Quite a life! Alienated, then stolen, then hidden, and finally, saved, even in death, for saying no. His life was also exemplary because it was an outrage, like all lives that are made, like all those which are manufactured today for young men. But his life was a conscious outrage and one which denounced itself publically.

Here is his first book. They thought they had obliterated him, but he comes back to life because a new public needs him. I hope that his two masterpieces will be returned to us soon: *Antoine Bloyé,* the most beautiful and lyrical of funeral orations, and *La Conspiration.* But it is not a bad thing to begin with this naked revolt: at the origin of everything is, first of all, refusal. Now, will the old men be so good as to move aside, and let this adolescent speak to his brothers: "I was twenty once, and I shall let no one say that it is life's most wonderful age."

The Paintings
of Giacometti

The Paintings of Giacometti

Seated at the back of a room at the Sphinx, I could see several nude women. The distance separating us (with the gleaming parquet floor seeming insuperable in spite of my yearning to cross it) impressed me as much as the women themselves.*

The result: four inaccessible figures seen vertically, balanced on an edge of background formed by the floor. He painted them as he saw them—*distant*. But these four tall whores are endowed with a cumbersome *presence*. They seem to surge from the floor, ready to fall on him in a heap, like the lid of a box. "I had often seen them, in a little room, rue de l'Echaude, but on one particular evening, they seemed threateningly close." Distance, in his eyes, far from being accidental, is part of the innermost nature of the object. These whores at twenty yards, twenty insuperable yards remove— are forever fixed in the glare of his hopeless desire. His studio is an archipelago, a disorder of diverse distances. Against the wall, a Mother Goddess retains all the proximity of an obsession. When I retreat, she advances, closest when I am farthest away. The small statue at my feet is a pedestrian seen in the rear-view mirror of an automobile—about to disappear. In vain do I approach him; he keeps his distance. These solitudes repell the visitor with all the insuperable length of a room, a lawn, a glade one dare not cross. They bear witness to the strange paralysis which grips Giacometti at the sight of a fellow creature. Not that he is a misan-

---

Concerning an exhibition of paintings by Giacometti at the Galerie Maeght. Published in Les Temps Modernes, *June, 1954.*

* Letter to Matisse, November, 1950.

thrope. This numbness is the effect of surprise mingled with fear, often admiration, and sometimes respect. True, he is distant, but distance, after all, was invented by man and has no meaning outside the context of human space; it separated Hero from Leander and Marathon from Athens, but does not separate one pebble from another. I first understood distance one evening in April, 1941. I had spent two months in a prison camp, which is like saying, in a sardine can, where I had experienced absolute proximity. My skin was the boundary of my living space. Day and night I felt the warmth of a shoulder or a thigh against my body. But it was never disturbing, as the others were a part of me. On my first night of freedom, a stranger in my native city, not having yet reached my friends of former days, I pushed open the door of a café. Suddenly, I experienced a feeling of fear—or something close to fear. I could not understand how these squat, bulging buildings could conceal such deserts. I was lost; the few drinkers seemed more distant than the stars. Each of them was entitled to a huge section of bench, to a whole marble table, while I, to touch them, would have had to cross a "gleaming wooden floor" that separated us. If these men, shimmering comfortably within their tubes of rarefied gas seemed inaccessible to me, it was because I no longer had the right to place my hand on their shoulder or thigh, or to call one of them "fat-head." I had rejoined bourgeois society, where I would have to learn to live once again "at a respectful distance." This sudden agoraphobia betrayed my vague feeling of regret for the collective life from which I had been forever severed. The same is true of Giacometti. For him, distance is not voluntary isolation, nor even a movement of withdrawal. It is a

requirement, a ceremony, a sense of difficulty, the product
—and he says this himself*—of powers of attraction and
forces of repulsion. If he was unable to cross those few feet
of shining wood separating him from the nude women, it
was because poverty or shyness nailed him to his chair. But if
he felt the distance insuperable, it was because he so yearned
to touch that luxuriant flesh. He rejects promiscuity, the casual relations of proximity, because he wants friendship and
love. He dares not take for fear of being taken. His figurines
are solitary, but when placed together, in whatever combination, they are united by their solitude, to suddenly form a
small magical society. "Looking at some figures which I had
set at random on the floor, in order to clear the table, I
realized that they formed two groups which seemed to cor-
respond exactly to what I had been seeking. I mounted the
two groups on bases, without making the slightest change.
. . ." An exhibition by Giacometti is a populace. He has
sculpted men who cross a square without seeing each other;
they pass, hopelessly alone, and yet, *they are together*. They
will lose each other forever, but this would not have happened had they not tried to find each other. However, he
has defined his universe better than I possibly could when he
wrote, of one of his groups, that it reminded him of "a
corner of a forest observed over the course of many years,
and whose trees, with naked slender trunks, seemed like
people, suddenly frozen in their tracks, speaking to one
another." And what is this circular distance—which only
words can span—if not the negative concept of *vacuum*.
Ironic, defiant, ceremonious and tender, Giacometti sees
empty space everywhere. Surely not everywhere, you will

* Letter to Matisse, November, 1950.

say, for some objects touch others. But this is exactly the point. Giacometti is certain of nothing, not even that. For weeks on end, he has been fascinated by the legs of a chair that did not *touch* the floor. Between things as between men, the bridges are broken, and emptiness seeps in everywhere, every creature concealing his own. Giacometti became a sculptor because he was obsessed by vacuum. Of one of his small statues, he wrote: "Me, hurrying down a street in the rain." Sculptors rarely do a bust of themselves; when they attempt a "portrait of the artist" they look at themselves from the outside, in a mirror—prophets of objectivity. But imagine a lyric sculptor. What he tries to convey are his internal feelings, the boundless void enclosing him, separating him from shelter and abandoning him to the storm. Giacometti is a sculptor because he carries his vacuum along with him, as a snail its shell, because he wants to retain his awareness of all its facets and dimensions. Sometimes both he and his minuscule portion of exile are companionable—at others, he cannot bear the sight of it. A friend once moved in with him. Pleased at first, Giacometti soon found his presence disturbing. "One morning I opened my eyes, and there were his trousers and jacket *in my vacuum.*" But at other times, he clings to walls, for the void surrounding him portends fall, landslides, and avalanches. In any case, he must bear witness to its presence.

Can he accomplish this through sculpture? The figure is already "ten paces," "twenty paces" away when it leaves his fingers, and whatever we do, it will remain there. It is the statue who decides from what distance it must be seen, like court protocol establishing the remove from which the king may be addressed. Reality engenders the no-man's land surrounding it. A figure by Giacometti is the artist himself producing his small pocket of nothingness. Yet all of these slight absences, as much a part of us as our names, our shadows are not enough to make a world. There is also Vacuum, that universal distance from everything to everything. The street is deserted in the sunshine, but *in the midst of this emptiness*, a figure suddenly appears. The sculpture creates vacuum, *starting from plenum.* * But can it show plenum arising where before there was only vacuum? Giacometti has tried a hundred times to answer this question. His composition *The Cage* represents his "desire to abolish the base and to utilize a *limited* space for the creation of a head and face." For this is the essence of the whole problem; vacuum will forever precede the beings who inhabit it, if it is first enclosed within walls. The *Cage* is "a room which I have seen. I have even seen the curtains behind the woman. . . ." Another time, he makes "a figurine in a box, between two other boxes which are houses." In short, he frames his figures. They keep an imaginary distance, in relation to us living within an enclosed space which imposes its own distances upon them, within a prefabricated vacuum they can never fill, and which they endure rather than create. And what is this framed and inhabited vacuum, if not a painting? Lyrical when he sculpts, Giacometti becomes objective when he paints. He tries to capture the features of Annette or Diego, just as they appear in an empty room, in his deserted studio. Elsewhere I have tried to show that he approaches sculpture as a painter, since he treats a plaster statuette as though it were a figure in a

* *plenum:* the whole of space regarded as being filled with matter. (*Trans.*)

painting.* He confers an imaginary and fixed distance upon his statuettes. But inversely, one could say that he approaches painting as a sculptor, because he wants us to consider the imaginary space defined by the frame as *true* vacuum. He would like us to perceive the seated woman he has just painted through varying thicknesses of empty space. He sees his canvas as a pool of still water, with the figures perceived *in* the painting, as Rimbaud saw a room in a lake—*in transparency*. Sculpting as others paint, painting as others sculpt, is he painter or sculptor? Neither, both: painter and sculptor because this era doesn't allow him to be both sculptor and architect. Sculptor in order to restore to each his circular solitude, painter to replace men and objects within the world, that is, within the great universal Void— at times he has sculpted what he had first planned to paint.† But at other times, he knows that only sculpture (or in other instances, painting) will allow him to "realize his impressions." In any case, these two activities are inseparable and complementary. They allow him to treat all aspects of his relationship to others, depending upon whether distance originates in them, in him, or in the universe.

How can vacuum be painted? Before Giacometti, it seemed that no one had attempted to resolve this problem. For five hundred years, painting had been crammed to the bursting point; the entire universe had been forced into them. Giacometti began first by expelling the world from his canvases. It would suffice to paint his brother Diego, all

---

* He was the first to think of sculpting man as he actually is seen, that is, from a distance. He confers upon his plaster figures an *absolute distance*, just as the painter does with the inhabitants of his canvas.

† For example, *Nine Figures* (1950): "Last spring, I had wanted very much to paint them."

alone, lost in a hangar. But he still had to distinguish this figure from all that surrounds him. Ordinarily, this would be achieved by outlining his contours. But a line is produced by the intersection of two surfaces; and space cannot be made to pass for surface, and still less for volume. A line is used to separate the container from the contained. But vacuum does not contain. Could we say that Diego "is in relief" against the partition behind him? Of course not: the figure-background relationship only exists for relatively flat surfaces. Unless he is actually leaning against it, the distant partition cannot serve as a "backdrop" for Diego, because he has no real connection with it. Or rather he does; since the man and the object are in the same painting, they must maintain an accord based upon pre-established principles (hues, values, proportions), which confer unity upon the painting. But these correspondences are at the same time cancelled out by the nothingness interposed between them. No, Diego is not in relief against the gray background of a bare wall. He is there, the wall is there, and that is all. Nothing encloses, supports or contains him: *he appears*, all alone, within an immense frame of empty space. With each of his paintings, Giacometti takes us back to the moment of creation *ex nihilo*. Each painting restates the old metaphysical questions. Why is there something rather than nothing? And yet there is something—this stubborn, unjustifiable, superfluous apparition. The painted figure is hallucinatory because it takes the form of an *interrogative apparition*.

But how can the artist place a figure on the canvas without enclosing him by means of line? Will he not explode into vacuum like a deep-sea fish propelled to the surface? Not at all. Line conveys arrested flight. Representing an

equilibrium between the external and internal, it fastens itself around the form which the object assumes under the
pressure of exterior forces. Line is a symbol of inertia, of
passivity. But Giacometti does not consider the finite in
terms of a limitation to which he is subjected. For him, the
cohesiveness of reality, as well as its plenitude and determination are but one and the same, the effect of its inner
powers of affirmation. "Apparitions affirm and circumscribe
themselves in the process of defining themselves. Similar to
those strange curves studied by mathematicians, simultaneously encompassing and encompassed, the object is its
own envelope. One day, as he was doing a sketch of me,
Giacometti exclaimed in surprise: "What density! What
lines of force!" And I was even more astonished than he,
since I have always believed my features to be flabby and
commonplace. But he saw each feature as a centripetal
force. The face coils, like a buckle, buckling itself. Turn
around; you will never see a contour, only completion. Line
is the beginning of negation, the passage from being to non-
being. But Giacometti maintains that the real is absolute
positivity. *Being is*, and then, all of a sudden, it is no longer.
But there is no transition conceivable from being to nothingness. Notice how his multiple lines are *interior* to the
form he is describing. See how they represent the intimate
relationship of being with itself, the folds of a jacket, the
wrinkles in a face, the protrusion of a muscle, the direction
of a movement—all these lines are centripetal. Their aim is
to condense, to oblige the eye to follow them, always leading it back to the center of the figure. The face seems to
have contracted under the effect of some astringent substance. In a few instants it will be no larger than a fist, like a

shrunken head. However, the boundary of the body is nowhere indicated. At times the heavy mass of flesh slyly and mysteriously comes to an end, in a vague brown nimbus, somewhere beneath the tangled lines of force—and at other times, it literally has no boundary. The contours of an arm or a thigh are lost in the flashes of light dissolving it. Without warning, we are witness to an abrupt dematerialization. We are shown a seated man with his legs crossed. When I only looked at his face and torso, I was convinced that he had feet, I even thought I saw them. But when I look at them now, they disintegrate, melting into luminous haze. I no longer know where vacuum begins and where the body ends. But this is not at all comparable to Masson's technique of disintegration, where, by scattering objects over the canvas he gives them a certain ubiquity. If Giacometti has failed to delineate the shoe, it is not because he believes it without limits, but because he is counting upon us to supply them. And the fact is that the shoes are there, heavy and dense. To see them, I must simply avoid looking at them directly. To understand this technique, we must examine the sketches which Giacometti sometimes makes of his sculptures. Four women seated on a base: so far so good. But now let us examine the drawing carefully. Here is the head and neck, drawn with clear strokes, then nothing, again nothing, then an open curve which sweeps around a point—the belly and the navel. Here again is a stump of thigh, then nothing, then two vertical lines, then lower down, two others. That is all. A whole woman. What did we do? We used our knowledge to re-establish continuity, and our eyes to reassemble these *disjecta membra*. But we saw shoulders and arms on the blank paper, and we saw them because we *recognized* the head and belly. These members were indeed there, although not indicated by lines, in the same way that we sometimes conceive lucid and complete thoughts which are not formulated by words. The body is a current passing between its two extremities. We are confronted by the pure reality, the invisible tension of blank paper. But doesn't the blankness of the paper also represent empty space? Exactly, for Giacometti rejects both the inertia of matter and the inertia of pure nothingness. Vacuum is plenum, expanded and unfolded, as plenum is oriented vacuum. Reality is flashes of lightning.

Have you noticed the superabundance of white lines that striate his torsos and faces. Diego is not solidly stitched, but, in the language of dressmakers, only basted. Or, could it be that Giacometti wants "to write luminously on a dark background"? This is almost correct, for the problem is no longer one of separating plenum from vacuum, but of painting plenitude itself. Plenitude, however, is both unity and diversity at the same time. How can it be differentiated without being divided? Dark lines are dangerous; they can strike out being, or mar it with fissures. If used to outline an eye or encircle a mouth, dark lines create an impression of fistulas of empty space in the heart of reality. These white striations are there to indicate without portraying. Guiding the eye, they determine its movements, and then melt from view. But the real danger lies elsewhere. We know how well Arcimboldo* succeeded with mounds of vegetables and piles of fish. Why do his tricks delight us? Isn't it

* Giuseppe Arcimboldo (1527–1593), Milanese artist famous for his bizarre paintings in which flowers, fruit, fish or shells were compressed in such a way that they could be read as both still lifes and portraits; court painter to Rudolf II in Prague. (*Trans.*)

because we have long been familiar with this procedure? And, in their own way, haven't all our painters been Arcimboldos? They no longer stoop to composing a human head with a pumpkin, some tomatoes and a few radishes. But they compose faces every day, using a pair of eyes, a nose, two ears and thirty-two teeth. What is the difference? Take a sphere of red flesh and puncture two holes in it. Stick an enameled marble into each hole. Draw a nasal appendix and paste it on, like a false nose, under the ocular globes. Pierce a third hole and garnish it with white pebbles. Isn't that the same as replacing the indissoluble unity of the face with an assortment of heterogeneous objects? Emptiness seeps in everywhere; between the eyes and eyelids, between the lips, into the nostrils. A face becomes an archipelago. Did you say that this strange assemblage conforms to reality, that an oculist could remove the eye from its orbit, and a dentist extract the teeth? Perhaps. But then, what should the painter paint? What is? What we see? But what do we see? Some have painted the chestnut tree beneath my window as a round quivering unity, while others have painted the leaves one by one, with every vein. Do I see a leafy mass or a multiplicity? Leaves or foliage? In reality, I see both, but not quite either one, with the result that I am tossed from one point of view to the other. I certainly do not see leaves, since I am incapable of seeing each one of them in its entirety. Just as I am about to apprehend them, they escape, and when I am about to apprehend the foliage, it decomposes. In short, what I see is teeming cohesion, contained dispersal. Now try and paint that! And yet, Giacometti wants to paint what he sees, and exactly as he sees it. He wants his figures, at the heart of their original vacuum, and on an immobile canvas, to fluctuate ceaselessly between continuity and discontinuity. And the head should, at the same time, be both isolated, as it is sovereign, and also reassumed by the body, becoming a mere telescope of the belly, in the sense that we speak of Europe as a peninsula of Asia. He wants to make the eyes, nose and mouth leaves within foliage, both separate and united at the same time. And he manages to do all this—that is his singular triumph. How does he do it? By refusing to be more precise than perception. His solution is not a *vague* style of painting. Quite the contrary, he suggests the absolute precision of being within the lack of precision of perception. In themselves, and for others with better eyesight—angels, for example—these faces conform rigorously to the principle of individuation. A first glance confirms them to be plotted down to the most minute detail. And furthermore, we can recognize Diego or Annette immediately. That alone would suffice, if need be, to clear Giacometti of any charges of subjectivism. At the same time, however, we are unable to confront the painting without a certain uneasiness. In spite of ourselves, we feel an urge to call for a flashlight, or at least a candle. Is it haze, oncoming twilight, or our tired eyes? Is Diego lowering or raising his eyelids? Is he dozing? Dreaming? Or is he spying on us? To be sure, we ask ourselves these questions even in an exhibition of the worst sort of trash, in front of some awful portrait, so flabbily painted that all answers are equally possible without any one of them being inevitable. But the indeterminate quality that comes from lack of skill has nothing in common with the calculated indetermination of Giacometti, which could more accurately be termed supra-determination. I turn once again to Diego, and from one moment to the next he is alternately asleep, awake, looking at the sky, or fixing his gaze upon me. All of these are true, all of them equally obvious. But if I bend my head slightly to one side, or shift the direction of my gaze, one truth vanishes, to be replaced by another. If, weary of the struggle, I attempt to adopt one opinion, I have no recourse but to leave as quickly as possible. And even then, my final opinion will still remain a fragile probability, like discovering a face in the firelight, in an ink blot, or in a wallpaper pattern. Appearing suddenly, the shape assumes an identity which imposes itself upon me, and even though I know that others will see it differently, I am incapable of seeing it in any other way. But the face in the flames has no intrinsic truth, while in Giacometti's paintings, we are both disturbed and enchanted by the awareness that *there is a truth*, and that we are certain of its being there—there, right under our nose, if we only look for it. My vision blurs and I give up. But I have begun to understand: Giacometti dominates us because he has inverted the facts by his formulation of the problem. Take, as another example, a painting by Ingres. If I look at the tip of the Odalisque's nose, the rest of her face becomes fuzzy, a pink lump of butter spotted by rosy red lips. But now, when I focus my attention on the lips, they emerge from the blur, moist and slightly parted, and the nose disappears, swallowed up by the amorphous background. But I am not disturbed by its disappearance, since I know that I can summon it back at will—thus I feel reassured. But with Giacometti, it is just the reverse. For a detail in one of his paintings to appear precise and reassuring, all I need do is refrain from making it the explicit object of my attention. My confidence is inspired by what I see out of the corner of my eye. The more I look at Diego's eyes, the less able I am to interpret them. But while looking at his eyes, I discover his slightly sunken cheeks, and a strange smile which hovers at the corners of his mouth. Yet as soon as my obsessive need for certainty makes me lower my gaze to his mouth, everything vanishes immediately. What is his mouth like? Hard? Bitter? Ironical? Wide open? Sealed? Against this, I now *know* that his eyes, almost outside my range of vision, are half-closed. Yet, nothing prevents me from turning away, obsessed by the phantom face which is constantly forming, unforming and reforming behind me. The remarkable part is that we believe in it, as we believe in hallucinations which begin with a fleeting awareness that something has grazed us obliquely. When we turn to that side, there is nothing there. But on the other side, of course. . . .

These extraordinary figures are so perfectly immaterial that they become transparent, so totally, so fully real that they assert themselves like a physical blow and cannot be forgotten. Are they appearing or disappearing forms? Both. At times, they seem so diaphanous, that we would not dream of questioning their features, but merely pinch ourselves to determine whether they really exist. But if we persist in scrutinizing these faces, the painting in its entirety begins to live; a dark sea rolls over and submerges them, leaving only a surface splashed with soot. Then the waves roll back and we see them once more, white and naked, glittering under the water. But as soon as they reappear, they assert themselves violently, like muffled shouts reaching us from a mountain peak, informing us that someone, somewhere, is in pain and crying desperately for help. This game of appearance and disappearance, of flight and provocation, gives Giacometti's faces a certain air of coquettishness. They remind me of Galatea, fleeing her lover among the willows, but wanting him to see her at the same time. Flirtatious, yes, and graceful, because they are all action, but sinister, too, because of the emptiness that surrounds them, these creatures of nothingness achieve the plenitude of existence because they steal away and confound us. Every evening a magician has three hundred accomplices; his spectators and their second natures. He attaches to his shoulder a wooden arm clothed in a bright red sleeve. But the audience requires that he have two arms in identical sleeves. When they see two arms and two sleeves, they are satisfied. But meanwhile, a real arm, swathed in black, and invisible, produces the rabbit, the playing card, and the explosive cigarette. Giacometti's art is close to that of the magician. We are both his dupes and his accomplices. Without our avid, unthinking gullibility, the traditional errors of our senses, and the contradictions of our perception, he could never succeed in making his portraits live. His technique is a form of guesswork, based upon what he sees, but as much, and more, upon what he thinks we will see. His object is not to present us with an exact image, but to produce simulacra which, at the same time as they make no pretense of being anything other than what they are, arouse in us feelings and attitudes generally produced by an encounter with real men. At the Musée Grevin we may be either annoyed or terrified to find that we have taken a wax dummy for the guard. And nothing would be easier than weaving elaborate practical jokes on this theme. But Giacometti is not particularly given to jokes of this kind. With one exception. The single exception to which he has devoted his life. For he has long understood that artists work in the realm of the imaginary, creating only illusions. And he knows further that "monsters imitated by art" only arouse an artificial terror in the spectator. But he still never gives up hope. One day, he is going to show us a portrait of Diego, exactly like the others in appearance. Forewarned, we shall know in advance that it is only a phantom, an empty illusion, prisoner within its frame. And yet, on that day, before this mute canvas, we shall feel just the slightest shock. The same shock that we feel returning home late at night and seeing a stranger coming towards us in the dark. Then Giacometti will know that his paintings have given birth to a real emotion, and that his simulacra, without ever ceasing to be illusory, have, for a few moments, been invested with *real* powers. I hope that he will bring off this memorable trick soon. If he does not succeed, it only means that no one can. In any case, no one can go further.

Nathalie Sarraute

One of the most curious features of our literary epoch is the appearance, here and there, of penetrating and entirely negative works that may be called anti-novels. I should place in this category the works of Nabokov, those of Evelyn Waugh, and, in a certain sense, *The Counterfeiters* of André Gide. By this I don't at all mean essays that attack the novel as a genre, such as *Puissances du roman* by Roger Caillois, which I should compare, with all due allowances, to Rousseau's *Lettre sur les Spectacles*. These anti-novels maintain the appearance and outlines of the ordinary novel; they are works of the imagination with fictitious characters, whose story they tell. But this is done only the better to deceive us; their aim is to make use of the novel in order to challenge the novel, to destroy it before our very eyes while seeming to construct it, to write the novel of a novel unwritten and unwritable, to create a type of fiction that will compare with the great compositions of Dostoievsky and Meredith much as Miro's canvas, "The Assassination of Painting," compares with the pictures of Rembrandt and Rubens. These curious and hard-to-classify works do not indicate weakness of the novel as a genre; all they show is that we live in a period of reflection and that the novel is reflecting on its own problems. Such is this book by Nathalie Sarraute: an anti-novel that reads like a detective story. In fact, it is a parody on the novel of "quest" into which the author has introduced a sort of impassioned amateur detective who becomes fascinated by a perfectly ordinary couple—an old father and a daughter

Originally the preface for Portrait of a Man Unknown, *by Nathalie Sarraute, translated by Maria Jolas (George Braziller, 1958).*

who is no longer very young—spies on them, pursues them and occasionally sees through them, even at a distance, by virtue of a sort of thought transference, without ever knowing very well either what he is after or what they are. He doesn't find anything, or *hardly* anything, and he gives up his investigation as a result of a metamorphosis; just as though Agatha Christie's detective, on the verge of unmasking the villain, had himself suddenly turned criminal.

Nathalie Sarraute has a horror of the tricks of the novelist, even though they may be absolutely necessary. Is he "with," "behind," or "outside" his characters? And when he is behind them, doesn't he try to make us believe that he has remained either inside or outside? Through the fiction of this soul-detective, who knocks against the shell of these "enormous beetles" from the "outside," sensing dimly the "inside" without actually touching it, Nathalie Sarraute seeks to safeguard her sincerity as a storyteller. She takes her characters neither from within nor from without, for the reason that we are, both for ourselves and for others, entirely within and without at the same time. The without is neutral ground, it is the *within* of ourselves that we should like to be for others and that others encourage us to be for ourselves. This is the realm of the *commonplace*. For this excellent word has several meanings. It designates, of course, our most hackneyed thoughts, inasmuch as these thoughts have become the meeting place of the community. It is here that each of us finds himself as well as the others. The commonplace belongs to everybody and it belongs to me; in me, it belongs to everybody, it is the presence of everybody in me. In its very essence it is generality; in order to appropriate it, an act is necessary, an act through which I shed my particularity in order to adhere to the general, in order to become generality. Not at all *like* everybody, but, to be exact, the *incarnation* of everybody. Through this eminently social type of adherence, I identify myself with all the others in the indistinguishableness of the universal. Nathalie Sarraute seems to distinguish three concentric spheres of generality: the sphere of character, the sphere of the moral commonplace, and the sphere of art—in particular, of the novel. If I pretend to be a rough diamond, like the father in the *Portrait of a Man Unknown*, I confine myself to the first sphere; if a father refuses to give money to his duaghter, and I declare: "He ought to be ashamed of himself; and she's all he's got in the world . . . well, he can't take it with him, that's certain," then I take my position in the second sphere; and if I say of a young woman that she is a Tanagra, of a landscape that it is a Corot, or of a family chronicle that it's like something from Balzac, I am in the third. Immediately the others, who have easy access to these domains, approve and understand what I say; upon thinking over my attitude, my opinion, and my comparison, they give it sacred attributes. This is reassuring for others and reassuring for me, since I have taken refuge in this neutral and common zone which is neither entirely objective— since after all I am there as the result of a decree—nor entirely subjective—since I am accessible to everybody and everybody is at home there—but which might be called both subjectivity of the objective and objectivity of the subjective. And since I make no other claim, since I protest that I have nothing up my sleeve, I have the right, on this level, to chatter away, to grow excited, indignant even, to display my own personality, and even to be an "eccentric," that is to say, to bring commonplaces together in a hitherto unknown way; for there is even such a thing as the "hackneyed paradox." In other words, I am left the possibility of being subjective within the limits of objectivity, and the more subjective I am between these narrow frontiers, the more pleased people will be; because in this way I shall demonstrate that the subjective is nothing and that there is no reason to be afraid of it.

In her first book, *Tropismes*, Nathalie Sarraute showed that women pass their lives in a sort of communion of the commonplace: "They were talking: 'They had the most terrible scenes and arguments, about nothing at all. All the same, I must say, he's the one I feel sorry for. How much? At least two million. And that's only what Aunt Josephine left. . . . Is that so . . . ? Well, I don't care what you say, he won't marry her. What he needs is a wife who's a good housekeeper, he doesn't even realize it himself. I don't agree with you. Now, you listen to what I say. What he needs is a wife who's a good housekeeper . . . housekeeper . . . housekeeper. . . .' People had always told them so. That was one thing they had always heard. They knew it: life, love and the emotions, this was their domain, their very own."

Here we have Heidegger's "babble," the "they," in other words, the realm of inauthenticity. Doubtless too, many writers, in passing, have brushed against the wall of inauthenticity, but I know of none who, quite deliberately, has made it the subject of a book: inauthenticity being anything but novelistic. Most novelists, on the contrary, try to persuade us that the world is made up of irreplaceable individuals, all exquisite, even the villains, all ardent, all different. Nathalie Sarraute shows us the wall of inauthenticity rising on every side. But what is behind this wall? As it happens, there's nothing, or rather almost nothing. Vague attempts to flee something whose lurking presence we sense dimly. *Authenticity*, that is, the real connection with others, with oneself and with death, is suggested at every turn, although remaining invisible. We feel it because we flee it. If we take a look, as the author invites us to do, at what goes on inside people, we glimpse a moiling of flabby, many-tentacled evasions: evasion through objects which peacefully reflect the universal and the permanent; evasion through daily occupations; evasion through pettiness. I know of few more impressive passages than the one which shows us "the old man," winning a narrow victory over the specter of death by hurrying, barefooted and in his night-shirt, to the kitchen, in order to make sure whether or not his daughter has stolen some soap. Nathalie Sarraute has a protoplasmic vision of our interior universe: roll away the stone of the commonplace and we find running discharges, slobberings, mucous; hesitant, amoeba-like movements. Her vocabulary is incomparably rich in suggesting the slow centrifugal creeping of these viscous, live solutions. "Like a sort of gluey slaver, their thought filtered into him, sticking to him, lining his insides." (*Tropismes*, p. 11.) And here we have the pure woman-girl, "silent in the lamplight, resembling a delicate, gentle, underseas plant, entirely covered with live, sucking valves" (*idem*, p. 50). The fact is that these groping, shamefaced evasions, which seek to remain nameless, are also relationships with others. Thus the sacred conversation, the ritualistic exchange of commonplaces, hides a "half-voiced conversation," in which the valves touch, lick and inhale one another. There is first a sense of *uneasiness:* if I suspect that you *are not*, quite simply, quite entirely, the commonplace that you are *saying*, all my flabby monsters are aroused; I am afraid: "She crouched on an arm of the chair, twisting her outstretched neck, her eyes bulging: 'Yes, yes, yes,' she said, nodding her head in punctuation of each phrase. She was frightening, mild and submissive, smoothed out flat, with only her eyes protruding. There was something distressing and disturbing about her, her very mildness was threatening. He felt that at any cost she must be pulled together and calmed, but that only someone with superhuman force would be able to do it. . . . He was afraid, on the verge of losing his head, and there wasn't a moment to spare for thinking things over. He started to talk, to talk without stopping, of anybody and anything, taking infinite pains (like a snake at the sound of a flute? like a bird in the presence of a boa constrictor? he no longer knew) he must hurry, hurry, without stopping, without a minute to lose, hurry, hurry, while there's still time, in order to restrain her, to placate her." (*idem*, p. 35.) Nathalie Sarraute's books are filled with these impressions of terror: people are talking, something is about to explode that will illuminate suddenly the glaucous depths of a soul, and each of us feels the crawling mire of his own. Then, no: the threat is removed, the danger is avoided, and the exchange of commonplaces begins again. Yet sometimes these commonplaces break down and a frightful protoplasmic nudity becomes apparent. "It seemed to them that their outlines were breaking up, stretching in every direction, their carapaces and armors seemed to be cracking on every side, they were naked, without protection, they were slipping, clasped to each other, they were going down as into the bottom of a well . . . down where they were going now, things seemed to wobble and sway as in an undersea landscape, at once distinct and unreal, like objects in a nightmare, or else they became swollen, took on strange proportions . . . a great flabby mass was weighing on her, crushing her . . . she tried clumsily to disengage herself a bit, she heard her own voice, a funny, too neutral-sounding voice . . ." Nothing happens, in fact: nothing ever happens. With one accord, the speakers draw the curtain of generality before this temporary weakness. Thus we should not look in Nathalie Sarraute's book for what she does not want to give us: for her the human being is not a character, not first and foremost a story, nor even a network of habits, but a continual coming and going between the particular and the general. Sometimes the shell is empty. Suddenly there enters a "Monsieur Dumontet," who having knowingly rid himself of the particular, is reduced to a delightful, lively assemblage of generalities. Whereupon everybody takes a deep breath and hope returns: so it was possible, so it was still possible! A deathly calm accompanies him into the room.

These remarks have no other aim than to guide the reader through this difficult, excellent book; nor do they make any attempt to present its entire content. The best thing about Nathalie Sarraute is her stumbling, groping style, with its honesty and numerous misgivings, a style that approaches the object with reverent precautions, withdraws from it suddenly out of a sort of modesty, or through timidity before its complexity, then, when all is said and done, suddenly presents us with the drooling monster, almost without having touched it, through the magic of an image. Is this psychology? Perhaps Nathalie Sarraute, who is a great admirer of Dostoievsky, would like to have us believe that it is. For my part, I believe that by allowing us to sense an intangible authenticity, by showing us the constant coming and going from the particular to the general, by tenaciously depicting the reassuring, dreary world of the inauthentic, she has achieved a technique which makes it possible to attain, over and beyond the psychological, human reality in its very *existence*.

(*Translated by Maria Jolas*)

The Artist and
His Conscience

The Artist and His Conscience

*M*y dear Leibowitz,

You have asked me to add a few words to your book, since, some time ago I had occasion to write on the subject of literary commitment, and you now hope, through the association of our names, to emphasize the solidarity which unites artists and writers in their common concerns in a given age. Had friendship alone not sufficed, the desire to declare this solidarity would have decided me. But now that I must write, I admit to feeling very awkward.

I have no specialized knowledge of music and no desire to make myself ridiculous by paraphrasing poorly and with the wrong terms what you have so well stated in the appropriate language: nor do I foolishly presume to introduce you to readers who already know you well, following you avidly in your triple activity of composer, conductor and music critic. I would really like to say how good I think your book is: clear and simple, it taught me so much, unraveling the most confusing and involved problems and accustoming us to see them with fresh eyes: And what of it? The reader doesn't need me to tell him the merits of your book, he has only to open it. All things considered, I think the best is to suppose that we are talking just as we have often done and that I unburden myself of the questions and anxieties raised by your book. You have convinced me, yet I still feel certain areas of resistance and uneasiness. I must share them with you. To be sure, I am one of the profane who dares to question an initiate, a pupil

Originally *the preface for* L'Artiste et sa Conscience, *by René Leibowitz (Éditions de l'Arche, Paris, 1950).*

who argues with the teacher after class. But the same is true of many of your readers and I can imagine that my feelings reflect theirs. Finally, this preface has no other purpose than to ask, in their name and mine, that you write a new book, or even an article, where you will dispel our last remaining doubts.

I cannot laugh at the nausea of the Communist boa constrictor, unable either to keep down or vomit up the enormous Picasso. In the C.P.'s indigestion, I see the symptoms of an infection which contaminates our entire era.

When the privileged classes are comfortably settled in their principles, when their consciences are clear, and when the oppressed, duly convinced of being inferior creatures, take pride in their servile state, the artist is at his ease. Since the Renaissance, you say, the musician has consistently addressed himself to a public of specialists. But who is this public, if not the ruling aristocracy who, not content with merely exercising military, judicial, political and administrative powers over the whole territory, made itself also a tribunal of taste? Just as that elite determined, by divine right, the human shape, so the cantor or choirmaster produced his symphonies or cantatas for the whole man. Art could call itself humanist because society remained inhuman.

Is the same still true today? This is the question which haunts me, and which, in turn, I put to you. For by now, the ruling classes of our western societies can no longer believe that they themselves provide the measure of man. The oppressed classes are conscious of their power, and possess their own rituals, techniques and ideology. Rosenberg, speaking of the proletariat, has put it admirably:

The Artist and His Conscience

On one side, the present social order is permanently threatened by the extraordinary virtual power of the workers; on the other, the fact that his power is in the hands of an anonymous category, a historical "zero," is a temptation to all the modern myth-makers to seize upon the working class as the raw material of new collectivities, by means of which the society can be subjugated. May not this proletariat without a history be as easily converted into anything other than itself? The pathos of the proletariat, holding in the balance the drama between revolution by the working class on its own behalf, and revolution as an instrument for others, dominates modern history.

Now, it is precisely music—to speak only of this one area—which has been metamorphosed. This art took its laws and limitations from what it conceived to be its essence. You have demonstrated brilliantly how, in the course of a free yet rigorous evolution, music wrenched itself from its alienation and set about creating its essence while freely providing its own laws. In its modest way, couldn't music thus influence the course of history by providing the working class with the image of a "total man," who also has wrenched himself from his alienation, from the myth of a human "nature" and who, through daily struggle, forges his own essence and values according to which he judges himself? As soon as it recognizes *a priori* limitations, music reinforces alienation in spite of itself, glorifies the *given* and, while proclaiming freedom in its own fashion, declares that this freedom receives its limitations from nature. It is not uncommon that these "myth-makers" use music to fool the listener by inspiring him with holy emotions, as witnessed by the use of martial music or choirs. But, if I understand you correctly, something akin to a show of the naked power of creation must be seen in the most recent forms of this art. I think I have grasped precisely what you would oppose to these Communist musicians who signed the Prague Manifesto. They want the artist to reduce himself to a society-object, they want him to sing the praises of the Soviet world as Haydn sang those of divine Creation. They ask him to copy what *is,* to imitate without transcending, and to set an example to his public of submission to an established order: if music is defined as a permanent revolution, doesn't it threaten, in its turn, to arouse in the listener the desire to carry this revolution into other areas? You, on the contrary, want to show man that he is not manufactured and never will be, that he will everywhere and always retain the freedom to make and to remake himself beyond everything which is ready-made.

But here is what disturbs me: haven't you established the fact that an internal dialectic has carried music from monody to polyphony and from the most simple to the most complex polyphonic forms? This means that it can go forward but not backward: it would be as naïve to hope for its return to previous figurations as to want industrial societies to return to pastoral simplicity. Very good. But by the same token, its increasing complexity reserves it—as you yourself recognized—for a handful of specialists, found, by necessity, among the privileged classes. Schoenberg is farther removed from the workers than Mozart was from the peasants. You will tell me that the majority of bourgeois understand nothing of music, and this is true. But it is equally true that those who can appreciate it belong to the

bourgeoisie, profit from bourgeois culture, bourgeois leisure, and in general, practice a bourgeois profession. I
know: amateurs are not rich; they are most often found in
the middle classes, and it is rare to find a big industrialist
who is a fanatic music lover. This does happen, however:
but I don't ever recall seeing a worker at one of your con-
certs. It is certain that modern music is shattering forms,
breaking away from conventions, carving its own road. But
exactly to whom does it speak of liberation, freedom, will,
of the creation of man by man—to a stale and genteel listener whose ears are blocked by an idealist aesthetic. Music
says "permanent revolution" and the bourgeoisie hear "Evolution, progress." And even if, among the young intellectuals, a few understand it, won't their present impotence
make them see this liberation as a beautiful myth, instead of
their own reality? Let us understand each other. This is neither the fault of the artist nor of art. Art has not changed
internally: its movement, negativity and creative power
remain what they have always been. What Malraux wrote
remains as true today as it was then: "All creation is at its
origin the struggle between a form in power and an imitated form." And so it must be. But in the heavens above
our modern societies, the appearance of those enormous
planets, the masses, upsets everything. Transforming artistic
activity from a distance, they rob it of its meaning without
even touching it and spoil the artist's tranquil conscience.
Because the masses are *also* fighting for man, but blind-
folded, since they are in constant danger of going astray, of
forgetting who they are, of being seduced by the voice of
the myth-maker, and because the artist has no language
which permits them to hear him. He is speaking of *their*

freedom—since there is only one freedom—but speaking of it in a foreign tongue. The difficulties of the cultural policy of the USSR suffices to prove that this is a question of historical contradiction inherent to our time and not one of bourgeois disgrace, due in part to the subjectivism of the artist. Of course, if we believe that the Soviet Union is the Devil, then it follows that its leaders find perverse pleasure in carrying out purges which overthrow and decimate the artistic ranks. Or if we believe that God is a Soviet, then things are just as easy: God does what is just. That is all. But if, for a moment, we dare to uphold this new and paradoxical thesis, that the Soviet leaders are men, men in a difficult, indeed, untenable position, who are nevertheless trying to bring about what they believe is right, who are often outstripped by events, and who are sometimes carried farther then they might like, in short, men like all of us, then everything changes. Then we can imagine that they are not overjoyed by these sudden jerks of the gear which threaten to derail the locomotive. By destroying classes, the Russian revolution set out to destroy the elite, that is, those refined and parasitic organisms which are found in all societies of oppression and which produce values and works of art like papal bulls. Wherever an elite functions, an aristocracy of the aristocracy outlining for aristocrats the shape of the whole man, new values and works of art, far from enriching the oppressed man, increase his absolute impoverishment. The productions of the elite are, for the majority of men, rejection, want and boundaries. The taste of our "art lovers" forcibly defines the bad taste or lack of taste of the working classes, and as soon as refined minds consecrate a work, there is one more "treasure" in the world which the worker will never possess, one more thing of beauty that he is unable to appreciate or understand. Values cannot be a positive determination for each man until they are the common product of all. Any one of society's new acquisitions, whether a new industrial technique or a new form of expression, being created for everyone, must be for each an enriching of the world and a way which opens before him, in short, his innermost potential. But instead, the whole man as defined by the aristocracy is the sum of opportunities taken away from everyone; it is he who knows what others do not know, who appreciates what they cannot appreciate, who does what they cannot do, who is, in short, the most irreplaceable of beings. By contrast, the individual in a socialist society is defined at birth by the totality of possibilities which all give to each one, and at his death, by still new possibilities—small as they may be—which he has given to all. Thus *all* is the road of each man towards himself and *each one* the way of all towards all. But the necessities of administration, industrialization and war forced the Soviet Union into first forming a policy of a trained elite. It needed engineers, bureaucrats and military leaders at the same time that it undertook to realize a socialist aesthetic. And from this follows the danger that this trained elite whose culture, profession and standard of living sharply affects those of the mass, produces in its turn values and myths, that "amateurs" bred in its midst create a special *demand* for artists. The Chinese text which you quote, revised and corrected by Paulhan, sums up quite well the threat hanging over a society in the process of construction: if horse lovers suffice to produce beautiful race horses, an elite which becomes a specialized public would suffice to give rise to an art for the elite. A new segregation threatens to take effect: a culture of *cadres* will rise with its whole procession of abstract values and esoteric works of art, while the mass of workers will again fall into a new barbarism which will be measured exactly by its incomprehension of the products destined for this new elite. This, I think, is the explanation of the infamous purges which revolt us. To the degree that the body of trained specialists is reinforced, in the measure that the bureaucracy threatens to become a class, if not an oppressive elite, to that degree will the artist develop a tendency towards aestheticism. And at the same time that they are obliged to depend upon this elite, the rulers must force themselves to maintain, at least in terms of an ideal, the principle of values produced by the community as a whole. Certainly, this drove them into contradictory actions, since they created a general policy of *cadres* and a cultural policy of the masses; with one hand they create an elite and with the other they are obliged to destroy its ideology which is incessantly reborn and which will always rise again. But there is, conversely, as much confusion in the minds of the enemies of the Soviet Union when they reproach its leaders, at the same time, for creating a class of oppressors and for wanting to destroy the class aesthetic. The truth is that the Soviet leaders and the artist in the bourgeois society are colliding against the same impossibility: music has developed according to its dialectic, becoming an art which depends upon a complex technique. This is a regrettable fact, but *it is a fact*, nevertheless, that it demands a specialized public. To sum up, modern music requires an elite and the working masses require music. How can this conflict be resolved? By "giving a form to the profound sensibility of the people"? But *what* form? Vincent d'Indy wrote serious music "On a French Mountain Air." Do you think the mountain dwellers would recognize their song? Besides, the popular sensibility creates its own forms. Folk songs, jazz and African chants don't need revision and correction by professional musicians. On the contrary, the application of a complex technique to the spontaneous products of this sensibility has the necessary consequence of distorting the products. This is the tragedy of Haitian artists who are unable to weld their formal training to the folk material they want to use. The Prague Manifesto states, more or less, that the level of music must be lowered, while the cultural level of the masses is being raised. Either this is totally meaningless, or it confesses that art and its public will meet in absolute mediocrity. You are right to observe that the conflict of art and society is eternal, stemming from the essence of the one and the other. But it has taken a new and sharper form in our time: art is a permanent revolution, and for forty years now, the fundamental situation of our societies has been revolutionary; but the social revolution calls for a conservative aesthetic whereas the aesthetic revolution demands, in spite of the artist himself, a social conservatism. Picasso, a sincere Communist, condemned by the Soviet leaders, purveyor by appointment to rich American collectors, is the image of this contradiction. As for Fougeron, his paintings have ceased to please the elite, without arousing the slightest interest on the part of the proletariat.

Further, the contradiction widens and deepens as soon as we begin to consider the sources of musical inspiration. The problem, states the Prague Manifesto, is "to express the feelings and loftiest progressive ideas of the people." So much for feelings. But as for "lofty progressive ideas," how on earth do you set them to music? For music is a *non-signifying* art. Slovenly minds have taken delight in speaking of a "musical language." But we are perfectly aware that the "musical phrase" has no designated object: it is in itself an object. How then can this mute evoke for man his destiny? The Prague Manifesto suggests a solution which for sheer naïveté is a joy: we shall cultivate "musical forms which allow these goals to be attained, above all, vocal music—operas, oratorios, cantatas, chorals, etc." Good God, these hybrids are nothing but babblers, making small talk to music. What they are really saying is that music should be only a pretext, a means of enhancing the glory of the word. *It is the word* of which Stalin will sing, the Five Year Plan, the electrification of the Soviet Union. Set to other words, the same music could glorify Petain, Churchill, Truman, the TVA. By changing the words, a hymn to the Russian dead of Stalingrad will become a funeral oration for Germans fallen before the same city. What do the sounds contribute? A great blast of sonorous heroism; it is the word which will speak. There can be no musical engagement unless the work of art is such that it can receive only one verbal commentary. In a word, the sonorous structure must *repel* certain words and *attract* others. Is this even possible? Perhaps, in certain special cases, and you give as an example, *The Survivor of Warsaw*. But even there, Schoenberg could not avoid recourse to words. In that "gallop of wild horses," how would we recognize the enumeration of the dead without the words? We would only hear a gallop. Poetic comparison doesn't reside in the music, but in the rapport of the music with the words. But here, at least, you will say, the words are a part of the work, they are not in themselves a musical element. True, but must we now reject the sonata, quartet and symphony? Must we devote ourselves to "operas, cantatas and oratorios," as urged by the Prague Manifesto? I know that you do not believe this. And I am completely in agreement with you when you write that "the chosen subject should remain a *neutral* element, something akin to raw material which is then subjected to a purely artistic treatment. In the final analysis, it is only the quality of this treatment which will prove or deny the adherence of extra-artistic feelings and concerns to a purely artistic design."

Only now I no longer know wherein lies musical engagement and I fear it has already escaped from the work of art to take refuge in the behavior of the artist, that is, in his attitude towards art. The life of the musician may be exemplary; exemplary of the chosen poverty, the refusal of easy success, the constant state of dissatisfaction and that permanent revolution which he wages against others and against himself. But I'm still afraid that his austere personal morality remains an external commentary to his work. The musical work of art is not, *by itself*, negativity, rejection of traditions, a liberating movement: it is the positive consequence of this rejection and this negativity. A *sonorous object*, it no more reveals the composer's doubts and fits of despair than the patent of an invention reveals the torments and anxieties of the inventor; it does not show us the dissolution of old rules, but makes us see others which are the *positive* laws of its development. Moreover, the artist *should not be* a commentator of his own work for the benefit of the public. If his music is committed, this commitment will be found in its intuitive reality, in the sonorous object as it will appear immediately to the ear, without reference to the artist or to previous traditions. Is this even possible? It seems to me that we simply stumble again upon the same dilemma which we found at first: by forcing music, a non-signifying art, to express predetermined meanings, it becomes alienated. But again, by rejecting the meaning which you call "extra-artistic" musical liberation runs the risk of leading to abstraction and of offering the composer in question that purely formal and negative freedom which Hegel characterizes as Terror. Slavery or Terror. Conceivably our era offers the artist no other alternative.* If a choice must be made, I confess that I prefer Terror: not for its own sake, but because, in this era of flux, it upholds the exigencies proper to the aesthetics of art, allowing it to await, without too much detriment, a more favorable time.

But I must admit that I was less pessimistic before reading your book. I shall now give you the feelings of a rather uncultured listener; whenever I heard a musical composition performed, I found no significance of any sort in the sequence of sounds, and it was a matter of complete indifference to me whether Beethoven composed one of his funeral marches on "the death of a hero" or that Chopin might have wanted to suggest Wallenrod's satanic laugh at the end of his first *Ballade*. Conversely, it did seem to me that this sequence had a *meaning* and it was this meaning which I liked. I have always really distinguished meaning from significance. It seems to me, an object signifies when

* To be precise: The artist, for me, differs from the man of letters in that he deals with non-signifying arts. I have elsewhere shown that the problems of literature are entirely different.

an allusion to another object is made through it. In this case, the mind ignores the sign itself; it reaches beyond to the thing signified; often it so happens that this last remains present when we have long since forgotten the words which caused us to conceive of it. The meaning, on the contrary, is not distinct from the object itself and is all the more manifest inasmuch as we are more attentive to the thing which it inhabits. I would say that an object has a meaning when it incarnates a reality which transcends it but which cannot be apprehended outside of it and which its infiniteness does not allow to be expressed adequately by any system of signs: it is always a matter of a totality, totality of a person, milieu, time or human condition. I would say that the Mona Lisa's smile does not "mean" anything, but that it has a meaning. Through it, that strange fusion of mysticism and naturalism, evidence and mystery which characterize the Renaissance is materialized. And I have only to look at it to distinguish it from that other smile, equally mysterious but more troubling, more rigid, ironic, naïve and holy, which hovers vaguely about the lips of the Etruscan Apollo, or from the "hideous," secular, rationalist and witty suspicion of a smile on Houdon's Voltaire. Certainly, Voltaire's smile was *significant.* It appeared at specific times, it *meant,* "I'm no fool" or "Just listen to that fanatic!" But at the same time, the smile is Voltaire himself, Voltaire as an ineffable totality. You can talk about Voltaire forever—his existential reality is incommensurate with speech. But let him smile and you *have* him completely and with no effort. Thus does music seem to me, a beautiful mute with eyes full of meaning. When I listen to a Brandenburg Concerto, I never *think* of the seventeenth century, of the austerity of Leipzig, of the puritan stolidity of the German princes, of that moment of the spirit where reason, in full possession of its techniques, nevertheless remained subject to faith and where logic of concept was transformed into logic of judgment. But it is all there, present in the sounds, just as the Renaissance smiles on the lips of the Mona Lisa.

Further, I have always believed that the "average" public who, like me, lacks precise knowledge of the history of musical composition could date to the minute a work of Scarlatti, Schumann or Ravel, even if mistaken in the name of the composer, because of this silent presence, inherent in all sonorous objects, of an entire era and its concept of the world. Isn't it conceivable that musical commitment might reside at this level? I know what you will reply to this: if the artist paints himself entirely into his work—and his century with him—he did so unintentionally: his only concern was to sing. It is today's public who, at a hundred years' remove, finds intentions in the object which were never placed there. The listener of the last century only perceived the melody. He found natural and absolute rules in what we, in retrospect, consider to be postulates reflecting the era. All this is true, but can't one conceive of a more conscious artist today who, by reflecting on his art, would try to endow it with his condition as a man? I only put the question to you: you are the one who is qualified to answer it. But even if, like you, I condemn the absurd Prague Manifesto, I also cannot help being disturbed by certain passages in Jdanov's heralded speech* which inspired the Soviet Union's whole cultural policy. You know it as well as I do:

* Delivered on August 17, 1934, to the First Soviet Writers' Congress.

the Communists are guilty because they are wrong in their means of being right and they make us guilty because they are right in their means of being wrong. The Prague Manifesto is the stupid and extreme consequence of a perfectly defensible theory of art and one which does not necessarily imply an aesthetic authoritarianism. Jdanov states: "we must know life in order to represent it truthfully through works of art, not just to represent it in a dead scholastic way, not only as objective reality, but to represent reality in its revolutionary development." What does he mean if not that reality is never inert, but always in the process of changing, and that those who understand or portray it are themselves in the process of changing. The profound unity of all these changes which come at will is the future meaning of the entire system. It is the artist who must break the already crystallized habits which make us see in the *present* tense those institutions and customs which are *already out of date*. To provide a true image of our time, he must consider it from the pinnacle of the future which it is creating, since it is tomorrow which will decide today's truth. In one sense, this concept rejoins yours—you have shown that the committed artist is *in advance* of his times and that he looks on the present traditions of his art with the eyes of the future. In you as in Jdanov, there is certainly an allusion to negativity and transcendence. But he is not satisfied with the moment of negation. For him, the work has value, above all, for its positive content: it is a block of the future fallen into the present, anticipating by several years the judgment we shall bring to bear upon ourselves. It releases our future possibilities, and in one move it follows, accompanies and precedes the dialectical progression of history. I have always thought that nothing was sillier than those theories which try to determine the mental level of a person or of a group. There is no such level: to be "his age" for a child, is to be simultaneously below and above that age. The same is true of our habits of intellect and feeling. "Our senses have an age of development which does not come from the immediate environment but from the moment of civilization," Matisse wrote. Yes, and reciprocally, they go beyond this moment and perceive confusedly a crowd of objects which will be seen tomorrow, they discern another world in this one. But this is not the result of some sort of prophetic gift: the contradictions and conflicts of the era stimulate them to the point of bestowing upon them a sort of double vision. Thus is it true that a work of art is at the same time an individual achievement and a social fact. It is not the religious and monarchical orders alone that we find in *The Well-Tempered Clavier:* to these prelates and barons, both victims and beneficiaries of oppressive traditions, Bach held up the image of a freedom which, at the same time as it appeared to be contained within a traditional framework, transcended tradition towards new creations. Against the closed traditions of little despotic courts, he opposed an open tradition: he taught how to find originality within an established discipline; actually—how to live. He demonstrated the play of moral freedom within the confines of a religious and monarchical absolutism and depicted the proud dignity of the subject who obeys his king and the devout who worships his God. Entirely at one with his era, whose prejudices he accepts and reflects, he is, at the same time, outside it, and judges it wordlessly according to the still-implicit laws of a pietistic morality which will give birth, half a century later, to the ethics of Kant. The infinite variations which he performs, the postulates which he constrains himself to respect, place his successors on the verge of changing the postulates themselves. His own life, certainly, was a model of conformism and I cannot imagine that he ever advocated any very revolutionary views. But from the point of view of a still-unborn individualistic rationalism, isn't his art simultaneously the exaltation of obedience and the transcendence of this same obedience which he *judges* at the same instant that he claims to demonstrate? Later on, without losing his noble audience, the artist will acquire another. By the reflection which he exercises upon the formulas of his art, by his continuous reworking of worn-out customs, the artist reflects, *in anticipation of* the bourgeoisie, that progression without obstacles or revolution which they hope to bring about. Your conception of musical commitment, my dear Leibowitz, seems appropriate to that fortunate era. The assimilation of the aesthetic needs of the artist to the political ones of his public was so perfect that one critical analysis serves to demonstrate the woeful inadequacy of custom duties, tolls, feudal laws and those of the prescriptions which traditionally regulated the length of the musical theme, the frequency of its recurrence, the mode of its development. At the same time, this critique respects the jurisdictions of art and of society: tonal aesthetics remain the natural law of all music as the law of property remains that of every community. You can be sure that I do not pretend to explain tonal music by the laws of property. I merely indicate that in each age, there are profound correspondences between the objects in every domain upon which negativity is brought to bear and between the limits reached by this negativity, at the same time and in every direction. "There is a human nature, don't touch it." This is the common meaning of the social and artistic injunctions of the eighteenth century. Rhetorical, moving, sometimes verbose, the art of Beethoven gives us, with some delay, the musical image of the Assemblies of the French Revolution. It is Barnave, Mirabeau, sometimes, alas, Lally-Tollendal. And I am not thinking here of the meanings he himself occasionally liked to give his works, but of their meaning which ultimately expressed his way of hurling himself into a chaotic and eloquent world. For in the final analysis, these torrential discourses and floods of tears seem suspended in the freedom of an almost mortuary calm. Without shattering the rules of his own art, without crossing its boundaries, we could say that he went beyond the triumphs of the Revolution, beyond even his own failure. If so many people find consolation in music, it seems to me that it is because it speaks to them of their sorrows in the same voice which they will use to speak of them when they are comforted, and because it makes them see these sorrows with the eyes of a future day.

Is it so impossible that an artist will emerge in the world today, and without any *literary* intention, or interest in *signifying*, still have enough passion, to love and hate it, to live its contradictions with enough sincerity, and to plan to change it with enough perseverance, that he will transform even this world, with its savage violence, its barbarism, its refined techniques, its slaves, its tyrants, its mortal threats and our horrible and grandiose freedom into music? And if the musician has shared the rage and hopes of the oppressed, is it impossible that he might be transported beyond himself by so much hope and so much rage that he could sing today of this world with the voice of the future? And if that were so, could one still speak of "extra-aesthetic" concerns? Of "neutral" subject matter? Of "significance"? Would the raw material of music be distinct from its treatment?

I put these questions to you, my dear Leibowitz, to you and not to Jdanov. His answer I know. For at the moment when I believed he would show me the way, I realized that he was lost. Scarcely had he mentioned this transcendence of objective reality, when he added: "Truth must unite with the historical and concrete character of the representation in the task of ideological transformation and education of the workers in the spirit of Socialism." I had thought he was asking the artist to live the problems of his times freely and intensely, *in their totality*, so that the work of art could reflect them to us in his way. But I see now that it was a question only of ordering didactic works of art from bureaucrats which they should execute under the supervision of the party. Since the artist is to have his concept of the future imposed upon him, instead of being allowed to find it himself, it makes little difference, politically, that this future is still to be created: for the musician, it is ready-made. The entire system founders in the past; Soviet artists, to borrow the expression so dear to them, are *passéistes.** They sing the future of Soviet Russia the way our romantics sang the past of the monarchy. Under the Restoration, it was a problem of balancing the immense glory of our revolutionaries by an equal glory which they pretended to discover in

---

* *passéiste:* one who lives in the past, who is incapable of adjusting to the present. (*Trans.*)

the first years of the Old Order. Today, the Golden Age has been displaced by projecting it ahead of us. But, in any case, this shifting Golden Age remains what it is: a reactionary myth.

Reaction or Terror? An art that is free but abstract, or an art that is concrete but indentured? A mass public that is ignorant or a learned listener who is bourgeois? It is for you, my dear Leibowitz, who live in full conscience, without compromise or mediation, to tell us whether this conflict is eternal, or whether it is a moment in history, and in the latter instance, whether the artist has today the means within himself to resolve it, or whether, before we see the outcome, we must wait for a profound change of social life and human relations.

Merleau-Ponty

I have lost so many friends who are still alive. No one was to blame. It was they. It was myself. Events made us, brought us together, separated us. And I know that Merleau-Ponty said the same thing when he thought of the people who haunted, and then left his life. But he never lost me, and he had to die for me to lose him. We were equals, friends, but not brothers. We understood this immediately, and at first, our differences amused us. And then, about 1950, the barometer fell: fair wind for Europe and the world, but as for us, a gale knocked our heads together, and a moment later, it tossed each of us at opposite poles of the other. Our ties, often strained, were never broken. If I were asked why, I would say that we had a great deal of luck, and sometimes, even virtue, on our side. We each tried to remain true to ourselves and to one another, and we nearly succeeded. Merleau is still too much alive for anyone to be able to describe him. Perhaps he will be more easily approached—to my way of thinking, in any case—if I tell the story of that quarrel which never took place, our friendship.

At the École Normale, we knew each other without being friends. He was a day student, I was a boarder. Each of these states took itself for a chivalric order, in which the other was the foot soldier. When we were drafted, I was an enlisted man, and he became a second lieutenant. Thus he was a knight twice over.* We lost sight of each other. He

---

Originally published in Les Temps Modernes, *October, 1961.*

* I don't know whether he regretted, in 1939, when he came into contact with what his chiefs referred to curiously as "the men," that he hadn't enlisted as a simple soldier. But I know that when I saw my

had a teaching post in Beauvais, I think, while I taught in Le Havre. Each of us, nevertheless, was preparing himself, without knowing it, for an encounter with the other. Each of us was trying to understand the world insofar as he could, and with the means at his disposal. And we had the same means—then called Husserl and Heidegger—since we were similarly disposed.

One day in 1947, Merleau told me that he had never recovered from an incomparable childhood. He had known that private world of happiness from which only age drives us. Pascalian from adolescence, without even having read Pascal, he experienced his singular selfhood as the singularity of an adventure. To be someone, is something which happens and unhappens, but not without first tracing the ribs of a future, always new and always begun anew. What was he, if not this paradise lost, a wild and undeserved piece of luck, a gratuitous gift transformed, after the fall, into adversity, depopulating the world and disenchanting him in advance? This story is both extraordinary and commonplace. Our capacity for happiness is dependent upon a certain equilibrium between what we refuse and concede to our childhood. Completely deprived or completely endowed, we are lost. Thus, there are an infinite number of lots we can draw. His was to have won too soon. He had to live, nonetheless. To the end, it remained for him to make himself as the event had made him. That way and other ways. Seeking the golden age, and with that as his point of departure

---

officers, those incompetents, I regretted for my part, my prewar anarchy. Since we had to fight, we were wrong to have left leadership in the hands of these conceited imbeciles. In any case, we know that Merleau remained an officer after the brief period of Resistance, which accounts for some of the difficulties between us.

he forged his myths and what he has since called his "style of life." It established his preferences—choosing, at the same time, the traditions which recalled the rituals of childhood, and the "spontaneity" which evoked childhood's superintended liberty. This naïveté, by starting from *what has happened*, also discovered the meaning of *what is happening*, and finally, it made a prophecy based on this inventory and its evaluation. This is what he felt as a young man, without as yet being able to express it. Through these detours, he finally arrived at philosophy. He wondered—nothing more. Everything is played out from the beginning, and we continue in spite of this. Why? Why do we lead a life which is disqualified by its absences? And what does it mean to live?

Futile and serious, our teachers were ignorant of History. They replied that these were questions which shouldn't be asked, or that were badly expressed, or (and this was a tic of every teacher's at that time) that "the answers were to be found in the questions." To think is to weigh, said one of them, who did neither. And all of them said: man and nature form the object of universal concepts, which was precisely what Merleau-Ponty refused to accept. Tormented by the archaic secrets of his own prehistory, he was infuriated by these well-meaning souls who, taking themselves for small airplanes, indulged in "high-altitude" thinking, and forgot that we are grounded from birth. They pride themselves, he was to later say, on looking the world in the face. Don't they know that it envelops and produces us? The most subtle mind bears its stamp, and we cannot formulate a single thought which isn't conditioned in depth, from the outset, by the being to which it claims to allude.

Since we are all ambiguous histories—luck and ill-luck, rational and irrational—whose origin is never knowledge, but the event, it is not even imaginable that we could translate our life, that unraveling mesh, in terms of cognition. And what can be the value of a human thought about man, since it is man himself who both makes the judgment and vouches for it? Thus did Merleau "ruminate" his life. But don't start thinking of Kierkegaard at this moment. It would be too soon. The Dane fled Hegelian knowledge. He invented opacities for himself from the dread of transparency. If daylight should penetrate him, Sören would be reduced to nothing. Merleau-Ponty is exactly the opposite. He wanted to understand, to understand *himself*. It wasn't his fault, if, through practice, he discovered the incompatibility between universalist idealism and what he would call his "primordial historicity." He never claimed to place unreason above rationalism. He only wanted to oppose History to the immobility of the Kantian subject. This is only, as Rouletabille said, "seizing reason by the right end," nothing more. In short, he was looking for his "anchorage." To begin at the beginning, we shall see what was missing for him: intentionality, situation, and twenty other tools which could be procured in Germany. About this time, but for other reasons, I needed the same instruments. I had come to phenomenology through Levinas, so I set off for Berlin where I remained for a year. When I returned, we had come to the same conclusion, without having any doubts of it. Until September, 1939, we each pursued our own reading and research at the same pace, but separately.

Philosophy, as we know, has no direct efficacity. It took the war to bring us close together. In 1941, intellectuals, more or less throughout the country, formed groups which claimed to be resisting the conquering enemy. I belonged to one of these groups, "Socialism and Liberty." Merleau joined us. This encounter was not the result of chance. Each of us had come from a *petit bourgeois* background. Our tastes, our tradition and our professional conscience moved both of us to defend freedom of the pen. Through this freedom, we discovered all the others. But aside from that, we were simpletons. Born of enthusiasm, our little group caught a fever and died a year later, of not knowing what to do. The other groups in the Occupied Zone met the same fate, and doubtless for the same reason. In 1942, only one of them remained. A little later Gaullism and the *Front National* reclaimed these first-hour Resistants. As for the two of us, in spite of our failure, "Socialism and Liberty" had at least brought us into contact with one another. The era helped us. There was then, among Frenchmen, an unforgettable transparency of heart, which was the reverse of hatred. Through this national friendship, which approved of each man in advance, provided he hated the Nazis, we recognized each other. The key words were spoken: phenomenology, existence. We discovered our real concern. Too individualist to ever pool our research, we became reciprocal while remaining separate. Alone, each of us was too easily persuaded of having understood the idea of phenomenology. Together, we were, for each other, the incarnation of its ambiguity. Each of us viewed the work being done by the other as an unexpected, and sometimes hostile deviation from his own. Husserl became our bond and our division, at one and the same time. On this terrain, we were only, as Merleau so rightly said of language, "differences without terms, or rather, terms engendered by the differences which emerge between them." His recollections of our conversations varied. Basically, he was only interested in developing from within, and discussions distracted him. And then again, I made too many concessions to him, and with too much alacrity. Later, in his darker hours, he reproached me for this, as well as for having exposed *our* point of view to third parties without taking into account *his* reservations. He attributed this, he told me, to pride and some sort of blind disdain for others on my part. Nothing could be more unjust. I have always considered, and still consider, the Truth to be a whole. On small issues, then, it seemed to me that I ought to relinquish my points of view if I hadn't been able to convince my interlocutor to relinquish his. Merleau-Ponty, on the contrary, found his security in a multiplicity of perspectives, seeing in them the different facets of being. And if I was silent on the subject of his reservations, it was in good faith. Or almost. Do we ever really know? My mistake was rather to have dropped the decimals, in order to achieve unanimity more quickly. In any case, he didn't hold this against me too much, since he continued in the affectionate idea of me as a conciliator. I don't really know whether he profited from these discussions. Sometimes, I doubt it. But I can't forget what I owe to them: ventilated thinking. To my mind, this was the purest moment in our friendship.

But he didn't tell me everything. We never talked politics except to discuss the BBC news. I had fallen into a state of disgust from which I emerged only when I could rally a solid organization. Merleau, at other times more reserved on the subject of our project, was less prone to ever forget about it. It offered to him the reflection of an event in miniature. It brought man back to himself, to the accident which he was, which he would continue to be and which he produced. What had they experienced, wanted, and finally, what had they done, these professors (including ourselves), these students, these engineers, so suddenly joined together, and just as suddenly separated by a whirlwind? Merleau-Ponty questioned perception. It was, he believed, one of the beginnings of the beginning. Through this ambiguous ordeal, our body is surrendered to the world and the world to our body. It is both the hinge and the anchorage. But the world is also History. Perhaps, before anything else, we are historical. In the margins of the book which he was slowly writing, he reflected upon that which, ten years later, would appear to him as the fundamental anchorage. *The Phenomenology of Perception* bears the traces of these ambiguous meditations, but I was unable to recognize them. He had needed these ten years in order to rejoin what he had sought since adolescence, this *being-event* of men, which can also be called existence. Perhaps I should say that phenomenology remained a "static" in his thesis, and that gradually, through a careful study, of which *Humanism and Terror* was the first stage, he was to transform it into a "dynamic." This would not be untrue: exaggerated, certainly, but clear. Let us say that this vulgarization at least allows us to penetrate the movement of his thought. Gently, carefully, inflexibly, it was turning back upon itself, in order to reach back to its primitive state. In those years which preceded the Liberation, he had not advanced very far. Nevertheless, he already knew that History could not look itself in the face, any more than nature, because it envelops us. How? How could this totality of future and past time enclose us? How can we discover the others within us as our profound truth? How can we perceive ourselves within them as the law of their truth? The question is already asked at the level of perceptive spontaneity and "intersubjectivity." It only becomes more urgent and more concrete when we replace the historical agent in the womb of universal flux. Work and anxiety, tools, governments, customs, culture—how can we "insert" the person into all of this? And inversely, how can he be extracted from that which he never tires of spinning, and which incessantly produces him?

Merleau had believed he would live in peace. A war had made him into a warrior, and he had made war. Suppose this strange merry-go-round were to define for us, both the limits and the scope of historical action? We had to examine it closely. Investigator, witness, defendant, and judge, he turned back and examined, in the light of our defeat, and the future German defeat (of which we were assured after Stalingrad), the false war which he had fought, the false peace in which he had thought he was going to live. And there he was, always, at the juncture of things, the briber bribed, the practical joker hoaxed, victim and accomplice, in spite of a good faith of which there could be no doubt, but which, nevertheless had to be questioned.* Everything happened in silence. He had no need of a partner to make this new day dawn upon the singularity of his era, upon his own singularity. But we have the proof that he never

* Not as I did, in 1942, by the eidetic imagery of bad faith, but by the empirical study of our historical fidelities, and of the inhuman forces which pervert them.

ceased to reflect upon his era. Even in 1945 he wrote: "In sum, we have learned history, and we maintain that we must not forget it."*

This was the polite "we." In order to learn what he already knew, I still needed five years. Overwhelmed at birth and then frustrated, he was destined, by his experience, to discover the force of things, the inhuman powers which steal our acts and our thoughts. Invested, enveloped, predestined, yet free, his primitive intuition disposed him to understand the event—that adventure which issues from everywhere—devoid of consistence or significance as long as it hasn't filled us with its hazardous shadows, as long as it hasn't forced us to give to it, freely and in spite of ourselves, its iron necessity. Then, too, he suffered in his relations with others. Everything had been too wonderful, too soon. The form of Nature which first enveloped him was the Mother Goddess, his own mother, whose eyes made him see what he saw. She was the *alter ego*. By her and through her, he lived this "intersubjectivity of immanence" which he has often described and which causes us to discover our "spontaneity" through another. With childhood dead, love remained, equally strong, but bereft. Certain that he would never again find this destroyed intimacy, he was only capable of demanding. All and nothing: sometimes too much, other times, not enough. He moved quickly from demands to disinterest, not without suffering from these failures which confirmed his exile. Misunderstandings, estrangements, separations due to mutual wrongs, his private life had already taught him that our acts become inscribed into our

* Merleau-Ponty, "La guerre a eu lieu," in *Les Temps Modernes,* October, 1945.

little world otherwise than we might have wished, and that they make us other than we were, by giving us, after the fact, intentions which we didn't have, but which we shall have from now on. After 1939, he lived within his miscalculations, within these incidental expenses which we have to accept because we weren't able to foresee them, and which are even peculiar to historical action. In 1945 he wrote: "We have been led to assume and to consider as our own, our intentions, the meaning which our acts have for us, but also the consequences which these acts have on the outside, the meaning which they take on within a certain historical context."* He saw his shadow "cast upon History as on a wall, this shape which found its actions on the outside, this objective Mind which was himself."† Merleau felt sufficiently involved to have the constant awareness of restoring the world to the world, sufficiently free to objectify himself in History through this restitution. He freely compared himself to a wave, a crest among other crests, and the entire sea pulled upwards by a hemstitch of foam. A mixture of singular probabilities and generalities, the historical man would appear when his act, made and predicted from its farthest point to its most unknown objectivity, would introduce a beginning of reason into the primitive unreason. To his enemies, Merleau replied, in all certainty, that his interpretation of existence didn't oppose him to Marxism, and in proof of this, the well-known phrase: "Men make History on the foundations of past circumstances," could have passed, in his eyes, for a Marxist version of his own thinking.

* *Ibid.*
† *Ibid.*

The intellectual Communists weren't wrong about us. As soon as the calm seas of 1945 were past, they attacked me. My political thinking was confused, my ideas were dangerous. Merleau, on the contrary, seemed close to them. A flirtation began. He often saw Courtade, Hervé, Desanti. His own traditionalism found company in theirs. After all, the Communist Party was a tradition. He preferred its rituals, its tough-mindedness, refired by twenty-five years of History, to the speculations of those without a party.

However, he was not a Marxist. It wasn't the idea which he rejected, but the fact that it was a dogma. He refused to acknowledge that Historical materialism is the unique light of History, or that this light emanates from an eternal source, which principle extracts from the vicissitudes of the event. He reproached this intellectualism of objectivity, as he did classical rationalism, for looking the world in the face, and for forgetting that it envelops us. He would have accepted the doctrine if he could only have seen it as phosphorescence, a shawl thrown upon the sea, billowed out, unfurled by the swells, and whose truth depended specifically upon its perpetual participation in the underwater surges. A system of references, yes: on condition that it is altered through the act of referring to it; an explanation, if you wish, but one which is deformed as it is explained. Should we speak here of a "Marxist relativism"? Yes and no. Whatever the doctrine might be, he distrusted it, fearing that it would only be another version of "high altitude thinking." Thus, a relativism, but a relativism of precaution. He believed only in this one absolute: our anchorage, life. In essence, for what did he reproach the Marxist theory of History? Only this—which is capital, and nothing else—

that it had not given contingency its rightful place. "Every historical undertaking has something of an adventure about it, as it is never guaranteed by any *absolutely* rational structure of things. It always involves a utilization of chance, one must always be cunning with things (and with people), since we must bring forth an order not inherent to them. Thus, there still remains the possibility of an immense compromise, of a corruption of History, or of the class struggle, powerful enough to destroy, but not enough so to construct, and where the guiding lines of History, as they have been drawn in the Communist Manifesto, will be erased." The contingence of each man and of all men, the contingence of the human venture, and within the womb of the latter, the contingence of the Marxist venture. Here we discover the fundamental experience of Merleau-Ponty. First he reflected upon the singularity of his life, then, turning back to his historical existence, he had discovered that the one and the other were made from the same cloth.

But given these reservations, he accepted historical materialism as a grid, as a regulating idea, or, if you prefer, as a heuristic scheme: "For fifteen years now, there have been too many writers who have bypassed Marxism falsely for us to bother distinguishing among them. To go beyond a doctrine, one must first have reached its level, and be able to explain it better than the doctrine itself could. If, confronted by Marxism, we raise a few questions, it is not because we favor a more conservative philosophy of History which would only be still more abstract." In short, Marxism *faute de mieux*.

Let us understand each other: Fundamentally, Marxism is a practice whose origin is the class struggle. If you deny this struggle, there is nothing left of it. In 1945—and as long as the Communist Party shared power with the bourgeois parties—this struggle was not clearly distinguishable. The young intellectuals of the Party believed in it faithfully. They weren't wrong. I say they *believed* in it, because they certainly couldn't see it under the phony mask of national unity. Merleau-Ponty often irritated them because he only half believed it. He had reflected upon the consequences of victory. No more allies, only two giants face to face. The latter, anxious to avoid friction, had redrawn the globe at Yalta. I'll take the East, you can have the West. But Peace didn't interest them in the slightest. There would be a Third World War—there was no doubt of that—and each of them, anxious to win as quickly as possible, would come to terms with the other only to postpone the war until the best bases had been secured. In any case, the balance of power temporarily remained in favor of the West. Thus, in that moment of History, revolution in Europe was impossible. Neither Churchill, nor Roosevelt, nor finally even Stalin would have allowed it. We know what happened to the Greek resistance and how it was liquidated. Today everything is clear. History became one for the entire world. And the result was this contradiction, undecipherable at the time: the class struggle was transformed, place by place, into a conflict between nations—thus becoming separate wars. Today, *le Tiers Monde** enlightens us. In 1945, we could neither understand, nor conceive of this metamorphosis. In short, we were blind. One-eyed, Merleau-Ponty came to conclusions which were shocking because

* *le Tiers Monde:* literally "the Third World," designating the politically nonaligned, underdeveloped countries. (*Trans.*)

they seemed self-evident. If the revolution could be stopped from the outside by the desire to maintain international balance, if exterior forces could crush it at birth, if the workers could no longer expect their emancipation to come from themselves, but from world conflict, then the revolutionary class had said its farewells. Only the bourgeoisie remained, surrounded by the immense mass of workers which it exploited and atomized. But the proletariat, that invincible force which brought sentence against capitalism, and whose mission was to overthrow it, the proletariat had simply left the stage. It was possible that he would return, perhaps tomorrow, perhaps in fifty years. It was equally possible that he would never return. Merleau-Ponty noted this absence, deploring it, as well he might, and suggested that we should organize ourselves without waiting, for as long as this absence might last. He went as far as to trace the guidelines of a program, in a text which I transcribe here from memory, but quite faithfully I'm sure: "While waiting, it is incumbent upon us that we do nothing which could prevent the rebirth of the proletariat, even better, that we do everything to help him to re-constitute himself. In short, we must carry out the policy of the Communist Party." I vouch for the last words, in any case, as I was so struck by them. Born of the class struggle, the Communist Party determines its policy on the basis of this struggle. In capitalist countries, the Party couldn't survive the disappearance of the proletariat. But Merleau-Ponty no longer believed in civil war, and by the same token, even challenged the legitimacy of the Communist organization. The paradox remains that he proposed at this same moment, that we ally ourselves with the Party.

There was still another paradox. Go find a bishop, and tell him, just to see what he will say: "God is dead. I doubt that he will be resurrected, but, in the meantime, I will go along with you." He will thank you for your gracious proposals, but he won't swallow them. But Merleau's Communist friends took just the reverse attitude. They gave him hell, but nicely, and without driving him away. If we really think about it, this wasn't surprising. The Party came out of the Resistance ahead. It was less strict in the choice of its fellow travelers. But, more than anything else, its intellectuals were in an uncomfortable position. Radical by the order of things, they would have wanted the proletariat to organize his conquests, continuing his march forward. The bourgeoisie, terrorized by the publicity given its betrayals, would have let them do anything. But, instead, the Communists procrastinated. They said: "Let's seize power." And they were answered: "The Anglo-Saxons might intervene at any minute." A new contradiction appeared in the movement of a "flying wedge": in order to save peace and the socialist countries, a revolution required by the masses from within could be countermanded from without. These young men who had come to the Party through the Resistance didn't retract their faith. Far from it. But there were doubts and disputes. After all, France was a bourgeois democracy. What was the C.P. doing in a tripartite government? Wasn't it the hostage of capitalism? They went on faithfully transmitting slogans which disturbed them: "We must know when to end a strike . . . The Revolutionary objective is the reconstruction of the country." But they couldn't prevent Merleau's conclusions from worrying them. At least at the edges. After all, he approved the

Party's policy of reform, this policy whose executors they made themselves through obedience. Could he be blamed for repeating outloud what they themselves occasionally whispered? Where is the proletariat? In point of fact, he was there, but bridled and muzzled. And by whom? Every day Merleau-Ponty, that Cassandra, irritated them a little more. And Merleau, in turn, was irritated by them. In both cases, unjustly.

What Merleau misunderstood was the fact that his friends had grown roots. He returned to this question fifteen years later in the preface to *Signes*. There, on the contrary, he insisted upon the status of a militant enveloped, involved, and who, nevertheless, would himself contribute through his fidelity and through his acts to making the party which had made him. This was ambiguous repentance, which led him, above all, to justify his denials. It is easy to laugh when you are serenely judging a policy from the outside. When those who create it from day to day, if only by their acquiescence, discover its meaning, and when they see their own shadow cast upon the wall, there is nothing left for them but to break with it. But the argument can be turned the other way, and I think that he knew it. For those young men who struggled between good faith and sworn faith, by means of acts which they daily assumed, and whose meaning they saw changed in their very hands, for them, more than once, the "high-altitude thinker" was Merleau-Ponty.

They, in turn, misunderstood him. They didn't know the road he had followed. From a few conversations which we had later, I was left with the feeling that before 1939, he had been closer to Marxism than he was ever to be subsequently. What made him withdraw from it? I imagine that it was the Trials. He must have been very upset by them, for he spoke of them at great length, ten years later, in *Humanism and Terror*. After the trials, he could hardly even be disturbed by the German-Soviet Pact. He amused himself by writing rather "Machiavellian" letters to "distribute the blame." Through friends and through the writings of Rosa Luxemburg, he had been converted to the idea of "the spontaneity of the masses," which was close to the general movement of his particular movement. When he saw "Reasons of State" smoldering behind the masses, he turned away.

A Christian at twenty, he ceased to be one because, as he said: "We believe that we believe, but we don't believe." More specifically, he asked that Catholicism reintegrate him in the unity of immanence, and this was precisely what it couldn't do. Christians love each other in God. I wouldn't go so far as to say that he moved from this idea to socialism: this would be too schematic. But the time came when he encountered Marxism and asked what it offered. He found this to be the future unity of a classless society and, in the meantime, the warm comradeship of battle. After 1936, there is no doubt. It was the Communist Party which disturbed him. One of his most constant characteristics was to seek everywhere for lost immanence, to be rejected by this immanence in favor of transcendence, and then, to vanish. Nevertheless, he didn't remain at this level of the original contradiction. From 1950 to 1962 he conceived gradually of a new link between being and intersubjectivity. But if, in 1945, he still dreamed of transcendence, he hadn't yet found it.

In short, he had come a long way, when, in spite of the disgusts he had endured, he proposed this hard-hitting, severe and disillusioned Marxism. And if it was true that he had "learned History" with no taste for it, from a sense of vocation and from obstinacy, it was equally true that he would never forget it. And this is what his Communist friends, more sensitive to unreserved adherence than to specific and limited areas of agreement, didn't see at the time. Solely concerned, as he was, with probing his relation to History, I imagine that their criticisms would have affected him very little, causing him, at most, to persist in his ideas silently, if, by chance, we hadn't started *Les Temps Modernes* just at that time. Now he had the instrument, and he was almost forced to express all the aspects of his thought.

We had dreamed of this review since 1943. If the Truth is one, I thought, we must, as Gide said of God, seek it not elsewhere but everywhere. Each social product and each attitude—from the most private to the most public—are its allusive incarnations. An anecdote reflects an entire era as much as the substance of a political Constitution. We would be hunters of meaning, we would speak the truth about the world and about our own lives. Merleau found me optimistic. Was I so sure that there was meaning everywhere? To which I might have replied that there is meaning in nonmeaning and that it was up to us to find it. And I know what he would have replied in turn: explain barbarism all you want, you still won't dissipate its mystery. But the discussion never took place. I was the more dogmatic, he the more subtle, but this was a matter of temperament, or as we said, of character. We were both motivated by the same desire: to emerge from the tunnel and to see clearly. He wrote: "Our only recourse is in a reading of the present which is as complete and faithful as possible, which doesn't distort its meaning, which even acknowledges its chaos and inherent non-meaning where they exist, but which doesn't refuse to discern there a direction and an idea."

This was our program. Today, after Merleau's death, it is still the program of the review. No, the real difference should be called our inequality. Since he had learned History, I was no longer his equal. While I still hung back, questioning the facts, he was already trying to make the events speak.

Facts *repeat* themselves. Of course, since they are always new—but what then? The annual play of a successful playwright is new. He had to invent the idea, and then reflect and work on it. Each word was a *trouvaille* and the actors, in turn, "struck" just the right note. For several days they had said: "I just don't feel the part," and then, suddenly: "I feel it." Then finally, on the day of the dress rehearsal, the unexpected happened. The play became what it was—which means—the same as all the others. The fact confirms and begins anew. It points to customs, old contradictions, sometimes, more profoundly, even to structures. The same adultery is committed every night, for fifty years, before the same bourgeois audience in the heart of Paris. By only seeking its permanencies, I hoped that we would unknowingly discover the ethnography of French society.

Merleau-Ponty didn't scorn permanencies. As a matter of fact, he loved the childish return of seasons and rituals. But for this same reason, hopelessly pining for his childhood, he knew that it would never return. If the adult, living in the world of adults, could be visited by the grace of his first years, it would be too wonderful. Life would be as round as the earth. Merleau, an exile, had very early *felt* what I could only *know*. We can't go backwards, the gesture cannot be reclaimed, the gentle contingency of birth is changed, by its very irreversibility, into destiny. I was not unaware that we proceed along the course of things and never retrace our steps. But for a long time, I cherished the illusion that each day we grow in value, trapped by the bourgeois myth of progress. Progress, that accumulation of capital and virtues. We keep everything. In short, I was approaching excellence. This was the mask of death. Today it is stripped away. But this mask repelled Merleau. Born to die, nothing could restore to him the immortality of his childhood. Such was his original experience of the event.

In the middle of the last century, he would have lived time in reverse, in vain, as did Baudelaire after the "break." The golden age over, there is only room for degradation. Merleau's virtue was to have avoided this reactionary myth. As much degradation as you like, but it is ours. We cannot be subjected to it, without bringing it about, which means without creating man and his works through it. The event falls upon us like a thief, it throws us into a ditch or perches us on top of a wall. We only hear his gunfire. But scarcely had he taken off, the police at his heels, than there we are, so profoundly changed that we no longer even understand how we could formerly have loved, acted, lived. But who, in 1945, remembered the 30's? They were quietly preparing for retirement, the Occupation had killed them, and only their bones remained. A few of them dreamed of a return to prewar life. Merleau knew this couldn't happen, and that it was foolish and criminal to desire it. When he asked himself, in 1945, whether the human venture would founder in barbarism, or whether it would be vindicated by socialism, he was interrogating world history as though it were his own life. Time past, time recaptured? Digression, deviation, drifting; a hundred times rewritten, these words from his pen bear witness to the fact that we gain nothing without loss, that the future, even the closest, most docile future, betrays our hopes and our calculations. But, for the most part, it betrays them by fulfilling them. Our past acts return to us, from the depth of future years, unrecognizable, and yet ours. We must either despair, or find the changing reason for the change, and being unable to restitute the old facts, we must institute new ones, at least in the heart of the event which disowns them. We should try to govern this strange drifting which we call History from the interior, by seeking the implicit objectives of men within the movement which carries us along, in order to propose them explicitly. This brought us back to questioning the event—and without distorting anything—in order to find within it a temporal logic. I would be tempted to call this logic a "dialectic" had not Merleau, from this time on, challenged the term, and if, ten years later, he hadn't more or less repudiated it.*

In sum, the prewar period denied the times. When our walls were blown down by a cyclone, we looked among the wreckage for the survivors, and we said to them: "It's nothing, really." The worst of it is that they believed us. Merleau-Ponty "learned history" more quickly than we did,

---

* In 1945 he didn't declare himself: He found the word too ambitious to be applied to the modest activity of *Les Temps Modernes*.

because he took a painful and unqualified pleasure in time as
it flowed by. This is what made him our political commentator without his even wanting to be, and without
anyone being aware of him as such.

At that time, *Les Temps Modernes* had an editorial staff
which lacked any homogeneity whatsoever: Jean Paulhan,
Raymond Aron, Albert Ollivier. Of course, they were our
friends. But—unknown to everyone, and first of all, ourselves—we didn't share any of their ideas. In fact, only the
day before, our inert coexistence had been a lively comradeship. Some of them had just come from London, others
from hiding. But the Resistance soon dispersed. Each of
them found his rightful place once again, whether it was *Le
Figaro*, the *R.P.F.* [*Rassemblement du Peuple Français*], or
the *Nouvelle Nouvelle Revue Française*. The Communists
themselves, having participated in the first issue through the
pen of Kanapa, took leave of us. It was a hard blow for
those who remained. We lacked experience. Merleau saved
the review by agreeing to direct it. He became editor-in-
chief and political editor. This happened naturally. He
didn't propose his services to me and I didn't allow myself to
"choose" him. We simply announced jointly, after a certain
time had elapsed, that he was going to assume this double job
and that he couldn't resign them without the review fold-
ing. We only argued about one point: since the editorial
staff had disappeared from the front cover, I suggested that
Merleau's name appear there next to mine, as we were its
two directors. He sharply refused. I repeated this request a
hundred times during the years which followed, using only
one argument. It would have been closer to the truth. A
hundred times, smiling, relaxed, he repeated his refusal, ex-

plaining it by circumstantial reasons which were never the same. As his explanations changed constantly, and as his position remained unchanged, I concluded that he was hiding his real motives from me. I told him this, and he defended himself rather laconically. He didn't want to deceive me, he simply wanted to cut short any discussion of the subject. But then again whatever the subject happened to be, he never liked the debate to go to the heart of the issue. And here he won. I know no more about it today than I did in 1945. Was it modesty? I doubt it. It wasn't a matter of sharing honors, but responsibilities. I have been told the contrary. "You were the more well-known at the time. He was too proud to accept the benefit of this fame." It was true that I was the better known, but I didn't boast of it. This was the time of the cellar rats, of existential suicides. The respectable papers covered me with dirt and the tabloids equally so. Notorious through misunderstanding. But, those who read, in *Samedi Soir*, the interesting account of a virgin whom I lured, so it would seem, to my room to show her my etchings, those people weren't reading *Les Temps Modernes*. They wouldn't have even known of its existence. To the real readers of the review, on the contrary, we were both equally well-known. They read both our essays, preferring those of one, or the other, or politely dismissed both of us on equal terms. Merleau knew this as well as I. We showed each other the letters we received. In general, his public, mine, and that of *Les Temps Modernes*, were one and the same, and the best we could have hoped for. They didn't shoot the piano player, but evaluated his work without concerning themselves with other matters. Merleau could neither suffer nor profit from my dubious renown.

Should one say that he was afraid of being compromised? Nothing could have been more foreign to him. He proved this in the review itself, by publishing articles which created a scandal. Well, then? Why did he insist upon signing T.M. under editorials which he had conceived and edited from the first to the last word? All these writings which he didn't sign have been attributed, willy-nilly, to me. That goes without saying, since I seemed to be the only captain of that vessel. And last year, while glancing through some foreign bibliographies, I discovered that I was the author of his article on the Soviet camps—the very same one which he had acknowledged and legitimized in his last book. Why hadn't he signed it in 1950, since he was to use it again later? Why did he go back to it ten years later if he hadn't been willing to sign it at first? Why did he leave all those bastards for the review, since it was entirely up to him to "regularize" them? That is the question. And I don't claim to answer it. I had to go on living, nonetheless, and I adopted the most convenient explanation. He insisted upon independence, and any chain would have weighed upon him, except this tacit agreement, renewed with each issue, which didn't commit anyone, and which either one of us could break within an hour. This is possible, and yet, today, I think that he distrusted me. He was aware of my incompetence, and he was afraid of my zeal. If I should ever start talking politics, where would we all end? I have no proof of this distrust, except the following: in 1947 I published in the review an essay, "What is Literature." He read the first proofs, and thought he had discovered a phrase which assimilated, as was the style then, fascism and "Stalinism" under the common heading of "totalitarianism." I was in Italy at the time, and on reading this, he wrote to me immediately. I received his letter in Naples, and I still recall my stupefaction. "If," he in substance said, "you really apply the same measuring rods to Communism and Nazism, I ask you to accept my resignation as of now." Happily, as I was able to prove to him, it only involved a typographical error. And the matter ended there. But when I think about it, this gives the measure of his distrust. First of all, in the state of proofs, the text was incomprehensible and visibly mutilated. Next, and Merleau knew this perfectly well, I had never indulged in that kind of foolishness. Finally, his resignation was tendered with a bit too much enthusiasm. In sum, everything indicates that he expected the worst. But what strikes me, above all, is the fact that he was afraid that I would bolt to the *Right*. Why? Did he believe me to be right wing by temperament? Or did he simply fear that this hyena with a fountain pen, having been dismissed by the jackals, would apply for admission to the Pen Club? In any case, he was taking precautions against any blunders on my part. If any one of them proved inexcusable, he could retreat within twenty-four hours. This fire alarm was still in place five years later, when a political disagreement separated us. But then, Merleau didn't make use of it. As long as he could still hope that our conflicts would be resolved, he remained. His letter of 1947 proves that he would have left the review within the hour if I had fallen into the clutches of the Right. When I moved further to the left, he accepted being compromised. He thought he already saw the ditch, the fall was imminent, and he nonetheless remained at my side, determined not to jump except as a last resort. For a long time, I believed that he had been wrong not to join me at the pillory. A public collaboration would have constrained us both, so I said to myself, to reciprocal concessions. We would have spared each other, to save the collective editorship. But for some time now, I am inclined to think that he was right. In 1952, our differences could neither be disguised nor destroyed. They didn't stem from our personalities, but from the situation. As long as the name of Merleau hadn't been pronounced, we could delay matters longer. The clandestine nature of our bond, planned to facilitate his retreat, gave us the means of remaining together until the very last minute. The separation was gentle. We felt no need to proclaim it, that is, to change it into a public dispute. That, perhaps, is what saved our friendship. In the circles close to both of us, these precautions gained him the reputation of an *éminence grise*. This was all the more untrue, as he was no one's adviser. Master of his party, as I was of mine, his role, like mine, was to decide and to write.

He made a great point, nevertheless, of insisting that I read his articles, both those signed T.M. and which involved the review as a whole, and those which bore his name and only committed him. Please understand me. This attitude *resembles* that of an employee, or a bureaucrat who sees to it that his actions are "covered" by his principal. In fact, it was just the reverse. Merleau had no other boss but himself. He was much better oriented than I in the ambiguous world of politics. I knew this. And it would be an understatement to say that I had faith in him. It seemed to me, reading him, that he revealed my own thoughts to me. But our "gentlemen's agreement" required that he consult me. Anonymous, he didn't want me to be saddled with his writings. He put all of his delicacy in them. I was still stammering in the new language he had already mastered. Aware of this, he had a horror of coercing or seducing me. Thus he brought me his manuscripts without any comment. In these first times, he took great pains just in order to be readable. I was lost in the political labyrinth. I approved everything he wrote in advance, and fled precipitously. He sought out my hiding place, trapping me there. I would suddenly find him before me, smiling, holding out his manuscript. "I accept it, I agree with you," I stammered. "I'm delighted," he said without budging. And indicating with his left hand the sheets of papers which he proferred me with his right, "All the same, you should read them," he added patiently.

I read, I learned, I ended by becoming an avid reader. He was my guide. It was *Humanism and Terror* which caused me to make an important decision. This small dense book revealed to me the method and object. It gave me the push I had needed to release me from my immobility. We know what a scandal it created everywhere. Communists vomited on it, who today, don't see a thing wrong with it. But above all, it caused a fine commotion on our Right. One sentence in particular, which assimilated the opponent to the traitor and inversely, the traitor to the opponent, set off the dynamite. In Merleau's mind, this applied to those disturbed and threatened societies which huddle together around a revolution. This was viewed as a sectarian condemnation of all opposition to Stalin. Within a few days, Merleau became the man with a knife between his teeth. When Simone de Beauvoir visited the editors of the *Partisan Review* in New York, they didn't bother to hide their dismay. We were being manipulated. The hand of Moscow held the pen of our father Joseph. Those poor people! One evening at Boris Vian's apartment, Camus took Merleau aside and reproached him for justifying the Trials. It was most painful. I see them still. Camus, revolted, Merleau-Ponty courteous and firm, somewhat pale, the one indulging himself, the other refusing the delights of violence. Suddenly, Camus turned his back and left. I ran after him, accompanied by Jacques Bost. We found him in the deserted street. I tried as best I could to explain Merleau's ideas, which the latter hadn't deigned to do. With the sole result that we parted estranged. It took six months and a chance meeting to bring us together again. This memory is not a pleasant one for me. What a foolish idea it was to offer my services in this affair. It is true. I was to the Right of Merleau, and to the Left of Camus. What perverse humor prompted me to become the mediator between two friends, both of whom, a little later, were to reproach me for my friendship for the Communists, and who are both dead, unreconciled?

In fact, by this little sentence which had everyone screaming, and which is now accepted by everyone as a basic truth, universally valid even beyond the limits intended by the author, Merleau did nothing but apply to other circumstances what the war had taught him. We will not be judged by our intentions alone. What reveals our worth as much and more than the intentional effects of our actions, are their involuntary results which we have guessed, exploited, or, in any case, assumed. "The man of action," he was to write later, quoting Hegel, "has the certainty that necessity, through his act, will become contingency, and contingency, necessity." And with that, he asked History the truly philosophic question: What is a detour? What is aimless drifting? We started out in foul weather, persevered stoically through strong winds, we grew old in grief, and now, here is the result. What is left of former objectives? What has gone overboard? A new society was born in midstream, created by the undertaking itself, gone astray through its deviation. What can this society permit? What must it reject at the risk of breaking its back? And whatever its heritage, who is to tell us whether we have taken the shortest route, or whether we should attribute the meanderings to all of our deficiencies?

Through this rigorously unjust justice which preserves the wicked through their works, and which condemns men of good faith to hell for acts committed in all purity of heart, I finally discovered the reality of the event. In a word, it was Merleau who converted me. At heart, I was a throwback to anarchy, digging an abyss between the vague phantasmagoria of collectivities and the precise ethic of my private life. He enlightened me. This reasonable, ambiguous and insane undertaking, always unpredictable and always foreseen, which attains its objectives when it has forgotten what they were, which bypasses when it wants to remain faithful to them, which annihilates itself in the false purity of failure and degrades itself in victory, which sometimes abandons the enterprise midway, and other times denounces it when it no longer feels responsible—Merleau taught me that I would find it everywhere, in the most hidden aspect of my life as well as in the broad daylight of History, and that there is only one, which is the same for all of us: the event which makes us by becoming action, action which unmakes us by becoming through us event, and which, since Marx and Hegel, we call *praxis*. In sum, he showed me that I was making History in the same way that M. Jourdain was speaking prose. The course of things made the last rampart of my individualism crumble, carrying with it my private life. I found myself in the same places where I was beginning to escape. I recognized myself, more mysterious in the harsh light of day than I would ever have believed, and two million times richer. The time had come. Our era required that all men of letters write their dissertation on French politics. I prepared myself for this examination. Merleau instructed me without lecturing, from his experience and from the consequences of his writings. If, as he said, philosophy must be "spontaneity which teaches," I can say that, for me, he was the philosopher of his politics. And as for the latter, I maintain that we could have had no other, and that ours was the right one. One has to have a good start in order to survive. My start came from him and it was excellent. The proof of this is that our readers took all the curves with us. It will soon be seventeen years since the first issue of *Les Temps Modernes* appeared. We have regularly gained subscribers, and we have lost a few dozen, at the very most.

In 1945 it was possible to choose between two positions. But no more than two. The first and better, was to talk to Marxists and to denounce, to them only, the fact that the revolution had been nipped in the bud, the Resistance murdered, the Left shattered. Several periodicals took this position and disappeared, unheeded. This was the happy era when people had ears not to hear and eyes not to see. Far from believing that this failure condemned their effort, I maintain that we could have imitated them without foundering. The strength and the weakness of these reviews was to have restricted themselves to political ground. Our own published novels, literary essays, *témoignages*, documents— these rafts kept it afloat. But, to be able to denounce the betrayal of the revolution, one first had to be a revolutionary. Merleau was certainly not one, and I wasn't one yet. We didn't even have the right to call ourselves Marxists, in spite of our affinities for Marx. For revolution is not a state of soul. It is a daily practice illuminated by a theory. And even if it doesn't suffice to have read Marx in order to be a revolutionary, one joins him sooner or later as an agitator of revolution. The result is clear. Only men formed by this discipline could criticize the Left with any efficacity. Thus, at the time, they would have had to belong, whether closely or loosely, to Trotskyite circles. But by the same token, and through no fault of their own, this allegiance disqualified them. In that bewildered Left which dreamed of unity, they were considered "divisionists." Merleau-Ponty, as well, saw the threat clearly. He watched the working classes marking time, and he knew the reasons for it. But if this *petit bourgeois* intellectual had pointed to the gagged, chained, confused workers, defrauded of their victory (even had he burst into tears, even had he squeezed tears from his readers' eyes), he would simply have been practicing a higher form of demagoguery. But when, on the contrary, he concluded that the proletariat was on vacation, he was sincere and true to himself, and I was true to myself when I approved his conclusions. Us, revolutionaries? Go on! Revolution then seemed the most pleasant of myths, a sort of Kantian idea. I mouthed the word respectfully, knowing nothing about it. Moderate intellectuals, the Resistance had pulled us to the Left, but not enough so. And

then again, the Left was dead. Left to our own devices,
what were we, what could we be, if not reformers?

The other attitude remained. We had no choice, it was
self-evident. Coming from middle-class backgrounds, we
tried to be the connecting link between the *petite bourgeoisie* and the Communist intellectuals. This bourgeoisie
had engendered us. We had received its culture and values
as our heritage. But the Occupation had taught us that
neither one nor the other should be taken for granted. We
asked our friends in the Communist Party for the necessary
tools to take humanism away from the bourgeois. We asked
all our left wing friends to do this work with us. Merleau
wrote: "We weren't wrong in 1939 to want liberty, truth,
happiness, transparent relations among men, and we didn't
renounce humanism. (But) the war . . . taught us that these
values remain nominal . . . without a political and economic
infrastructure which makes them part of existence." I can
well see that this position, which one might call eclectic,
wasn't viable in the long run, but I also see that both the
French and international situation made it the only possible
one. Why should we be more royalist than the king? We
had forgotten the class struggle, this was a fact, but we
were not the only ones to have done so. The event chose
us to bear witness to what the *petit bourgeois* intelligentsia
wanted in 1945, at that moment when the Communists had
lost the means and the intention of overthrowing the
regime. This intelligentsia, so its seems to me, paradoxically
wanted the Communist Party to make reformist concessions
on the one hand, and on the other, they wanted the French
proletariat to find his revolutionary aggression once more.
The paradox is only one in appearance. This chauvinist

class, exasperated by five years of occupation, was afraid of the Soviet Union, but would have been assuaged by a revolution which was "really our own kind." In any case, there are always degrees of being and thinking. Whatever the entreaties of this revolutionary and chauvinistic reformism, Merleau had no interest in being the mouthpiece of a flag-waving tricolor proletariat. For his part, he had begun—as had many others in other countries at this same moment—an immense labor of confrontation. He set about wearing down our abstract concepts into a Marxism which was transformed within him as soon as he had assimilated them.

Today the task is easier, and the Marxists—whether Communist or not—have taken it up in turn. In 1948, it was thornier, inasmuch as the Communist Party intellectuals had no qualms about sending these two suspect bourgeois on their way, empty-handed, since they had announced themselves fellow-travelers without anyone's having invited them on the trip. We had to defend Marxist ideology without hiding our reservations and our hesitancies. We had to go a part of the way with people who, in turn, treated us like police-intellectuals. We had to thrust and parry without being insulting or severing relations; criticize freely but with moderation these cadavers who didn't tolerate a single disagreement; affirm, in spite of our solitude, that we were marching along at their side, at the side of the working class—(reading us, the bourgeois laughed derisively)—but without forbidding ourselves, when necessary, to take sides hastily with the Communist Party, as we did at the beginning of the war in Indo-China, or to fight for peace and the lessening of tension, within the confines of our confidential review, as though we were publishing a popular daily. They didn't forbid us to refrain from every virtuous passion, particularly self-importance and anger, to speak in the desert as though before a gathering of the nation, but without losing sight, of course, of the fact that we were utterly inconsequential, and finally, they didn't forbid us to remember at each moment, that one doesn't need success in order to persevere, but that nevertheless, perseverance has success as its goal. In spite of these jeers and low blows, Merleau-Ponty did the work properly, unfalteringly and with taste. It was his job. He didn't unveil—and who did?—the reality of the years around 1945, but he profited from the illusory French unity to remain as close to the Communists as possible, in order to broach impossible but necessary subjects of discussion, and to lay the foundations, beyond Marx, for what he sometimes called "Left-wing thought." In one sense, he failed. Left-wing thought is Marxism, nothing more, nothing less. But, History recuperates from everything but Death. If Marxism is today in the process of becoming *all of Left-wing thought,* we owe this, in the first place, to a handful of men, of which he was one. The *petits bourgeois,* as I have said, were moving towards the Left. The stop signal was heard everywhere, but this movement had already achieved advanced positions. Merleau gave the most basic expression to the common desire for democratic union and for reform.

Two years of clear sailing and then came the declaration of the Cold War. Merleau could see through Marshall's homilies, and denounced them as the generosity of an ogre. This was the time of shifting alliances. The Communist Party got tough, the Right took off towards the center, and at the same moment, we began to hear the death rattle of the R.P.F. The bourgeoisie lifted its head, christened itself the third force and enunciated the doctrine of the *cordon sanitaire*. We were pressed to take sides, but Merleau refused. Sometimes he needed to stand his ground: "the blow from Prague," one strike following another, the fall of the tripartite government, the Gaullist tidal wave in the municipal elections. He had written: "The class struggle is masked," and he unmasked it. Nevertheless, we persisted with our offers of mediation which no one took seriously, all the more certain that we could, in our two persons, effect the unity of the Left since, at this time, it had no other representative. The *R.D.R.* [*Rassemblement Démocratique Révolutionnaire*] was born, a mediating neutrality between two power blocs, between the advanced segment of the reformist *petite bourgeoisie* and the revolutionary workers. They asked me to join them, and allowing myself to be persuaded that it shared our goals, I accepted. Merleau, solicited elsewhere, nevertheless joined in order not to disavow me. I wasn't long in discovering that I had made a mistake. In order to live as closely as possible to the Communist Party, to force it to accept certain criticisms, we had, first of all, to be politically ineffective, so that they could envision another use for us. Merleau-Ponty was just their man. Solitary, without partisans or zealous disciples, his thinking, always new and renewed, had faith only in itself. The *Rassemblement*, on the contrary, however small it was and admitted itself to be, was counting on force of numbers. And thus it opened hostilities, even though it hoped to stop them at once. Where else could it have recruited advocates of revolution except in Communist or near-Communist circles? The Party, bristling, treated this group as an enemy from the very first day, to their great shock. The ambiguity of this situation was at the origin of our internal divisions. Some of them, disgusted, turned towards the Right. In general these were, the "organizers." The others, the majority, claiming to be unshakable, aligned themselves with the social action of the French Communist Party. The latter, which included us, reproached the others for having abandoned the initial program. "Where is your neutralism?" we asked them. They in turn, retorted with, "And where is yours?"

Did Merleau discover before I did that political thought is not easily integrated unless carried to its extreme, when it is taken up elsewhere by those who need it? Or, rather, isn't it that he was as little able in 1948 as in 1941 to restrain himself from showing a certain scorn for these groups which he found too young, which lacked roots and tradition? The fact is, that he never attended the meetings of the governing board, of which he was, nevertheless, a founding member. At least, this is what I was told, as I didn't go very often myself. He may also have rightly feared that we would pervert the meaning of his undertaking, and that *Les Temps Modernes* would become the monthly organ of the *R.D.R.* He said nothing to me about all this—perhaps because he shared my imprudence, perhaps because he did not want to reproach me for it, counting on the event to open my eyes. In short, he directed the review as usual, leaving me to wage war alone, intermittently, under the banner of neutrality.

In any case, by the spring of 1949, we were in agreement: the *R.D.R.* wasn't viable. The Movement for Peace, then headed by Yves Farge, was scheduled to hold a congress in Paris. As soon as the *Rassemblement* was informed of this, they hastily invited some well-known Americans, and decided to devote a few days after the congress as "study days" for peace. We had evidence that the right-wing press could be counted upon to spread the news. In brief, these days devoted to pacifism were only a ploy, encouraged, if not inspired by the Americans. Richard Wright came to see me. He was worried. He had been too openly solicited by the American Embassy for him to want to speak. "Where are we going?" he asked. Merleau joined us. The three of us decided not to appear at any of the meetings, and we wrote a joint letter explaining our abstention. The war of the two peaces was waged without us. At the *Vel d'Hiv*, they heard an American brag about the atom bomb, but they didn't see us there. The militants were outraged. In June, 1949, they went to the leaders and told them what they thought of them. I joined my voice to theirs. We assassinated the *R.D.R.* and I left for Mexico, disillusioned but reassured. Merleau hadn't appeared at the congress, but there was no doubting his opinion. I told myself that I had needed this unpleasant experience in order to share his beliefs entirely. And from this, it had taken nothing but the perfectly reasonable irrationality of politics to make us fall into an anti-Communism which we vomited, but which we nevertheless had to adopt.

When I saw him again in the fall, I told him that I had finally understood him. No more active politics. The review and the review only. I submitted various projects to him. Why not devote an issue to the Soviet Union? Our accord, it seemed to me, was total. We had become interchangeable.

So I was all the more astonished when my suggestions found so little echo. It would have been one thing if he had simply pointed out their absurdity to me. But, no, he just let them drop, silent and grim. It was because he had had wind of the Soviet camps. We had been told of the documents at the same time as Rousset, but through another source. Merleau's editorial appeared in the issue of January, 1950. You can also read it in *Signes*. This time I allowed my zeal to go as far as asking him to let me read it, even before he offered it to me. I didn't skip a word, approving everything, and first of all, the faithfulness of the author to himself. He exposed the facts and concluded his first paragraph with this sentence: "If the concentration camps number ten million, while, at the same time at the other end of the Soviet hierarchy, salaries and standards of living are fifteen to twenty times higher than those of free workers, then the entire system is changing its course and its meaning; in spite of the nationalization of production, and although private exploitation of man by man and unemployment don't exist, we ask what reason we still have to speak of socialism in connection with that country?" How could the Soviet workers tolerate this offensive return of slavery on their own soil? The explanation, he answered, is that it happened gradually, "without deliberate planning, from crisis to crisis, from expediency to expediency." The Soviet citizens know the code, they know that the camps exist. What they don't know, perhaps, is the extent of the repression. When they discover it, it's too late. They have become accustomed to it through gradual doses. "A great many young heroes . . . gifted bureaucrats, who had never known, in the sense of 1917, a critical mind and open discussion, will continue to believe that these prisoners are mad men, asocial beings, men of ill will . . . Communists throughout the world expect that through a kind of magical emanation so many factories and so much wealth must one day produce the whole man, even if, in order to create him, ten million Russians must be reduced to slavery." The existence of the camps, he said, make it possible to measure the illusions of today's Communists. But, he immediately added: "It is just this illusion which forbids us to confuse Communism with Fascism. If our Communists accept slave labor camps and oppression, it is because they are waiting for the classless society. . . . A Nazi was never encumbered with ideas such as the recognition of man by man, or internationalism, or a classless society. And while it is true that these ideas only find an unfaithful transmitter in Communism today, they are still inherent in it." And he added, more explicitly, "We have the same values as a Communist . . . We may think that he compromises them by incorporating them into today's Communism, but they still remain ours, while, on the contrary, we have nothing in common with the majority of Communism's enemies . . . The USSR is, *grosso modo,* on the side of those forces which are fighting against the forms of exploitation familiar to us . . . . We must not be indulgent towards Communism, but neither must we, in any case, make pacts with its adversaries. The only healthy criticism is that which aims, both within and without the Soviet Union, at destroying exploitation and oppression."

Nothing could be clearer. Whatever its crimes, the Soviet Union has this enormous advantage over bourgeois democracies: revolutionary aims. An Englishman had observed: "The camps are their colonies." To which Merleau an-

swered: "In that case, our colonies are—*mutatis mutandi*—
our slave labor camps." But our camps have no other goal
than to further enrich the privileged classes. Those of the
Russians are perhaps still more criminal since they betray
the revolution. The fact remains that they began with the
idea of serving it. It may be that Marxism has been bastard-
ized, that interior problems and external pressure have
warped the government, distorted institutions, and deflected
socialism from its course. Russia is not comparable to other
countries. It is only permissible to judge it when one has
accepted its undertaking, and then only in the name of that
undertaking.

In brief, five years after his first article, in a moment of
extreme danger, he returned to the principle of his politics:
on the side of the Party, right next to it, but never within.
The Party was our only pole, outside opposition our only
attitude towards it. To attack only the USSR was to absolve
the West. You may well find an echo of Trotsky in this
unyielding statement. If, said Trotsky, the Soviet Union is
attacked, we must defend the foundations of socialism. As
for the Stalinist bureaucracy, it is not for capitalism to settle
its count, the Russian proletariat will take care of that.

But Merleau's voice had grown somber. He spoke coldly,
even his anger lacked passion, almost lacking life, as though
he had already begun to feel the first symptoms of that
lassitude of the soul which is our common disease. Go back
to the texts of 1945, make the comparison. You will gauge his
disappointments, the wearing down of his hopes. In 1945:
"We will carry out, without illusions, the policy of the
C.P." In his article of 1950: "We have the same values as a
Communist," and, as though he were pointing out the weak-

ness of this purely moral bond: "People will tell me that the Communists have no values . . . They have them *in spite of themselves.*" To be in accord with them, we had to credit them with our maxims, knowing all the while that they rejected them. As for political agreement, it wasn't even a question of that anymore. In 1945 he forbade himself any thought, any action which might be harmful to the resurrection of the proletariat. In 1950, he simply refused to attack oppression in Russia alone. Either it must be denounced everywhere or nowhere. The fact was that the USSR of 1945 had seemed "ambiguous" to him. He found in it "signs of progress and symptoms of regression." This nation was emerging from a dreadful ordeal, it was possible to hope. In 1950, after the revelation of the concentration camp system: "We ask what reason we still have to talk of socialism." A single concession: The USSR is *grosso modo* on the right side of the barrier, with forces which are fighting against oppression. Nothing more. The revolutionary objective "to produce the whole man" is reduced, in the context of 1950, to being only an illusion of the Communist Parties. One could say that, about this time, Merleau found himself at the crossroads and that he was still loath to choose. Would he continue to favor the USSR in order to remain true to himself and to the underprivileged classes? Or would he detach himself from this society of concentration camps? If it should be proved to him that both are made from the same clay, why should one ask more of him than of the opposing powers of prey? A final scruple restrained him: "The decadence of Russian Communism doesn't make the class struggle a myth, nor more generally, does it make Marxist criticism null and void."

Were we so sure that we could reject the Stalinist regime without rejecting Marxism? I received an indignant letter from Bloch-Michel, which said, in substance: "How can you not understand that the Soviet economy needs manual slave labor, and that it systematically recruits millions of underfed and overexploited workers every year?" If he was right, Marx had thrown us from one barbarism into another. I showed the letter to Merleau, who didn't find it convincing. We found legitimate rage in it, and reasons of the heart, but not of the Reason. No matter. Better thought out, substantiated by proven facts, by arguments, how did we know that it wouldn't have dissolved our loyalty? The problems of industrialization, a period of socialist accumulation, being surrounded on all sides, the resistance of the peasants, the necessity of assuring adequate food production, demographic problems, suspicion, police terror and dictatorship—this combination of facts and consequences amply sufficed to overpower us. But what could we have said, what could we have done, even had it been proven to us that the concentration camp system had been required by the infrastructure? We would have had to know much more about the USSR and its production quotas. Several years later, I was able to acquire this knowledge, and I was liberated from my fears at the very hour when the camps opened their gates. But throughout the winter of 1950 we lived in grim uncertainty. The fact was that we couldn't be disturbed by the power of the Communists without being disturbed about ourselves. However inadmissible may have been their policies, we couldn't disavow them, at least not in the old capitalist countries, without resigning ourselves to a kind of betrayal. And it is the same thing to ask "Just how

far can they go," as "How far can I follow them?" There is
a morality of politics—a difficult subject, and never clearly
treated—and when politics must betray its morality, to
choose morality is to betray politics. Now, find your way
out of that one! Particularly when the politics has taken as
its goal bringing about the reign of the human. At the same
moment as Europe discovered the camps, Merleau finally
came upon the class struggle unmasked: strikes and repression, the massacres in Madagascar, the war in Vietnam, Mc-
Carthyism and the American Terror, the reawakening of
Nazism, the Church in power everywhere, sanctimoniously
protecting the rebirth of Fascism with her cloak. How
could we not smell the stench of the bourgeois cadaver?
And how could we publicly condemn slavery in the East
without abandoning, on our side, the exploited to their exploitation? But could we allow ourselves to work with the
Party, if this would mean putting France into chains and
covering it with barbed wire? What should we do? Should
we mercilessly strike those giants to the Left and the Right
who wouldn't even feel our blows? This was the solution of
despair. Merleau suggested this, for lack of a better one. I
saw no other solution either, but I was worried. We hadn't
budged an inch, the yes had simply changed to no. In 1945
we said: "Gentlemen, we are everybody's friend, and above
all, the friend of our dear C.P." And five years later: "We
are the enemies of all, the only privilege of the Party is that
it still deserves our severity." Without even speaking of it,
we both had the feeling that this "high altitude" objectivity
wouldn't take us very far. We hadn't chosen when choice
had been imposed upon everyone, and we had been right.
Perhaps now, our universal surliness could delay the choice

for a few more months. But whether publishers of a daily paper, or a weekly magazine, it was high time that we take the plunge or simply fold. The somewhat confidential character of our review gave us some respite, but our position, at first political, was in danger of gradually becoming moralistic. We never descended to the level of Beautiful Souls, but Fine Sentiments were flowering in our vicinity, at the same time that manuscripts were becoming scarcer. We were slowing down, people no longer wanted to write for us.

Once in China, I was shown the statues of two traitors in the bottom of a ditch. People had spat on them for centuries. They were all shiny, eroded by human saliva. We weren't shiny yet, but erosion had started. We wouldn't be forgiven for refusing Manicheism. On the Right, they hired butchers' boys to insult us. Everything was permitted them. They showed their behinds to the critics, who discovered that this was the "new generation." All of the fairies had been present at their cradle, but one. They disappeared for lack of talent. They lacked a certain zest, nothing more, but it had been denied them at birth. They would be dying of starvation today if they weren't fed by the Algerian War. Crime pays. They made a lot of noise, but did little damage. On the Left, things were more serious. Our friends in the Party hadn't been able to digest the article on the camps. Right was on our side and this was our feast. Their insults didn't bother me in the least: rat, hyena, viper, polecat—I rather liked this bestiary. It took me out of myself. Merleau was more upset by it, still recalling the comradeship of 1945. There were two times of day to be abused: first he was insulted in the early morning news sheets; then, by the end of the evening, he received the clandestine apologies of his Communist friends. This lasted until it was found simpler for these same people to take on more work. They wrote the articles at dawn and apologized at twilight. Merleau suffered less from being insulted by those close to him, than from the fact of being no longer able to respect them. Today, I would say that they were possessed by a violence which was literally mad, born of an exhausting war which wore them out, which took place elsewhere, but whose effects made themselves felt even in the depths of our province. They tried to believe they were others and they couldn't quite succeed. Merleau, I think, saw their faults and not their disease, this provincialism. This is conceivable as he knew them in their day-to-day life. In short, he kept his distance since this was what they wanted. The Communist Party had tolerated these fringes of critical sympathy on its edges without liking them. Beginning in 1949, it decided to annihilate them. Outside friends were kindly requested to keep their mouths shut. Should one of them make public his reservations, they would disgust him into becoming an enemy. Thus the Party proved to every militant (and each militant thought he proved to himself) that free examination of dogma is the beginning of treason. What Merleau's friends hated in him was *themselves*. What anguish there was in all that, and how it exploded after the electric shock of the XX Congress! Merleau knew the music. Communist tantrums didn't reduce him to anti-Communism. He took the blows without giving them. He did the right thing and let them talk. In short, he went on with his undertaking. No matter. They cut off his oxygen, exiling him once more to the combustible gas of solitary

life. Born of historic upheaval, the Communist Party with
its traditions and restraints, had formerly seemed to him,
even from afar, as a possible society. Now he had lost it. To
be sure, he had numerous friends who weren't Communists,
and who remained loyal to him. But what could he find in
them except the affectionate indifference of the prewar period? They sat around a common table, eating together, in
order to pretend for a moment that they had a common
task. These completely diverse men, still in a state of shock
from the intrusion of History into their private lives, had
nothing in common but a bottle of Scotch and a leg of
lamb. And of course these reunions came to the same thing
as death certificates. The Resistance had crumbled, he finally realized that. But these aperceptions have no profound
truth unless we feel them as a creeping form of our own
death. I saw Merleau often during the winter and spring.
He showed hardly any sign of nerves, but he was extremely
hypersensitive. I felt that, little by little, he was dying. Five
years later he was to write: "The writer knows full well
that there is no common denominator between the rumination of his life and what this life might have given his work,
making it clearer and more precise." This is true. Everyone
ruminates. We mull over insults suffered, disgust swallowed, accusations, recriminations, pleading; and then we
try to piece everything together, end to end, fragmented
material with neither head nor tail. Merleau, like each of us,
was familiar with these tedious repetitions, occasionally
pierced by a flash of lightning. But that year, there was
neither thunder nor light. He tried to take his bearings, to
go back to that crossroads where his own history intersected
the history of France and of the world, where the course of
his thinking had been born from the course of things. This

was what he had tried and succeeded in doing between 1939 and 1945. But in 1950, it was too late and too soon. "I would like," he said to me one day, "to write a novel about myself." I replied: "Why not write an autobiography?" "There are too many unanswered questions. In a novel, I could give them imaginary resolutions." Don't be deceived by this recourse to imagination. Let me remind you here of the role assigned to imagination in phenomenology, within this complex movement which realizes itself through the intuition of an essence. It was nonetheless true that this life was running out, but through meditation, it was discovering shores of shadow, solutions of continuity. In order then, to have launched, in spite of himself, into this conflict with old friends, wouldn't he have to have made a mistake at the very beginning? Or else, wasn't he forced to assume, at the risk of destroying himself, the deviations and digressions of an immense movement which had produced him and yet whose inner mechanism remained out of his reach? Or else —and as he himself had indicated in 1945, as a simple conjecture—hadn't we all fallen, for a time at least, into nonmeaning? Perhaps there was nothing else for us to do but *endure,* by holding fast to a few rare values. He kept his office at *Les Temps Modernes* and refused to change any of his activities. But, while it brought him closer to his origins, the "rumination of his life" slowly turned him away from day-to-day politics. This was his good fortune. When someone leaves the marginal zone of the Communist Party, they have to go somewhere. They walk for a while, and suddenly find themselves on the Right. Merleau never committed this treason. When he was dismissed, he took refuge in his inner life.

Summer came. The Koreans had begun fighting among

themselves. We were separated from one another when the news reached us, and each of us, by himself, made his own comments on the situation. We met again for a day, in August, in Saint-Raphael. Too late. We were overjoyed to rediscover our respective gestures, voices, all those familiar singularities which all friends throughout the world love in their friends. A single flaw: our thoughts, already formed, were incommunicable. From morning to night, we only talked of war, lying by the water's edge, immobile, then at a table, then at the terrace of a café, surrounded by naked vacationers. We argued while walking, we were still arguing at the station as I waited for my train. Two deaf men—we needn't have bothered. I talked more than he did, I'm afraid, and not without vehemence. He replied calmly, briefly. His flickering, thin smile with its childlike malice, made me hope that he still hesitated. But no. He had **never** trumpeted his decisions. I was forced to recognize that **he** had made up his mind. He repeated quietly: "The **only** thing left for us is silence."

"Who is 'us'," I said, pretending not to understand.

"Well, us. *Les Temps Modernes.*"

"You mean, you want us to put the key under the door?"

"No, not that. But I don't want us to breathe **another** word of politics."

"But why not?"

"They're fighting."

"Well, all right, in Korea."

"Tomorrow they'll be fighting everywhere."

"And even if they were fighting here, why should we be quiet?"

"Because brute force will decide the outcome. Why speak to what has no ears?"

I leaned out of the window and waved, as one should. I saw that he waved back, but I remained in a state of shock until the journey's end.

Very injustly, I reproached him for wanting to muffle criticism just at the moment when the cannons were beginning to rumble. This was the farthest thing from his mind. He had simply come across an overwhelming piece of evidence. The Soviet Union, he believed, had wanted to compensate for its inferior position in the arms race by assuring itself of strategic superiority. This meant, first of all, that Stalin considered war inevitable. It was no longer a question of preventing it, but of winning. And it merely sufficed that things should appear fatal to one of the powers, for things to become so in effect. This would be one matter if the capitalist forces were the first to attack. The world would be blown to pieces but the human venture, even shattered, would still have meaning. Something would die, which at least, would have tried to be born. But since preventative aggression was coming from the socialist countries, History would only be the shroud of mankind. The end of the game. For Merleau-Ponty, as for many others, 1950 was the crucial year. Then he believed he had seen the Stalinist doctrine without its mask, and it was nothing more than Bonapartism. Either the USSR was not the country of socialism, in which case socialism didn't exist anywhere and doubtless, wasn't even possible; or else, socialism was *that*, this abominable monster, this police state, the power of beasts of prey. In short, Bloch-Michel hadn't been able to convince Merleau-Ponty that socialist society was based upon slavery, but Merleau had convinced himself that it had engendered—whether by chance or necessity, or the two combined—imperialism. This didn't mean, of course, that he took sides with the other monster, capitalist imperialism. "But what difference is there," he said to himself, "one equals the other." Such was the metamorphosis. He refused to be outraged by the Soviet Union. "Outraged in the name of what? Throughout the world, they exploit, they pillage, they slaughter. So let's not blame any one party." The Soviet Union had simply lost, in his eyes, any privileged status. It was nothing more nor less than the other powers of prey. At this period, he believed that the internal reactions of History had definitely perverted its course. It would continue paralyzed, deflected by its own wastes, until the final fall. Thus, any reasonable words could only lie. Silence, the refusal of complicity, was all that remained. At first he had hoped to salvage what he considered to be of value in the two systems. To the better of the two, he wanted to make a gift of what the other had acquired. Disappointed, he next resolved to denounce exploitation everywhere. But after a new disappointment, he calmly decided not to denounce anything, anywhere, until a bomb from the East or West would put an end to our brief histories. Affirmative, then negative, then silent, he hadn't moved an inch. In any case, we shall misunderstand this moderation completely if we only see it as exterior positions held together by a suicide. I have said before that his worst rages were like underwater torpedoes which only damaged him. Hope remains in the wildest fury, but in this calm funereal refusal, no hope remained.

My reflections didn't go as far as his, which is what saved me from melancholy. Merleau made light of the Koreans, whereas I saw nothing but them. He moved too quickly on to world strategy, whereas I gazed hypnotized at the blood.

The fault lies, I thought, with those horse traders at Yalta, who had sliced Korea in two. We were both wrong, through ignorance, but not without good reason. Where, at that time, could we have found our knowledge? Who could have revealed to us that a military cancer was consuming the United States and that, already in the Truman era, the civilians were fighting with their backs to the walls? How, in August, 1950, could we have guessed MacArthur's plan, and his intention to profit from a conflict in order to return China to the Nationalist Chinese lobby? Did we know anything about Syngman Rhee, this feudal prince of a state reduced to poverty, or about the designs of the agricultural South upon Northern industry? The Communist press hardly mentioned any of that. It knew nothing more about it than we did and was satisfied with denouncing the crimes of the imperialist powers, that is, the Americans, without carrying the analysis any further. And then again, it discredited itself with a lie, before going any further. The only established fact was that the Northern troops had been the first to cross the dividing parallel. But the Communist press persisted in claiming the opposite. Today we know the truth, which is that the American troops, in conjunction with the feudal warriors of Seoul, set a trap for the Communists which the latter fell into. There were daily frontier incidents and the South Koreans profited from them, making such provocative moves that the North Koreans, outwitted, made the enormous mistake of attacking first, to forestall a blow which the others had no desire to strike. But the fault of the Communist Party everywhere was to think it would reveal the people's opinion, the only profound and true one, by offering them doctored truths. No, I have no further doubts about it. In this whole miserable business, the real warmongers were the feudalists of the South and the American imperialists. But neither do I doubt that the North attacked first. The task of the C.P. was not an easy one. If it acknowledged the facts, even for the purpose of interpreting their real meaning, its enemies everywhere would cry that it had been reduced to confessions. If denied these facts, its friends would discover the lie and withdraw. It had been less than a year since the existence of the Soviet camps had been revealed to us. We were still suspicious, ready to believe the worst. But in fact, the Soviet Union deplored this conflict which threatened to drag it into a war which it was not the least prepared to win. Nevertheless, it had to support North Korea under pain of losing its influence in Asia. But, on the contrary, young China entered the fray, knowing itself to be the object of American covetousness. Then, too, Communist China's revolutionary sense of brotherhood, its permanent interests, its international policy, all these demanded its intervention. But our information, in the summer of 1950, was too meager to permit us to distribute the blame. Merleau believed in Stalin's guilt because he had to believe in it. I didn't believe anything. I was swimming in uncertainty. This was my good luck. I wasn't even tempted to think that midnight had struck for our century, nor that we were living in the year 1000, nor that the curtain was about to rise on the Apocalypse. I viewed this scene of vast conflagration from afar, and saw only some fire.

In Paris, I saw Merleau once again. He was colder, more somber. Certain of our friends, his wife informed me, devoutly hoped that I would blow my brains out the day the

Cossacks crossed our borders. It went without saying that they were also howling for Merleau's brains. Suicide didn't tempt me. I laughed. Merleau-Ponty watched me without laughing. He was imagining war and exile. He seemed light-hearted, with that boyish air which I always knew him to assume when matters threatened to turn serious. He would be an elevator man in New York. A disturbing joke. This was another version of suicide. If war broke out, it wouldn't suffice that he cease to write, he would have to refuse to teach. Imprisoned in a cage, he would only press buttons and would mortify himself through silence. This gravity is so rare, that it takes one by surprise. However, it was his, ours, it is mine still. On one point, we were in agreement with those decent people who wanted our death. In politics, one must pay. We weren't men of action, but wrong ideas are crimes as much as wrong acts. How did he judge himself? He didn't tell me, but he seemed disturbed and disturbing. If ever, I said to myself, he should come to pass sentence upon himself, his hidden violence will make him proceed immediately to execution. Later, I often wondered how his icy anger towards the USSR could have turned into this morose attitude towards himself. If we had fallen into barbarism, we couldn't say a word, or even be silent without conducting ourselves as barbarians. Why did he reproach himself for these sincere and judicious articles? The absurdity of the world had stolen his thought from him, nothing more. He replied to that in *Signes*, with an explanation of Nizan, which is also valid for him. "Today we understand the objections which Sartre makes to the Nizan of 1939, and why they do not hold up against him. Nizan, he said, was angry. But is this anger a circumstance of mood? It is a mode of knowledge which is not inappropriate to fundamental issues. For someone who became a Communist and who acted within the Party, day after day, there is a burden to be borne of things said and done, since he, too, said and did them. To have taken the events of 1939 as he should, Nizan would have had to be a wooden dummy, to be broken . . . I remember having written prophetic letters in October, 1939, which, redistributed, in Machiavellian fashion, the blame between the Soviet Union and us. But I hadn't spent those years in preaching Soviet alliance. Like Sartre, I was without a Party—a good position from which to dispense justice serenely to the toughest side." Merleau-Ponty, far from being a Communist, had never even tried to be. It was not even a question for him of "acting within the Party," but he lived its life daily through the friends he had chosen. He didn't reproach himself for "things said and done," but for the commentaries which he had written about these things, for his decision never to propose a criticism without having tried to understand and to justify. Still, he had been right, for one does not know unless one gives. But the consequence was that he suffered because he gave for nothing. He had said: "Historic man has only one way of submitting to barbarism, and that is to create it." He was the victim of those whom he had so patiently defended, because he had made himself into their accomplice. In short, he abandoned politics at that moment when he decided that it had mislead him: with dignity and guilt. He had tried to live, now he walled himself up. To be sure, he was to change his mind later about all of this, and come to other conclusions, but that was in 1955. For five years, this stone of sorrow weighed upon his heart.

There was no lack of people to explain this turnabout by his class: he was a *petit bourgeois* with liberal ideas, he went as far as he could and then stopped. How simple it all is! And those who said this were themselves *petits bourgeois*, raised in liberalism and who, notwithstanding, opted for the Manicheism which Merleau refused. In fact, it was the fault of History that the thread was broken. She wears out the men she uses, riding them to death, like horses. She chooses the actors, transforming them to the marrow by the roles she imposes upon them, and then, at the slightest change, she casts them aside for brand new ones, whom she then hurls into the fray with no preparation. Merleau began work in the milieu which the Resistance had produced. When it died, he thought that this union would eminently survive through some sort of future humanism which the classes, by their struggle itself, could construct together. He "carried out the policy of the Communist Party," but refused, nevertheless, to condemn *en bloc* the cultural heritage of the bourgeoisie. Thanks to this effort to hold on to both ends of the chain, the circulation of ideas in France never stopped entirely. Here as everywhere, people detest intelligence, but before 1958, intellectual McCarthyism was unknown. Moreover, the official thinkers of the Communist Party condemned his ideas, but their betters always knew that they would have to be revived, and that Marxist anthropology had the duty to assimilate them. Without Merleau-Ponty, do you think for a minute that Tran Duc Tao would have written his thesis, which tried to annex Husserl to Marx? In many archaic religions, there are holy persons who exercise the function of *lieur*.* Everything

---

* *lieur:* literally, *binder* or *trusser*. (Trans.)

Situations

must be attached and tied by them. Merleau-Ponty played their part politically. Born of union, he refused to break it and his function was to bind. The ambiguity of his heuristic Marxism, of which he said, at the same time, that it couldn't suffice and that we had nothing else, was, I think, that it made possible meetings and discussions which will be continuous. Thus did he, for his part, make the history of this postwar period as much as it can be made by an intellectual. But, inversely, History made him while being made by him. Refusing to ratify the ruptures, hanging on with each hand to continents which were moving apart, he finally found, but without illusions, his old idea of catholicity. On both sides of the barricade, there are only men. Thus the human invention is born everywhere. We shall not judge it in terms of its origin, but on its content. It sufficed that the _lieur_ use all his strength to keep the two terms of the contradiction together, to delay the explosion for as long as he could. The creations, daughters of chance and of reason, will bear witness that the reign of man is possible. I can't decide whether this idea was late or early in October, 1950. One thing only is certain. It was not on time. The entire world was being shattered.

Every thought translated a prejudice, or tried to be a weapon; not a tie was formed without others being broken. To aid his friends, each man had to spill the blood of his enemies. Others besides the _lieur_ condemned Manicheism and violence, but they condemned it precisely because they were Manicheistic and violent: in a word, to serve the bourgeoisie. Merleau-Ponty was the only one not to hail the triumph of discord, the only one who did not agree—in the name of our "catholic" vocation—that love everywhere was

_282_

to become the other side of hatred. History had given him to us; but, well before his death, it took him away.

In *Les Temps Modernes*, we underplayed politics. It must be confessed that our readers weren't aware of this immediately. Sometimes we just procrastinated for so long, that when we finally got around to discussing an issue, everyone had forgotten it. But in the long run, people got angry. Uncertain, they asked for enlightenment. It was our bounden duty to provide them with explanations, or to admit that we were as stymied as they. We received angry letters; the critics became involved. I recently found in an old issue of *L'Observateur* a "Review of Reviews" which severely took us to task. We were aware, one and the other, one through the other, of these reproaches, but never said a word about them. This would have started the argument all over again. I was quite irritated. Did Merleau realize that he was *imposing* his silence on us? But then, as I reasoned to myself, the review belonged to him. He had defined its political orientation, and I had followed him. Even if our mutism was the ultimate consequence of this orientation, I still had to go along with him. It was harder for me to bear his smiling gloominess. He seemed to reproach us for having accompanied him in this wretched business and sometimes for having embarked on it. The truth was that he felt our growing discord and it hurt him.

We emerged from this stalemate without having decided anything, without speaking. Dzelepy and Stone sent us good, well-informed articles which revealed the war from day to day under a new light. These articles confirmed my opinions, and Merleau felt that they didn't disprove his. Thus, we didn't go back to the origins of our conflict. He didn't care much for the articles in any case, but he was too honest to reject them, and I didn't dare insist that we print them. I won't claim that we published them: they were published. We next saw them in the review. Others followed, finding the way to the printers by themselves. This was the beginning of an astonishing transformation. Although it had lost its political editor, *Les Temps Modernes* persisted in obeying him in spite of himself. In other words, the review indicated its radicalism all alone. Our colleagues there had been with the review for a long time. Most of them didn't see us very often. They had changed in order to remain as close as possible to the Communist Party, believing that they were following, when, in fact, they were leading us. Young men had joined the review because of the reputation Merleau had given it. It was, so they believed, the only publication in this iron age which held, at the same time, both to its preferences and its lucidity. Of these newcomers, none were Communists, but none wanted to draw away from the Party. Thus, in more brutal circumstances, they restored to *Les Temps Modernes* the position which Merleau had given it in 1945. But now, this came to the same as turning everything upside down. In order to remain so close to the Communists, we were forced, in 1951, to break with the remains of what still called itself the Left. Merleau kept silent. Or rather, with a certain degree of sadism, he gagged himself, and for the sake of our friendship and our professional conscience, forced himself to let pass a stream of tendentious articles which talked above the readers' heads and revealed, even through the mailing wrapper, through everything, even a film review, a vague, confused, impersonal point of view neither his nor entirely

mine. Thus, in the course of those six years, we each discovered that the review had acquired a kind of independence, directing us as much as we directed it. In short, during
the interregnum, between 1950 and 1952, a vessel without a
captain recruited, by itself, the officers who saved it from
perdition. If Merleau, upon contemplating this sardine rush-
ing in the wake of a whale could still say to himself, "This is
my work," he must have swallowed several fine draughts of
gall. For he was deeply attached to the review, that life
born of himself, and which, day after day, he kept alive. I
think he suddenly viewed himself as a father who, having
just the day before treated his son as a child, suddenly discovers a sullen, almost hostile adolescent "warped by bad
influences." Sometimes I tell myself that our common error
was to have kept silent, *even then*, when we were uncertain
and undecided. But no. The dice were cast.

The world had a war psychosis and I had a bad conscience. Everywhere in the West, people, nonchalant in
tone but wild-eyed with fear, asked what the Russians
would do with Europe when they took over. "It's inevitable," said the parlor strategists. The same people smugly
evoked the "corner of Brittany" which the United States
would maintain in Finistere to facilitate future debarkations.
Fine. If the fighting was on our soil, there would be no
problem. But other prophets believed that the US would
seek its real battlefields on other continents. What would
we do in that case?

One answer was given by bourgeois young virgins. An
entire class of a girls' *lycée* in Paris made a vow of collective
suicide. The black heroism of these poor children said a
great deal about the terror of their parents. I heard very

dear friends, former members of the Resistance, coldly declare that they would take to the woods and wage guerrilla warfare. This time, I told them, you will be more likely to be shooting Frenchmen. I saw from their eyes that this didn't perturb them in the least, or rather, that hysteria had made them fixate on this unrealistic resolve. Others chose realism. They would take a plane for the New World. In those years, I was a little less insane than the others. I didn't believe in the Apocalypse, if for no other reason than a lazy imagination. But I became more depressed. In the subway a man cried "Vivement les Russes!" I stared at him. An entire life was written on his face. Perhaps in his place, I would have said the same. I told myself: "And suppose this war really does take place?" People repeated to me: "You must go. If you stay, you will either make speeches on the Soviet radio or be silenced for good in a camp." These predictions hardly frightened me as I didn't believe in the invasion. Nevertheless, they did impress me. I saw them as intellectual games which, by pushing things to extremes, revealed to each man the necessity to choose, and the consequences of his choice. To stay, I was told, was to collaborate or die. And what about leaving? Living in Buenos Aires among rich Frenchmen while abandoning my poorer countrymen to their fate—wasn't that collaborating? And with the enemy class? It *was* your class, people will say. So what? Does that prove it wasn't the enemy of men?

If we must betray, let it be, as Nizan said in *Les Chiens de Garde*, the smallest number for the greatest good. In these morose fantasies, I felt my back to the wall. Everyone had chosen. When my turn came, I tried to hang back with neutrality. Several of us supported Rivet's candidacy, but the Communist Party had frightened away those to his Right. He was beaten.

Some Communists came to see me about "L'affaire Henri Martin."* They were trying to unite intellectuals of every variety, polished, slimy or slippery, to bring the matter to the public's attention. As soon as I had even a whiff of the story, it struck me as so stupid that I unreservedly joined my name to those protesting. We decided to write a book about it, and I left for Italy. It was spring. I learned from the Italian newspapers of Duclos' arrest, the theft of his diaries, the farce of the carrier pigeons. These sordid, child-ish tricks turned my stomach. There may have been more ignoble ones, but none more revelatory. An anti-Communist is a rat. I couldn't see any way out of that one, and I never will. People may find me very naïve, and for that matter, I had seen other examples of this kind of thing which hadn't affected me. But after ten years of ruminating, I had come to the breaking point, and only needed that one straw. In the language of the Church, this was my conversion. In 1950, Merleau too, was converted. Each of us were condi-tioned, but in opposite directions. Our slowly accumulated disgust made the one discover, in an instant, the horror of Stalinism, and the other, that of his own class. In the name of those principles which it had inculcated into me, in the name of its humanism and of its "humanities," in the name of liberty, equality, fraternity, I swore to the bourgeoisie a hatred which would only die with me. When I precipi-tously returned to Paris, I had to write or suffocate. Day

* *L'affaire Henri Martin,* Paris, 1953. Commentary by Jean-Paul Sartre, with texts by Hervé Bazin *et al.,* a *cause célèbre* which involved the court martial of Henri Martin, a naval officer, during the war in Indo-China. (*Trans.*)

and night, I wrote the first part of *Les Communists et la Paix*.

Merleau was not one to harbor any indulgence for the police methods of a dying regime. He seemed surprised by my zeal, but he strongly encouraged me to publish this essay, which, at first, was to have been only an article. When he read it, one glance was enough for him. "The USSR wants peace," I said. "It has to have peace. The only threat of war comes from the West." I didn't say a word about the Korean conflict, but in spite of my precautions, it seemed as though I had planned a systematic refutation of our political editor, opposing, point by point, my views to his. In fact, I had simply written at top speed, with rage in my heart, gaily, tactlessly. When even the best prepared conversions explode, the joy of the storm is unleashed where before there had been only total darkness, without a glimmer of light. I had never thought for a moment of sparing his feelings. But because of his affection for me, he chose to be amused by my wrath, instead of angered. However, a little while later, he pointed out that certain of our readers didn't agree with me. They shared my feelings about the tactics of our government—that went without saying—but to their mind, I made too many allowances for the Communists. "How will you reply?" I asked. It so happened that "to be continued" was printed at the end of this first study. "I'll answer them," he said, "after the next issue." Around 1948, in fact, the non-Communist Left elaborated the outline for a dissertation which became classic. #1. Thesis: They demonstrated the degradation of the government, its wrongs against the working classes, showing that here the Communist Party was right. #2. Antithesis:

They revealed the vileness of the Politburo and its mistakes, showing how it, too, had injured the masses. #3. Conclusion: They dismissed each of them on equal terms, indicating a middle course, without failing to cite the Scandinavian countries in their support. In Merlcau's view, I had only developed the thesis. He was still hoping—without too many illusions—that the antithesis was yet to come.

It never came. Nor did the continuation of the article appear in the following issue. The truth was that I was out of breath. I realized that I didn't know anything. Giving a Chief of Police hell wasn't enough to acquire insight into the whole century. I had read everything, but I had to re-read it all. I only had Ariadne's thread, but it sufficed, as it was the inexhaustible and difficult class struggle. I re-read. I still had a few cells left in my brain, and I racked them to exhaustion. I met Farge, I joined the Movement for Peace. I went to Vienna. One day I brought my second article to the printer which was, in fact, only a rough draft. The outline for the dissertation entitled, "The Third Force" was definitively cast aside. Far from attacking the Communists, I declared myself a fellow-traveler. At the end of the article, I once again noted "To be continued," but there was no further doubt permissible. Merleau only saw the article in the final proofs. The fact that I didn't give them to him myself was an aggravating circumstance. He read them at just that moment when he had to make up the issue. Why hadn't I submitted my manuscript to him, since he had never failed to submit his to me? Was I taking myself seriously for good now? I don't think that was it. Nor do I think I was fleeing from his remonstrances or objections. Rather would I blame that heedlessness of rage which, refusing all caution, heads straight for its object. I believed, I knew, I was disenchanted. Consequently, I would not go through all that again. In our all but confidential review, one had to shout to be heard. I would shout. I would stand on the side of the Communists and I would proclaim it. I am not going to give the objective reasons for my attitude. They aren't important here. I will only say that they alone counted, that I considered them urgent ones and that I still do. As for the heart's reasons, I find two. I felt that I was being prodded by our new staff, which was waiting for us to take the step. I knew that I could count on their approval, and again, I realize now that I rather resented Merleau for having imposed his silence upon me in 1950. The review had been floating for two years. I wasn't going to stand for it any more. Let each one judge. I have no excuse, I don't want any. What may be of interest in this adventure—which each of us lived painfully—is that it shows the sources from which discord may spring in the heart of the most loyal friendship and closest agreement. New circumstances and a disintegrating institution—our conflict had no other causes. The institution was our unspoken contract. Valid when Merleau talked and I was silent, this accord had never precisely defined our respective areas of specialization. Each of us, without even admitting it to himself, had appropriated the review. On one side, as in "The Caucasian Chalk Circle," there was my official and nominal paternity (for in everything concerning politics, mine was only that) and, on the other side, Merleau's paternity by adoption, five years of jealous care. Everything came to a head abruptly, in exasperation. We learned that each of us, by mutism as well as speech, had compromised the other. We only survived when we had but one thought, which was the case as long as I didn't think for myself. When two heads are under the same hat, how is the right one to be chosen? Seen from the outside, one could say that things had determined their own course. This is true, but it is too easy an explanation. It is true in general that empires crumble and parties die when they are no longer moving in the direction of History. And we must still further acknowledge that this idea, perhaps the most difficult of all, is carelessly handled by most writers. But how can someone who, even cautiously, applies the great social forces to himself, make use of them to explain the growth, life and death of micro-organisms like *Les Temps Modernes?* Would he say that a collective movement doesn't proceed without partial disasters? And then, whatever may have been the case, we had to live out this adventure by ourselves, bear the sentence pronounced upon us, execute it, and, as Merleau later said, institute it. And in all of this, there were wrongs on both sides, and in both our hearts, a futile good will.

Merleau could have ended things then and there. He could have provoked a quarrel or written against me. Eloquently, he abstained from either of these. For a time we remained this strange couple: two friends who still loved one another, each persisting in his opposition to the other, with but one voice between them. I admired his moderation all the more since, at this same time, we had some loudly announced defections. One of our oldest collaborators left us in haste for the *Nouvelle Nouvelle Revue Française* where he immediately began putting "the Hitlero-Stalinists" on trial, plaiting a martyr's wreath for Lucien

Rebatet. I wonder what is left of that one—possibly a dust speck of boredom off in the provinces, nothing more.

During the following years, I had the delight of witnessing several similar disintegrations. In order to fill the gaps and to solicit some articles, I held a meeting of our associates on alternate Sundays at my apartment. Merleau-Ponty came assiduously, the last to arrive, the first to leave, conversing in a low voice with everyone about everything except the review. He nevertheless had allies there, such as Claude Lefort, who disapproved of my position; Lefevre-Pontalis, who wasn't interested in politics; Colette Audry, who feared my excesses; and Erval. Merleau would not have had any trouble becoming the head of a strong opposition. He refused on grounds of principle—a review isn't a parliamentary assembly—and friendship. He refused to influence the group, while observing without pleasure that the group was influencing me. The majority was orienting itself towards this critical comradeship which he was just abandoning. Even in the face of virulent anti-Communism, it proposed to put a damper on the critics by insisting upon this quality of association. Above all, I think that Merleau found these meetings ridiculous and wholly unproductive. So they were after a while, not without his mutism making its contribution. But what should he have said? I never failed to ask for his opinions. He never gave them. It was as though he wanted to make it clear to me that I had no business asking his views on details, since I hadn't deigned to consult him on the essentials. He probably felt that I was appeasing my conscience cheaply and had no desire to come to my aid. My conscience, in fact, was clear, and I reproached Merleau for refusing his help. This complaint will seem unfair. All considered, it was asking him to collaborate in an enterprise which he openly disavowed. I realized this. But, after all, he was still one of ours, and from time to time, he still couldn't help taking the initiative—in general, a happy one. If, beginning in 1950, he had resigned his post as political editor, he was still editor-in-chief. In all ambiguous situations—prolonged to avoid a rupture—everything we do, in one direction or the other, makes matters worse.

But our misunderstanding had more serious causes, of an altogether different order. I thought that while I was being faithful to his thought of 1945, he was abandoning it. He thought he was remaining true to himself and I betraying him. I claimed to be carrying on his work, he accused me of spoiling it. This conflict didn't stem from us, but from the world, and both of us were right. His political thought was born of the Resistance, which means from a united Left. Within this union, it would have slid towards the most extreme radicalism, but it needed this atmosphere of triple entente. The Communist Party guaranteed him the practical efficacity of common action. The allied parties of the Left assured him that they would preserve humanism and certain traditional values by giving them real content. When, about 1950, everything exploded, he saw only debris. In his eyes, my madness was to hang on to a piece of flotsam while waiting for the rest to reconstruct the vessel automatically. For my part, I took sides when the Left crumbled because I believed its reconstruction was up to us. And certainly not from the top, but from the bottom. To be sure, we had no contact whatever with the masses, and we were, consequently, without any power. But our job was no less clear. Faced with the unholy alliance of the bourgeoisie and the socialist leaders, we had no other alternative but to stay as close to the Communist Party as possible, and implore the others to join us. We had to attack the bourgeoisie without let-up, laying bare its politics, tearing its pitiful arguments to shreds. We certainly wouldn't refrain from criticizing the Communist Party or the Soviet Union, but without it being a question—impossible task—of changing them. In the eyes of our readers, we hoped to prefigure future agreements by setting this minuscule example: an accord with the Communists which took nothing away from our freedom of judgment. Thus was I able to imagine, without bad faith, that I was continuing Merleau-Ponty's attitude.

In fact, however, the contradiction was not in us, but, beginning with 1945, in our position. To be for the whole is to refuse to choose among its parts. The privileged status which Merleau accorded the Communists was not an option: he considered their regime barely preferable. When the moment to choose came, he remained true to himself, and jumped ship so as not to survive the unity which had gone under. I, a newcomer, chose the Party precisely in the name of that unity. I believed that this unity couldn't be recreated, unless in proximity to the Party. Thus the same idea of union, at a few years' remove, had led one of us to reject the very choice which it had imposed upon the other. Everything comes from structure and from event at the same time. France is so constituted that the Party couldn't take power by itself. So, first of all, we had to think in terms of alliances. In the tripartite government, Merleau could still see the successor to the Popular Front. But in 1952, without any change in the demographic structure of the country, I could no longer confuse the Third Force—a simple Right-wing front—with the union of the masses. We would never be able to seize power from the Right, however, without first bringing together all the forces of the Left. The Popular Front remained the necessary means of conquest at just the moment when the Cold War made it an impossibility. While waiting for a regrouping which seemed very far away, we still had to keep its possibility alive from day to day by concluding alliances with the Party on a local basis. To choose or not to choose. After only five years, these two attitudes aimed at the same objective. Two attitudes? A single one, rather, opposing us like two adversaries, by forcing each of us to insist upon choosing one of his two contradictory components. In order to remain true to his refusals, Merleau forgot his desire for union. And to give future unity a chance, I forgot my universalism and chose to begin by accumulating disunity.

These words may seem abstract, but in fact, we had to live these historical determinants, which means that we lent them our life, our passions, our skin. I made fun of Merleau's "spontaneity." Indeed, in 1945 union did seem complete. He had a good head start to carry him along. He, in turn, made fun of my naïveté, and *volontarism.** But by 1952, union was over. And banking on false hopes didn't suffice to bring it back. The truth was that we were each recruited according to our aptitudes: Merleau when it was the time of subtleties, and I, when the time of the assassins had come. Lefort and I had some lively discussions. I proposed that he criticize me in the review itself. He accepted and submitted quite a nasty article. Angered, I replied in kind. Merleau, as a mutual friend, witnessed his becoming,

* *volontarism:* Sartre's term for the belief in the will. (*Trans.*)

despite himself, burdened with a new job. He had to volunteer as mediator. Lefort had the courtesy to submit his article to Merleau. I did the same with mine. It was my article which exasperated him. He informed me, with his usual gentle manner, that he would resign for good if I didn't cut a certain paragraph, which, as I think about it now, was unnecessarily violent. I seem to recall that Lefort made some sacrifices on his part. This didn't prevent both articles from exuding ill will. Merleau was devoted to both of us. All the blows which we dealt each other fell upon him. Without entirely agreeing with Lefort, he was closer to his point of view than to mine. Suddenly his tongue loosened. And so did mine. We launched into a long and futile explanation which bounced from one subject to another and from one discussion to another. Is there a spontaneity of the masses? Can groups find their cohesion from within? Ambiguous questions which at times took us back to politics, to the role of the Communist Party, to Rosa Luxembourg, to Lenin, and at other times, back to sociology, to existence itself, which means, to philosophy, to our "style of life," to our "anchorage," and to ourselves. Each word brought us back to the way of the world and to our own temperaments, and vice versa. Beneath our intellectual divergences of 1941, so calmly accepted when Husserl alone was the cause, we discovered, astounded, that our conflicts had, at times, stemmed from our childhood, or went back to the elementary differences of our two organisms; and that, at other times, they were between the flesh and the skin; in one of us, hypocrisies, complicities, a passion for activism hiding his defeats, and, in the other, retractile emotions and a desperate quietism. Of course, none of these were completely true or completely false. We quarrelled because we put the same ardor into convincing, understanding and accusing ourselves. This passionate dialogue which started in my office, midway between good and bad faith, continued in Saint Tropez, was resumed again in Paris, on the benches of the Café Procope, and continued still in my apartment. I went on a trip and he wrote me a long letter. I answered it when the temperature was 95° in the shade, which didn't help matters. What were we hoping for? At heart, nothing. We were carrying out the "labor of rupture" in the sense in which Freud has so aptly shown that mourning is labor. I think that the object of this dismal rumination *à deux,* this reassessment which made us lose our way, was to break our ties, one by one, with small jolts of anger, to cloud the transparency of our friendship until it had made us strangers. This undertaking, had it completed its course, would have ended in complete estrangement. One incident, however, intervened.

A Marxist whom I met by chance proposed writing on "the contradictions of capitalism" for the review. As he said, it was a familiar subject, but one which was poorly understood and upon which he could throw some new light. He didn't belong to the Party, but was a Party in himself, and one of the most rigid. He was so filled with the awareness of doing me a favor, that I was convinced. I warned Merleau, who knew the man, but he didn't say a word. As I was obliged to leave Paris, the article was submitted in my absence. It was a complete zero. As editor-in-chief, Merleau couldn't bring himself to let it appear without prefacing it by a "heading" which he wrote, and which presented, in so many words, our apologies to the readers.

He also took this occasion to reproach the writer in two lines for not having even mentioned the contradictions of socialism; that would have to wait for another time, wouldn't it? On my return, Merleau said nothing about any of this. Warned by a colleague, I had a look at the proofs and read the article under his heading, all the more irritated by the former as I found the latter still less defensible. Merleau, having "locked up" the issue, had in turn, gone away and couldn't be reached. Alone, in a state of joyous rage, I deleted the heading and the article appeared bareheaded. You can guess the rest. A few days later Merleau received the final proofs of the review, and realizing that his text had been omitted, took it all as badly as possible. He rushed to the telephone and gave me his resignation, this time for good. We were on the telephone for more than two hours. Jean Cau, grimly listening to half of this conversation, perched on an armchair near the window, thought he was witnessing the last moments of the review. We accused each other mutually of abusing power, I suggested an immediate meeting, I tried in every way possible to make him change his mind. He was unshakable. For several months I didn't see him. He never again appeared at the offices of *Les Temps Modernes,* and never had anything to do with it again.

If I tell this idiotic story at all, it is, first of all, because of its very futility. I think it over and say to myself, "It's heartbreaking," and at the same time, "It had to end that way." Just that way, badly, stupidly, inevitably. The canvas was ready, the end established in advance, like the *commedia dell'arte.* The only thing left for us to do was to improvise the rupture. We did it badly, but good or bad, we played the scene out, and others took our place on stage. I don't know which of us was the more to blame, and I have no consuming interest in that aspect of it. For in fact, the final guilt was written into our two roles. It had long been established that we would separate because of mutual wrongs, on a childish pretext. Because our collaboration couldn't continue, we had to break with each other, or the review dissolve.

Without *Les Temps Modernes*, the events of 1950 would not have had that much influence on our friendship. We would simply have fought over politics more often, or taken greater care never to discuss them. The fact is that the event generally touches people on one side, and they feel nothing except a dull shock, an unfathomable anguish. Unless, on the other hand, the event leaps at their throat and bowls them over in passing. In either case, they don't know what hit them. But scarcely has chance placed in our hands the most infinitesimal means of influencing or expressing historical movement, than the forces leading us are immediately stripped bare, causing us to discover "our cast shadow" on the blinding wall of objectivity. The review was nothing: just a sign of the times, like a hundred thousand others. But no matter. It belonged to History. Through it, both of us experienced our substance as historical objects. It was our objectivization. Through it, the course of things gave us our map and our double function; at first more united than we would ever have been without it, and then more divided. That goes without saying. Once we are caught in the gears, we are dragged in all the way. The little freedom left us is resumed in the instant where we decide whether or not to put our finger in. In a word, our beginning belongs to us. Afterwards we can only will our destiny.

The beginning wasn't bad—for this one reason, still mysterious to me. Contrary to the desire of all our colleagues, Merleau had, from the very first day, claimed the weakest position on the review. Doing everything, with no names mentioned, refusing any status which might defend him against my vagaries or my shifts of gear, it was as though he only wanted to receive his power from a living accord, as though his most useful weapon would be its fragility, and as though his moral authority alone must guarantee his functions. Nothing protected him, and because of that, he was not bound by anything or anyone. Present among us, as much in command as I was, and yet light and free as air. Had he agreed to having his name on the cover, he would have had to combat me, perhaps overthrow me. But he had envisaged this possibility from the first day, and refused on principle to wage a battle which would have demeaned us both and for no good reason. When the day came, a telephone call sufficed. He had made his decision, informed me of it, and disappeared. There was a sacrifice, nonetheless: the sacrifice was himself, *Les Temps Modernes*, and me. We were all victims of this purifying murder. Merleau mutilated himself, leaving me in the clutches of these fearful allies who, so I thought, would gnaw me to the bone, or reject me as they had rejected him. He abandoned *his* review to my incompetence. This aggressive expiation must have absorbed the greater part of his resentment. In any case, it allowed us to interrupt the labor of rupture and to save our friendship.

At first, he avoided me. Did he fear that the sight of me

would awaken his pain? Perhaps. But it seems to me more likely that he wanted to give our common future a chance. I would run into him on occasion. We always stopped to talk for a minute. When we were on the point of going our separate ways, I would suggest that he come and see us tomorrow, next week. He would reply with a firmly courteous, "I'll call you," and he never called. But another labor had begun—the liquidation of grudges, *rapproche-ment*—all that was ended by grief. In 1952 Merleau lost his mother.

He was as devoted to her as to his own life. More exactly, she *was* his life. He owed his infant happiness to the care which she lavished upon him. She was the lucid witness of his childhood, and because of that, when exile came, she remained its guardian. Without her, the past would have been swallowed up in the sands. Through her, it was preserved—out of reach, but alive. Until his mother's death, Merleau-Ponty lived that golden age by mourning it, like a paradise each day a little more distant, and in the carnal and daily presence of she who had given it to him. All the connivance of mother and son aimed at taking them back to old memories. Thus, for as long as she lived, Merleau's banishment retained its gentle quality, and occasionally, was just reduced to the naked difference which separates two inseparable lives. As long as they were two to reconstruct, and sometimes to revive the long prehistory of his gestures, his passions, his tastes, he still had the hope of reconquering this immediate accord with all those things which are the good fortune of children who are loved. But when his mother died, the wind slammed all the doors shut, and he knew that they were closed forever. Memories *à deux* are rituals. The survivor finds only dead leaves, only words. When, a short time later, Merleau-Ponty met Simone de Beauvoir, he said to her casually, with that sad gaiety which masked his most sincere moments: "But I am more than half dead." His childhood had died, and for the second time. As a young man, he had dreamed of finding his salvation through the Christian community, as an adult, through political comradeship. Twice disappointed, he suddenly discovered the reason for these defeats: "To be saved," on all levels, on all orders, would be to begin our first years anew. We repeat ourselves incessantly, we never start again. Seeing his childhood founder, he understood himself. His only yearning had been to find it again, and this impossible desire was his particular vocation, his destiny. What was left of it? Nothing. For some time now, he had been silent. Silence wasn't enough, he became a recluse, only leaving his office for the *Collège de France*. I saw no more of him until 1956, and even his best friends saw him less.

I should at least indicate what was going on in his mind in the course of the three years which separated us. But, as I have warned my readers, my only object here is to tell the story of a friendship. For this reason, I am more interested in the development of his ideas, than in the ideas themselves. Others will analyze the latter in detail, and much better than I could do. It is the man whom I want to re-establish, not as he was to himself, but as he lived in my life and I lived in his. I don't know to what degree this can be truthful. People will find me a questionable character, painting me negatively because of the way that I paint Merleau. Very well. In any case, I am sincere. I am describing things as I understood them.

Pain is emptiness. Other people would have remained hollow simulacra of hermits. But his pain, at the same time as it severed him from us, led Merleau back to his first meditation, to that good fortune which made him so unfortunate. I am struck by the unity of this life. Well before the war, this young Oedipus turned back upon his origins, trying to understand the rational unreason which had produced him. At just the moment when he was approaching it and writing *La Phenoménologie de la Perception*, History was at our throats, but he struggled against it without interrupting his research. Let us call that the first period of his reflection. The second period begins with the Occupation and continues until 1950. His thesis finished, he seemed to have abandoned his investigation in order to interrogate the History and politics of our time. But his concerns had changed in appearance only. Everything coalesced since History is a form of envelopment, since we are "anchored" in it, since we have to be placed historically, not *a priori*, nor by some sort of "all-surveying system of thought," but by the concrete experience of the movement which carries us along. If we really read them, Merleau's commentaries on politics are only a political experience in the process of becoming, by itself and in every sense of the word, the *subject* of meditation. If writings are acts, we can say that he acted in order to appropriate his action and to find himself in depth. Viewed in the general prospective of History, Merleau is an intellectual of middle-class background, made radical by the Resistance and carried away by the breakdown of the Left.* Trapped from within, his life turned back upon itself to seize the advent of the human in all its singularity. And

---

* It goes without saying that we could all define ourselves in the same way, save that our drifting varies, taking us sometimes in opposite directions.

however cruel, it is also obvious that his disappointment of 1950 must have been of help to him. It removed him from our grim fields of battle, but, by the same token, it presented him with an enigma—*the self*—neither quite the same nor quite another. Unlike Stendhal, he was not trying to understand the individual he was, but rather, in the manner of Montaigne, to understand the person, that incomparable mixture of the particular and the universal. It didn't suffice, however. Knots still remained to be untied. And he was still trying when his mother's death intervened to cut them. One can only admire how, through his grief, he appropriated this stroke of bad luck, converting it into his most rigorous necessity. Although signs of it had appeared for several years before, the third period of his meditation began in 1953.

Initially, this period was one of renewed inquiry and of mourning, at the same time. Thrown back upon himself for the third time by this death, he wanted it to enlighten his birth. *Something must happen* to the newborn infant, this seer-made-visible, who appears in the visible world: something, anything, even if it is only dying. He called this first tension between appearance and disappearance "primordial historicity." It is in it and through it that everything happens. From our first moment, we are precipitated into irreversible inflexibility. To survive birth, even for an instant, is an adventure, as it is an adventure not to survive. We do not escape this unreason which he calls our contingency. It is not enough to say that we are born to die, we are born at the moment of death. But at the same moment, the fact of his being alive prevented his mother from disappearing entirely. Not that he believed in our survival. His refusal to be considered an atheist in the last years wasn't out of consideration to his brief surge of Christianity in the past, but was simply to give the dead a chance. This precaution wasn't enough. What was he really doing by reviving a dead woman through ritual? Did this revive her by a dream, or was it *instituting* her?

Life, death, existence, being: he had to stand at their crossroads in order to carry on his dual investigation. In one sense, none of the ideas which he had advanced in his thesis had changed. But in another sense, they were all changed beyond recognition. He buried himself in the night of non-knowledge, in search of what he then called "the fundamental." For example, we read in *Signes:* "What is of interest to the philosopher (in anthropology) is precisely that it takes man as he is, in his effective situation in life and knowledge. The philosopher interested in anthropology is not one who wants to explain or construct the world, but he who aims at inserting us more deeply into being.*"

At the level of presence and absence, the philosopher appears, blind and clairvoyant. If *knowledge* claims to explain or construct, he doesn't even want *to know*. He lives within this mixture of oxygen and combustible gases which we call the True, but he doesn't deign to package truths, not even for distribution in the schools or textbooks. He does nothing but dig deeper, nothing but allow himself to flow, alive, without interrupting his endeavors, into the ludicrous abyss, the only one accessible to him, in order to seek within himself the door opening on to the night of what is not yet the self. This is to define philosophy as meditation, in the Cartesian sense of the word, which means

---

* "De Mauss à Lévi-Strauss."

as endlessly sustained tension between existence and being. That ambiguous rib is the origin. In order to think, he must be. The slightest thought transcends being by instituting him for others. This happens in a twinkling. It is the absurd and definitive birth, an indestructible event which changes into advent and defines the singularity of a life by its vocation for death. Savage and opaque, it is the work which retains being within its recesses. This unreason is the undertaking which will subsist in the community as its future *raison d'être*. And above all, it is language, that "fundamental," for the Word is only Being in the heart of man thrown out to exhaust itself within *meaning*. In short, it is man, burst forth in a single spurt, transcending his presence in being, to reach towards his presence in the other, transcending the past to reach towards the future, transcending each thing and his selfness to reach towards the sign. For this reason, Merleau, towards the end of his life, was inclined to give an ever more important place to the unconscious. He must have agreed with Lacan's formula: "The unconscious is structured like a language." But, as a philosopher, he stood at the opposite pole from psychoanalysis. The unconscious fascinated him, as being at once the chain and the hinge of being and existence.

One day Merleau-Ponty became furious with dialectic and maltreated it. Not, as he explains in *Signes,* that he would have agreed to its omission. The positive always has its negative corollary and vice versa. Consequently, the one will flow eternally through the other in a circular motion. As it turns, the philsopher turns as well. He must follow the circuitous route of his object scrupulously, and in a spirit of discovery, must penetrate his night as a spiral. Thus,

Merleau-Ponty developed the habit of following each No until he saw it transformed into Yes, and each Yes until it changed into No. He became so skillful at this *jeu de furet**that he virtually developed it into a method which I would call reversal. Through it, he jumps from one point of view to another, denying, affirming, changing more to less and less to more. Everything is contradictory and also true. I shall give only one example of this: "At least as much as Freud explains adult behavior by an inherited fatality of childhood, he also points out a *premature* adult life within childhood, as exemplified by . . . a first choice in relating to others in terms of generosity and avarice."† *At least as much:* for him, contradictory truths never fight one another. There is no danger of their blocking movement or provoking an explosion. Moreover, are they, strictly speaking, contradictory? Even if we accept this, we must recognize that contradiction, weakened by circular motion, loses its function as a "mobile of History," appearing in Merleau's view as the indication of a paradox, the living sign of fundamental ambiguity. In short, Merleau-Ponty accepts thesis and antithesis. It is synthesis which he rejects, reproaching it for changing dialectic into a building game. Spirals, on the contrary, are never allowed to conclude. Instead, each one manifests in its own way, the merry-go-round of being and existence. Children of the primordial slime, we shall be reduced to impressions in clay, if we don't begin with its denial. Let us turn things around. We, whose

---

* *jeu de furet:* Children's game in which the players, standing in a circle, hold a string around which a ring is passed from one to another. The game is played to a song which refers to the *furet*, the ferret, who runs around in a circle. (*Trans.*)

† *Signes*, p. 270.

very existence is the negation of that which is, what do we do from the first to the last instant, if not presage being, institute and restitute it by means of and on behalf of others, within the milieu of intersubjectivity? Instituting and presaging being is all very well, but as for seeing it face to face—we cannot count on that. We only know it through signs. Thus, the philosopher never stops going around in circles, nor stops the treadmill from turning. "This being, perceived through the stirrings of time, always sighted by our perception, by our carnal being, but towards which there can be no question of traveling, because the distance covered would remove his consciousness of being, this 'being of far-off distances,' as Heidegger says, always proposed for our transcendence, is the dialectical idea of being, as defined by Parmenides, beyond the multiplicity of things which are, and by this principle, sighted through them, since separated from them—this being would be only a flash of lightning and night sky."*

Merleau was still flirting. In this text he again speaks of dialectic, but he is not referring to Hegel, but to Parmenides and Plato. The role of meditation is to trace a line of circumference around its *subject* passing incessantly through the same points. But just what does this line perceive? An absence? A presence? The two together? Refracted through a prism, exterior being is broken down, multiplied,

* *Signes*, p. 197. The problem there was one of characterizing the *present moment* of philosophical research. Merleau gave it these two characteristics: "existence and dialectic." But some months earlier, he had given a lecture at the *Rencontres Internationales de Genève* on philosophy in our time, and it is remarkable that he never mentioned Dialectic there to describe our problems. On the contrary, he avoided the word *contradiction* and wrote: "Incarnation and the other are the *labyrinth* of reflection and sensibility for our contemporaries."

placed out of reach. But by the same movement, it interiorizes itself, becoming being from within, present entirely, forever, without losing its intangibility. And naturally, the inverse is also true. Interior being, this dangerous and miserly coil within us, does not cease to manifest its assimilation to Nature, the indefinite unfolding of exterior being. Thus, turning, and meditating, Merleau remained true to his spontaneous thought, to slow rumination pierced by rays of light. This is what he was discreetly erecting by means of a method which takes the form of a decapitated dialectic.

This descent into Hell at last allowed him to find the most profound merry-go-round of all—a discovery of the heart. And its proof is that it strikes with a somber density. I shall now tell how he informed me of it, almost two years ago today. Merleau painted himself in his subject matter, subtle and laconic, tackling problems head on when he seems to touch them only obliquely. I asked him whether he was working. He hesitated. "I may possibly write on Nature," and then, to lead me on, he added, "I read a sentence in Whitehead which struck me: 'Nature is in tatters.'" As you may have already guessed, he didn't add another word. I left him without having understood this. I was studying "dialectical materialism" at the time, and the word "Nature" evoked for me our psycho-chemical perceptions. Still another misunderstanding. I had forgotten that, in his view, Nature was the sensory world, this "decidedly universal" world where we encounter things and creatures, our own bodies and those of others. To understand him, I had to await the publication of his last article: "l'Oeil et l'Esprit." I imagine that this long essay must have formed part of the book he was writing. It was, in any case, related to it, and constantly refers to an idea which is going to be expressed, but which remains unformulated.

More hostile than ever to intellectualism, Merleau interrogated the painter and his savage, manual thinking. Through his paintings, he tries to seize the meaning of painting. At these times, Nature reveals her tatters to him. That far off mountain, he asks us in so many words, how does it manifest itself? By discontinuous, at times intermittent signals, slivers of scattered phantasmagoria, reflections of light, plays of shadow. This dust surprises us by its inconsistency. But our eye is precisely a "computer of being." With these air-borne signs it will produce an accumulated heap of the heaviest terrestrial mass. Our gaze is no longer content "to perceive being through the motion of time." We could say that its present mission was to erect from this motion the ever-absent unity starting from multiplicity. "Doesn't this unity exist?" we will ask. It is and it is not, like the dead clothes which haunt the tatters, like Mallarmé's rose, "absent from each bouquet." Being is through us who are through it. All of this, to be sure, does not work without the Other. This is how Merleau explains Husserl's difficult affirmation. "The transcendental conscience is intersubjectivity." Nothing, he thinks, can see without its being at the same time visible. How could we grasp what is if we were not? Here it is not a question of simple "noesis" producing its noetic correlative through these apparitions. Once again, to think we must be. The thing which is constituted through everyone, by means of each one, always an endlessly beveled whole, returns us, each through all, to our ontological status. We are the sea.

Having floated to the surface, every piece of flotsam is as innumerable as the waves, through them and like them absolute. The painter is the privileged artisan, the best witness of this mediated reciprocity. "The body is caught in the fabric of the world, but the world is made of the stuff of my body." A new spiral, but more profound than the others because it touches upon the "labyrinth of incarnation." Through my flesh, Nature is made flesh. But, inversely, if painting is possible, then the ribs of being which the painter perceives within the thing, and which he fixes on canvas must designate within himself the "flexions" of his being. "The painting . . . doesn't relate to anything among empirical things, save on condition of being autofigurative: it is only a show of things by being a show of nothing, demonstrating how things become things and the world, the world." This is precisely what gives "the occupation of painter an urgency which surpasses every other urgency." Through its figuration of being from the outside, it presents being to others from the inside, *his* flesh and theirs. It is not even enough to say that it presents. For, as Merleau says, "Culture is advent." Thus the artist has the sacred function of instituting being within the milieu of men, which means going beyond "the layers of brute being of which the activist is unaware" towards this eminent being which is *meaning*. And this is not only true of the artist, but of each one of us as well. "Expression," he says, "is the fundamental of the body." And what is there to express if not *being*. We do not make a move without restituting, instituting and bringing about its presence. Primordial historicity, our birth at the moment of death, is that surge from the depths through which the event becomes man, who, by naming things, declines his being. Such is also the history of the group, in its most basic sense. "How should we define this milieu where a form burdened with contingency suddenly opens a cycle of the future and governs it with the authority of the established, if not as History?"

This was the point of departure for his final thoughts. I have told how his last philosophy, "weighed down by contingency," patiently gnawing at chance and by chance interrupted, began with a discovery of the heart. Against grief and absence, it is he, in turn, who discovers himself. Merleau was the real "computer of being." He was left with a handful of relics and memories, but our gaze doesn't have far to go before it brings forth being from the mountain. With the rags and tatters of memory, the heart tears being from the dead. With the event which killed them, it brings about their advent. It is not only a question of restoring their eternity to the smiles and words which have disappeared. To live is to deepen them, to transform them, by our smiles and words into themselves, a little more each day, endlessly. There is a progress of the dead and this is our history. Thus Merleau made himself into his mother's guardian as she had been the guardian of his childhood. Born of her at the moment of death, he wanted death to be her rebirth. For this reason, he found more real powers in absence than in presence. "L'Oeil et l'Esprit" contains a strange quotation. In *Marianne*, Marivaux, reflecting upon the force and dignity of the passions, sings the praises of men who remove themselves from life rather than deny their being. What appealed to Merleau in these few lines was their revelation of an indestructible slab beneath the transparency of the shallow stream which is life. But don't think that he was returning to Cartesian substance. Hardly had he closed the quotation marks and taken up his pen again on his own account, than the slab crumbled into discontinuous sparks, again becoming that ragged being we must continue to be, perhaps only a disorderly imperative, and one which, at times, may be better ordered by suicide than by a living victory. But, by the same movement, since that is our rule, we shall institute within the human community, the being of the dead through our death, our being through that of the dead.

How far did he go in those somber years which changed him into himself? Reading him at times, it would seem that being invents man in order to make itself manifest through him. Didn't Merleau, from time to time, think he perceived some sort of transcendent mandate "hidden in immanence" within us? In one of his articles, he congratulates a mystic for having written that God is below us, and Merleau added, in so many words, "Why not?" He dreamed of this Almighty who would need men, who would still be called into question in each one's heart, and yet would remain total Being, unceasingly, infinitely instituted by intersubjectivity, the only one who we shall lead to the fount of our being, and who will share with us all the insecurity of the human adventure. Here we are obviously dealing only with a metaphorical indication. But the fact that he chose this metaphor is not without significance. Everything is there: the discovery and the risk of being is below us, a gigantic beggar-woman clad in rags, we need only an imperceptible change for her to become *our task*. God, the task of man? Merleau never wrote this, and forbade himself even to think it. Nothing says that he may not, at times, have dreamed it, but his method of inquiry was much too rigorous to allow him to advance anything which he hadn't established. He worked without haste. He was waiting.

People have claimed that he came closer to Heidegger. This is doubtless true, but it must be qualified. As long as his childhood was assured him Merleau felt no need to go back to the roots of his research. When his mother died, and childhood was abolished with her, absence and presence, Being and Non-Being, flowed into one another. Through phenomenology, and without ever departing from it, Merleau hoped to rejoin the imperatives of ontology. That which is no more, is not yet, and never will be.

It is for man to give being to beings. These tasks evolved from his life and from his bereavement. Through them, he found occasion to re-read Heidegger and to understand him better, but not to be influenced by him. Their paths crossed, that was all. Being is the only concern of the German philosopher. And in spite of a philosophy which they at times share, Merleau's principal concern remained man. When the former speaks of "the opening towards being," I feel a sense of alienation. I am certainly not denying that disturbing words come from Merleau's pen as well, for example: "Henceforth, the irrelative is not nature itself, nor is it the system of seizure of absolute conscience, nor is it even man, but rather, this 'teleology' which is written and thought between quotation marks—the joints and framework of a being which effects itself by means of man." The quotation marks have nothing to do with the problem. But it doesn't matter. This was said in passing. It is unfortunate that a man can still write today that the absolute is not man; but what he denies our domain, he accords to no other. His irrelative is really a reciprocal relationship closed in upon itself. Man is designated by his fundamental vocation which is to institute being, but equally so, being is designated by its destiny which is to effect itself through man. I have told how, at least twice—in the Christian community and in the brotherhood of political struggle—Merleau had sought envelopment within immanence, and had collided against the transcendent. More than ever avoiding any recourse to Hegelian synthesis, his last thoughts attempt to resolve the contradiction which he had lived. He lets transcendence flow into immanence, there to be dissolved at the same time as it is protected against annihilation by its very impalpability. It will be only absence and supplication, deriving its all-encompassing power from its infinite weakness. And, in a certain sense, isn't this the fundamental contradiction of humanism? Can dialectical materialism—in whose name many will try to criticize this meditation—do without an ontology? Looking at this more closely, however, and brushing aside the absurd theory of a reflection, don't we see, discreetly implicit, the idea of a layer of brute being which produces and sustains action and thought?

No. For the man who wrote this a few months before his death never stopped being a humanist: "In that instant where *l'homme-éclair* is kindled, everything is explained." And then what? To effect being is to consecrate it, which to be sure means to humanize it. Merleau doesn't maintain that we must perish in order for being to be, but just the contrary, that we shall institute being by that same act which causes us to be born human. Pascalian more than ever before, he repeats to us again: "Man is absolutely distinct from the animal species precisely in that he has no original equipment whatever, and is the dwelling-place of the contingent, sometimes taking the form of a kind of miracle and other times, the form of an adversity without motive." That suffices for man never to be the animal of a species, or the object of a universal concept, but rather, as soon as he appears, he is the explosion of event. But he finds the same lesson in the humanist Montaigne. "The explanations which define man as metaphysics or physics are those which Montaigne rejects in advance, since it is still man who 'proves' philosophies and science, and they are explained by him, rather than he by them . . ." Man will never think man. He makes him at every instant. And isn't this real humanism? Man will never be the total object of knowledge, for he is the subject of History.

The philosopher had grown somber, but it is still not hard to find a certain optimism in his last works. Nothing comes to an end, nothing is lost. An endeavor is born, instituting with one stroke *its* man—all man in a flash—and dies with him, or insanely survives him, only to end, in any case, in disaster, and at this same instant of disaster, it opens a door to the future. Spartacus fighting and dying is all of man. Who can say it better? A word is all words gathered up in a few sounds: a picture is all of painting. "In this sense," he says, "progress both is and is not." History constantly moves into our prehistoric environment. With each flash of light, the whole is illuminated, instituted, unravels and vanishes, immortal. Apelles, Rembrandt, Klee have each, in turn, *revealed being* within a defined civilization, with the means at hand. And well before the first of these was born, all of painting was already manifest in the caves of Lascaux.

Precisely because he is ceaselessly resumed in this ever-renewed flash of light, there will be a future for man. And there will also be the contingency of Good and of Evil.

Merleau no longer favored or condemned anyone. Adversity had placed us within a hairsbreadth of barbarism. The miracle, always and everywhere possible, could make us emerge from it. Since each gesture of our body and our language, each act of political life "spontaneously" takes into account others, transcending the singular within itself to reach towards the universal, so, although it is in no sense inevitable or promised, and although we ask less that it improve us in our being than that it clean up the wastes of our life, a *relative progress* has to be the most likely conjecture. "Very probably, experience will end by eliminating the wrong solutions." It was, I think, in this hope that Merleau agreed to write a few political commentaries for *L'Express*. The East and West, two growing economies, two industrial societies, each of them torn by contradictions. He would have hoped, above and beyond their regimes, to extricate their common needs at the level of their infrastructure, or, at least, their lines of convergence. This was his way of remaining true to himself. Again, it was a matter of refusing the Manichean option. There had been unity once. Before the loss of this minor paradise, he had wanted to denounce exploitation everywhere. Then he had shut himself away in silence. He emerged from this silence to seek everywhere for reasons to hope. Without any illusions; *la virtú,** nothing more. We are entangled. The ties uniting us to others are false ones. There is no regime which, by itself, would suffice to disentangle them, but perhaps the men who come after us, all men together, will have the power and the patience to take up this work where we left it.

The directions of our thinking separated us from one

---

* *virtú*: besides the concept of virtue, the Italian word also implies courage and manliness. (*Trans.*)

another a little more each day. His grief and voluntary seclusion made any reconciliation more difficult. In 1955 we all but lost each other through abstractions. He wrote a book on Dialectic, where he strongly took me to task. Simone de Beauvoir replied to him in *Les Temps Modernes* in terms no less strong. This was the first and last time that we fought in writing. By publishing our dissensions, we almost made them irremediable. But, on the contrary, at just the moment when our friendship seemed dead, it imperceptibly began to flower once more. Undoubtedly, he had taken too many pains to avoid violence. He needed some of it to liquidate his remaining grudges, to tell me once and for all what was in his heart. In short, the matter ended there and we saw each other again soon afterwards.

This was in Venice, in the first months of 1956. *La Société Européenne de Culture* had organized a meeting there of writers from the East and West. I was present. As I sat down, I noticed that the chair next to mine remained unoccupied. I leaned over and read Merleau-Ponty's name on the place-card. They thought we would be pleased to be seated next to one another. The discussion began but I was only half-listening. I was waiting for Merleau, not without dread. He came in, late as usual. Someone was speaking, he came in behind me, on tiptoe, lightly touched my shoulder and when I turned around, he smiled at me. The talks continued for several days. We didn't entirely agree, he and I, except to both be irritated when an Italian spoke who was too eloquent, or an Englishman who was too naïve, both of whom had as their mission to make the whole project fail. But in the presence of many diverse men, some older, others younger than ourselves, from the four corners of Europe, we two felt united by one culture, and one experience which was only valid for us. We spent several evenings together, with a certain awkwardness, never alone. It was better that way. Our friends who were present insured us against ourselves, against the temptation to re-establish our intimacy prematurely. As a consequence of this security, we only spoke to one another. Each of us were without any illusions about the significance of the meetings, but we each still hoped—he because he was a *lieur;* I, to "favor" the Left—that they would resume the following year. When it came time to edit the final minutes, we discovered that we were of the same opinion. It was nothing, yet it proved that a common labor could reunite us.

We met again in Paris, in Rome and again in Paris. Alone: this was the second step. The awkwardness remained, then seemed to disappear. Another emotion was born, tenderness. This gently funereal affection brings exhausted friends together again, friends so torn by strife that they have nothing left in common but their quarrel, and even that had ceased, one fine day, for lack of an object. The object had been the review. It had united, then divided us. Now it didn't even divide us any more. Our precautions had just missed estranging us. Forewarned, we took care never to spare each other again. Too late. Whatever we might do, each of us now only committed himself. When we took our bearings, I felt rather as though we had come to the point of exchanging family gossip: Aunt Marie is going to have an operation, nephew Charles has received his *bachot* . . . and that we were seated side by side on a park bench, with rugs over our knees, tracing figures in the dust with the tips of our canes. What was missing? It was not affection or esteem, but the undertaking. Buried, having been unable to separate us, our past activity took its revenge by making us pensioners of friendship.

We had to wait for the third step without forcing things. I waited, sure that we would find our friendship again. We were agreed in condemning the Algerian war unreservedly. He had returned his red ribbon [of the *Légion d'Honneur*] to Guy Mollet. Each of us were opposed to the rough draft of dictatorship which was Gaullism. We may not have shared the same point of view as to the means of fighting it. That would come. When fascism returns, it finds its old friends again. I saw Merleau again in March of that same year. I gave a lecture at the École Normale and he came. This touched me. For years it had always been me who urged that we get together, who suggested our meetings. Now, for the first time, he went out of his way spontaneously. Not in order to hear me elaborate ideas which he knew by heart, but to see me. At the end of the lecture, we gathered with Hippolyte and Canguilhem. This was a happy moment for me. But later I learned that Merleau still felt an awkwardness which persisted between us. There wasn't the shadow of it on my part, but unfortunately I was groggy with a case of grippe. When we parted, he hadn't said a word about feeling disappointed, but for a split second, it crossed my mind that his face had saddened. And then I forgot about it. "Everything is just as it was," I told myself. "Everything will begin anew." A few days later I learned of his death. Our friendship had ended upon this final misunderstanding. Alive we would have dissipated it, starting with my return. Maybe. Absent, we shall always be for one another what we have always been. Strangers.

There is no doubt about it. His readers may know him. He "met them in his works." Each time I become his reader, I shall get to know him—and myself—better. One hundred fifty pages of his future book are saved from oblivion, and then there is also "L'Oeil et l'Esprit" which says it all, providing one can decipher it. For all of us, we who shall "institute" this system of thought in tatters, it will remain one of the prisms of our "intersubjectivity." At this moment, when M. Papon, the Chief of Police, sums up public opinion by declaring that nothing surprises him, Merleau provides the antidote—being surprised by everything. He is a child scandalized by our futile grown-up certitudes, who asks shocking questions which the adults never answer. Why do we live? Why do we die? Nothing seems natural to him—neither that there should be a History or a Nature. He does not understand how it can happen that necessity turns into contingency and that all contingency terminates in necessity. He says this, and we, in reading him, are sucked into this spiral from which we shall never again escape. But he is not interrogating us. He is too afraid that we will hang on to dogmatisms which reassure us. He will be this interrogation of himself because the "writer has chosen insecurity": our fundamental situation as well as the difficult attitude which unveils this situation to us. It is not fitting that we ask him the answers. What he teaches us is the method of a preliminary inquiry. He recalls, after Plato, that the philosopher is he who is never astonished, but more rigorous than his Greek master, he adds that the philosophic attitude disappears as soon as astonishment ceases. The inverse of all those who predicate the "becoming-world" of philosophy, he replies that man, even were he to be one day happy, free and transparent to his fellow-man, would be astonished by this suspect happiness inasmuch as we are engaged, for the present, in creating our unhappiness. If he hadn't felt that this word had been debased by overuse, I would freely say that he was able to discover the internal dialectic of the questioner and the questioned, and that he applied it to the fundamental question which, for all our pretense of answers, we avoid. To follow him, we must renounce these two contradictory securities between which we incessantly oscillate. For we generally reassure ourselves through the use of two opposing but parallel universal concepts, each of which we take for objects. The first tells each of us that he is a man among men, and the second that he is *other* among others. But the latter is worthless since man makes himself unceasingly, but can never quite think himself. And the former deceives us since we are precisely alike in that each differs from all. Leaping from one of these ideas to the other, like monkeys from branch to branch, we avoid singularity, which is not so much a fact as a perpetual postulation. Severing our ties with our contemporaries, the bourgeoisie imprisons us within the cocoon of private life and defines us, with snips of the scissors, as *individuals*, which means, as molecules without history who drag themselves from one instant to the next. In Merleau, we discover ourselves through the contingency of our anchorage in Nature and History, that is, through the temporal adventure which we are in the womb of the human adventure. Thus History makes us universal in the exact measure which we make it particular. This is the important gift which Merleau offers us, through his desperate struggle to keep digging in the same place. Setting out from the well-known universality of the singular, he arrives at the singularity of the universal. It is he who unearthed the capital contradiction: Every history is all History, when *l'homme-éclair* is kindled, all is said. Every life, every moment, every era—contingent miracles or contingent failures—are *incarnations*. The word becomes flesh, the universal is only established by the living singularity which deforms it by singularizing it. Do not read this simply as a new chopped-up form of "tragic conscience." It is just the opposite. Hegel is describing the tragic opposition of two abstract notions, those same ones which I have said were the poles of our security. But for Merleau, universality is never universal, except in high-altitude thinking. It is born along with the flesh, flesh of our flesh. It retains in its most subtle degree our singularity. Such is the warning that Anthropology—Psychoanalysis or Marxism—should never forget; nor, as do the Freudians too often, that each man is Everyman, and that in all men, we must take into account the *flash of light*, the singular universalization of universality. Nor, should we forget, as novice dialecticians, that the Soviet Union is not the simple beginning of universal revolution, but its incarnation as well, and that 1917 gives future Socialism its indelible characteristics. This problem is a difficult one. Neither ordinary anthropology nor historical materialism will deliver us from it. Merleau didn't pretend to supply the solutions—quite the contrary. Had he lived, he would have buried himself, always turning, always deeper, until he had gone to the root of the givens of the question, as we can see from what he says of primordial historicity in "L'Oeil et l'Esprit." He hadn't come to the end of his philosophy, or at least, he hadn't the time to express it completely. Is this a failure? No, it is simply a continuation of the contingency of birth by the contingency of death. Singularized by this double absurdity, and meditating upon singularity from the beginning of his thought until his death, this life assumes an inimitable "style," and justifies the monitions of the work. As for the latter, which is inseparable from his life, a flash of light between two risks, illuminating the middle of our night, we could apply to him word for word the statement which he wrote at the beginning of this year [1961]:

If we cannot establish a painting, nor even elsewhere, a hierarchy, nor even speak of progress, it is not some sort of destiny which keeps us back. It is rather that, in one sense, the first painting went straight to the heart of the future. If no painting completes painting, if no one work of art completes itself absolutely, each creation changes, alters, enlightens, deepens, confirms, exalts, recreates or creates all the others in advance. If creations are not previous knowledge, it is not only that they pass away, like everything else, but also that they have almost their whole life ahead of them.

Question without an answer, *virtú* without illusion, the creation enters universal culture in the singular, but lodges there as a universal in the singularity of History. Changing, as Hegel has said, the contingent into the necessary and the necessary into the contingent, it has as its function to incarnate the problem of incarnation. For you, the *rendez-vous* is in his work.

But I had other *rendez-vous* with him, and I don't want to lie about our relationship, nor end on a note of lofty optimism. I still see his last melancholy expression—as we parted, at the rue Claude Bernard—disappointed, suddenly closed. He remains inside me, a painful sore, infected by sorrow, remorse and some bitterness. Changed from within, our friendship is there summed up forever. I neither accord any privilege to its last moments, nor do I believe that these moments contain the truth about a lifetime. Yet in that life, everything had been gathered up: all the silences with which, starting in 1950, he opposed me, are frozen in that silent expression, and reciprocally, I still feel to this day the eternity of his absence as a deliberate mutism. It is clear to me that our final misunderstanding—which would have been nothing had I seen him alive again—was made of the same fabric as all the others. It compromised nothing, revealing our mutual affection, our common desire not to spoil anything between us, but it also showed our lives were out-of-phase, causing our initiatives to be out-of-step; and then joined later by adversity, which suspended our dealings without violence, but forever. Death is an incarnation like birth. His death was non-meaning, full of a meaning which remained obscure, but fulfilled in all that concerned us, the contingency and necessity of a friendship without joy. Nevertheless, there had been something for which to strive. With our good qualities and our failings, the public violence of the one and the secret outrage of the other, we weren't so badly suited after all. And what did we do with it? Nothing, except avoid total estrangement. Each of you may blame who he will. In any case, we weren't really very guilty, so little, in fact, that sometimes all I can see in our adventure was its necessity. That is the way men live in our time. That is the way they love. Badly. This is true, but it is also true that it was us, we two, who loved each other badly. There is nothing to be concluded from this except that this long friendship, neither done nor undone, obliterated when it was about to be reborn, or broken, remains inside me, an ever-open wound.

Of Rats and Men

"*T*hey cured his squint with glasses, his lisp with a metal brace, his stammer with mechanical exercises, and he spoke perfectly, but in such a low and rapid voice that, 'What's that you're saying?' his mother would say, 'Speak up. What are you mumbling now?' and they nicknamed him the Mumbler. . . ."

This hushed, level, polite voice is what you will hear and from now on you will recognize it from all others. To whom does it belong? To nobody? One would say that language had begun to speak by itself. From far off, the word "I" happens to be pronounced, and we think we catch a glimpse of the Speaker of the Word, of the subject who is choosing his terms. A pure mirage: the subject of the verb itself is only an abstract word: the sentence has followed its customary route, assuming this personal turn only for convenience. But in fact, *someone is there*, "a thin fellow with hollow eyes and cheeks, a receding chin and forehead, a long protruding turtle's neck stretched in front of him, slightly round-shouldered: he seems to evaporate with his meager gestures, as though trying to contain himself within his being. But he is silent. He is an object. Each statement reconstructs and shapes him. Without this mute, the voice would be deserted. The mute inhabits it, spreading his verbal body across the words. It informs us that *he* is troubled, that *he* has completed a work on philosphy, that *he* is about to leave it with a certain Morel.

"What is it to us," you will say, "this anonymous whispering? We want well-made books by real authors: in liter-

---

Originally the foreword to Le Traître, *by André Gorz (Éditions du Seuil, Paris, 1958).*

ature, as in the flying trapeze our sole pleasure is in the enjoyment of the artist's skill: we attach no more importance to shudders racking an abandoned language than to the wind shaking the reeds." Well, then, close this book: only at the last page, in fact, does a certain Gorz, risen from the primordial slime, assert his retrospective rights to the discourse which bore him. "I didn't want to make a work of art," he says, and you will gladly believe him: scarcely have you heard this forlorn voice, then you perceive in it, all at once, the uncertain flabbiness of natural things, of some unknown arid quest, unconscious of itself, and always on the verge of running aground in words. But art is the calm reflection of movement. As soon as you begin reading a novel, or a confession, everything has long since been consumed. The before and after are only operational signs, the birth and death throes of a love exist at the same time, each spreading over the other in the eternal indistinction of the moment. To read is to make a transfusion of time. The hero lives on our life, our ignorance of the future. The dangers surrounding him are our own; with our reader's patience, he constructs a parasitic duration whose strand we break and resume at the pleasure of our moods. As for style—that great flourish of the arrogant—it is death. Its illusory speed carries us towards the author's past. The latter may well lament and torture himself. As soon as he takes pen in hand, the dice have long since been cast, his friend has already betrayed him, his mistress left him, his decision to hate them or the human race made; he writes to communicate his hatred. Style is a hammer which bludgeons our resistance, a sword which slashes our reasoning, it is all ellipse, syncopation, sleight-of-hand, fake connivance. Rhetoric supplies the terror, the rage, the insolence, the ruminative humiliation. The proud victor commands the attack and the shape of the sentences. This wild maniac, the great writer, hurls himself upon language, subdues, chains and mistreats it, all *faute de mieux;* alone in his study, he is an autocrat. If he spears his paper with a thunderous roar that will be the marvel of twenty generations to come, it is merely that he hopes to find in this verbal *ukase* the symbol of respectability and the modest powers which his contemporaries persist in denying him. A dead man's revenge. Contempt killed him ages ago. Behind these flashes of lightning lurks a dead child who prefers himself to everything else: the child Racine, the child Pascal, the child Saint-Simon, there are our classics. We like to stroll among the tombs of literature, this calm cemetery, deciphering its epitaphs, reviving for an instant their eternal meanings. What reassures us, is that these phrases *have* lived, their meaning is fixed forever, they will not take advantage of the brief survival which we deign to accord them by marching off unexpectedly, dragging us towards an unknown future. As for those novelists who aren't yet fortunate enough to be in their coffins, they play dead. They go looking for words in their fish ponds, they kill them, open them, drain them, and then prepare them *au bleu, meunière,* or grilled.

The Traitor will find its place beyond and apart from the literary undertaking. This Gorz is not dead. In the beginning, he carries his impertinence to the point of not even being born. Thus, no rhetoric at all: who would be persuading us? And of what? Neither is it a question of capturing our time span to nourish a fictitious hero, nor of directing our dreams with words. There is this voice, and that is all:

this voice which searches without knowing what it is searching for, which doesn't know what it wants, which speaks into the void, in darkness, perhaps to give a meaning *through words* to the words which escape from him, or perhaps, only to hide his fear.

For, it is afraid: we can no longer doubt it. It says: "*He* is afraid, *he* is anxious, because *he* has finished his book." This voice aspires to impassivity. In itself only a sound chamber where objective meanings are gathered together, it enumerates the passions of a thin fellow with a hollow gaze, but it doesn't feel them. We aren't taken in. Enclosed, at first, in this foreign body, *in the individual about whom they are speaking,* these passions burst from their wrappings. They can no longer be localized. The entire voice is impregnated with anguish. This is what causes the lifeless urgency of that mumbling, of those groping, scrupulous, modest words. They are feverish: it is the voice of worry that we hear. This time we have understood—the one *about whom they speak,* is *the one who is speaking.* But the two cannot manage to become one. There exists on earth at least one man who drinks, eats, sleeps, works, who, in short, resembles us like a brother, and who is condemned by a mysterious curse to remain *another* in his own eyes.

Have they so ground and crushed his inner life that there remains only a rumbling of words in a decomposed body? Or else, is his conscience intact, but so deeply buried that it must peer at him from afar, as a stranger, and not recognize him? No one knows yet, because this shattered being is nobody. This dummy with hollow eyes is all there is, this pure object which doesn't know itself, this little tumult of words unraveling into the empty night. To whom, in fact, is this voice speaking? Certainly not to us. In order to address men, you have to be one of them. It doesn't care about being heard. It is the fissure itself which deepens while trying to become whole, a tissue of language which has started unraveling. Without bearings, stirred by a nameless anguish, the words labor: if they are furiously trying to denote this carcass of a man, it is because they are humbly attempting to take possession of it, to dissolve it in themselves. The voice is born of a risk: either to lose oneself or win the right to speak in the first person.

This is the reason why the soliloquy disconcerts us: we are eavesdropping. You will laugh at my naïveté, you will tell me: but after all, Gorz published his book. Yes, *when there was* a Gorz to make decisions about it. But he neither added nor subtracted anything from this beginning which seems to go nowhere, and which was meant for no one. When I rambled on as a child, I was told, "Be quiet, you stream of warm water!" A stream of warm water will run through you: it will be made of those long undulant phrases like caterpillar trains, broken by parentheses, swollen by qualifications which they themselves have engendered in retrospect, struck out by doubts and regrets, turned upside down by going abruptly backwards. Where is the Order? Where is the Ceremony? Where the common politeness? You will try in vain to hang on to previous declarations; they are incessantly transformed by the declarations which follow: you will learn on page 80 that *we* really didn't think what was written on page 30, that *we* only believed we thought it on page 150, that *we* didn't even believe it, page 170, that what is more, *we* didn't even write it, that in fact, we had written a particular sentence dreaming that we had written another, page 200, that the dreamed and written meanings are strictly interchangeable and that both of them, moreover, are false. But we must not imagine ourselves to be witnesses of a confession which is, first of all, a lie, and which invents its sincerity as it goes along: there is neither confessant, nor confessor, nor confessional, nor anything to confess: when the voice was raised—I know, for I have been a witness—it had nothing to say and its truth did not exist. It spoke words at random, and because it had to start somewhere. These words are transparent, referring only to themselves. And above all, do not look for an expository device in this defenseless stammer: nothing is more sincere, less artificial than this undertaking. It begins in anguish, in want, there, right under your very eyes, with the same words. It goes astray, and we along with it. It is true that it is lost and that it will find itself: *it is true* that it disappears and grows rich.

Accustomed to the play of the intellect, we believe, from the first words, that we grasp the movement of this thought, the intention which presides over the construction of a paragraph: these rapid anticipations, these implicit conjectures, these prophecies which normally allow us to understand the course of the world and the actions of men. Thus, feet together, we jump on top of developments to come, to await this language on the march, comfortably settled at the last period. But in this instance, the procedure is worthless; we discovered a purpose, and, in this fact, we were not mistaken; it simply changes in midstream; there is nobody there to sustain it. "The Master is in the Styx" or rather, in limbo. There remain these knick-knacks of sonorous emptiness which are metamorphosed into flesh, each one of which, by its presence alone, modifies the others. Leaning against the final milestone, we watch this verbal flood roll towards us and then suddenly, it gathers itself up, contracts, changes direction, slides down another slope, and gives us the slip. This limitless recurrence of our disappointments makes us see chattering disorder in what will emerge later as an order in the process of construction.

For it is an order, this slow unpredictable progression. It is a truth in the process of becoming, of minutely organizing itself. It is an entire human existence which moves from the abstract to the concrete, from poverty to riches, from the universal to the particular, from anonymous objectivity to subjectivity. There are reasons for our astonishment: books are dead men. Here now is one which, scarcely in our hands, becomes a living creature. To be sure, we had to open it and awaken the signs, but the reader's slightest movement will precipitate an unforeseen event, neither its duration nor end is given in advance. You think you are lending it your continuity and it imposes its own. You will discover the laws of this perilous discourse as they are engendered, but you will know, at the same time, that they will not cease changing, and that the entire system will transform them in the same measure that it is based upon them.

This muted harsh voice, this voice which sheds itself, will resound in your ears. Its slowness is truly speed, since it guides us towards a *true* future, the only one which is not a dumb-show of memories, towards a place unknown to all, which does not exist yet which, nevertheless, *will be*. It strips away appearances. Neither warm, soft, nor fluid, it discovers for us the inflexible order of *enrichment*. Each sentence gathers unto itself all those preceding it, each the living atmosphere where the others breathe, live, and are transformed, or rather, there is only one, driving on over every terrain, nourished by every soil, always thicker, rounder, more dense, swelling to the bursting point, until it becomes a man. At every moment, it runs a real risk. It could explode, halt pitifully to fall back upon itself, an inert and frozen ball in the desert of the present. We feel this danger within ourselves, we read on anxiously. Of course, the book seems finished, after this page, others follow. But what does this prove? Everything could end in nothingness, or worse, could sink into the sands. What reassures us, however, is that we perceive, behind the hesitations of life and language, an arid, trenchant and frozen passion, a steel wire stretched between the lacerations of the past and the uncertainty of the future. An inhuman passion, ignorant of itself, an uneasy seeker, a lunatic silence within the heart of language. It bores a hole through the reader's time, dragging this stream of words behind. We shall have faith in it.

Since the work of art cries the name of the artist (that great corpse who has settled everything) to the four winds, *The Traitor* is not a work of art: it is a "happening," a sudden rush, a welter of words which dispose themselves: you hold in your hands that amazing object, a work in the act of creating *its* author. For about the latter, we know nothing save this negative characteristic: he will not, he cannot, be that sacrosanct monster we call the Writer. If he is there, at the end of his efforts, he will be anyone at all, a man like all the others. Because the voice is in search of a man, not a monster. So do not expect that *gesture* which is style: everything is *in action*. But if, in our great writers, you like a certain savor of the words, a particular air of the phrase, a physiognomy of feelings and thoughts, read *The Traitor. You will begin by losing everything,* but all will be restored to you; its weariness, its passionate quest, its breaking, give this voice an inimitable tone: in this writing without a subject, the radical impossibility of the style becomes finally a transcendence of all known styles, or, if you prefer, the style of death gives way to a style of life.*

The undertaking will be distasteful. We love those who love us: if you want to be read, you have to give of yourself, pinch the words slyly until they quiver, become hoarse with tenderness. But *him,* the object, the third person, the third knife, how could he love us? How could it love us, this voice? We are confronted by a severed man, trying to graft his stumps together. Work of this type leaves no time for leisure, tomorrow for whoring, if you still can. To which you will doubtless reply that your time is also limited, and that problems of grafting do not interest you. But what do you know about them? I read science-fiction occasionally, and always with pleasure. These stories give the exact degree to which we fear ourselves. One tale among others delighted me: men land on Venus. These future colonizers have hardly left their space ship when they joyously set off to hunt the natives of the planet, their future subjects, who, at first, do not appear. We can imagine the pride of these lords of creation, drunk with triumph and new freedom. But soon everything crumbles in the face of intolerable evidence: the conquerors are in a cage. Their

---

* I am not trying to establish the superiority of Gorz, but his originality. Like everyone, I love death as much as life, since both the one and the other are part of our lot.

every move has been charted, the roads they discover have been marked out for them. Bent over this glass cage, invisible, the inhabitants of Venus are subjecting these superior mammals to intelligence tests. This, it seems to me, is our common condition, with this difference—we are our own Venus dwellers and our own guinea pigs. Open *The Traitor* and you are a colonizer, nodding, you contemplate a strange animal—a native, perhaps—who runs panic-stricken over the ground of Venus. But I don't give you two minutes to perceive that the native is a rat and the rat none other than yourself. The book is a trap and we have fallen into it. At the moment, we scurry through the corridors of this too-large labyrinth under the gaze of the experimenters, that is, under *our* gaze. The experiment is under way: it consists of determining whether, in this debased world, there exists a sole act of which we can safely say, "I did it." Do we recognize our own pursuits? By fulfilling themselves, don't they become something *else?* Don't *others* carry them out in our place? Others who are dearer to us than ourselves, and who are sustained by our blood? Scarcely has this stranger, in my most secret council, decided my actions for me, when I hear the roars of the mob which inhabits me: a wild agitation takes on the form of all those people whom I do not know. They condemn my effort, protesting that it only concerns me. I am another, says the voice of the Traitor. I find this modest indeed. In its place, I would say that I am *others*, speaking of myself in the third person plural. Each of my acts, by inscribing itself into the passivity of my being, becomes a tourniquet whose imperious inertia defines *his man* in me, *his slave,* in other words, this other whom I must be in order to give it the first impetus and to renew it incessantly. My slightest gestures, my most sincere commitments produce lifeless shapes: I have to slip into these treadmills turning inside, like a circus horse, to make them go around. *He,* the author who is writing this preface, is, even at this moment, *Another,* and one whom I dislike. The book appealed to me and I said yes, that I would preface it, because we must always pay for the right to love the things we love. But as soon as I seized the pen, an invisible carousel began turning just above the paper. It was *the Forward as a literary genre,* which was seeking its specialist, a serene and handsome old man, an Academician. I *was not* an Academician. Never mind. *He* would become one for the occasion. How does one dare introduce another's book without being on the brink of death? *He* placed himself in that person's skin, he became august-transparent-and-astonished Elder. *He* wrote the preceding with the fingertips of a long pale hand which manipulated my thick-set one, he plunges his tentacles into me, breathing into my words and ideas to draw from them his quaint graces. If I try to break away from his grip, to write naturally, it only makes matters worse: I have no naturalness left. *He* filters it, transforming it into amiability. He will hold the pen until the end of this exercise and then take off. But, whatever I may subsequently undertake—pamphlet, lampoon or autobiography—other vampires await me, future intermediaries between my conscience and the written page.

Can I hope, at least, that the interloper will go away? But it so happens that he stays, and that I am the victim and the accomplice of his tenancy. One day, *Mirandole* found himself obliged to publish, under the pseudonym of *Jouvence,* one of those wholesome and angry books which exhort their readers to courage, and which, for this reason, are called courageous. The work had a great success. Sad and weary men saw an austere and holy figure between the lines who gave them hope. In short, Mirandole's work, by getting cold, created Jouvence, its real author. Today, Jouvence is heralded as a public service, his virtues are taught in the primary schools, he is part of our national wealth, and often represents France abroad: he lives on Mirandole and Mirandole dies from him. The other day, at some gala opening or other, only a miserable jump seat had been reserved for them. Mirandole, modest, almost shy, took hold of himself, however, and made a scene, trembling all the while. "Personally, I would have said nothing," he explained at the door, "but I *couldn't* let them do *that* to Jouvence."

Where is his error? Where is yours? After all, we didn't invite these undesirable guests: it is the *Others* who impose them upon us—the others or tools of the others, those rigid fingers pointing incessantly at us. The instrument case and the patient make out of a silly fat man, *The Doctor*, this angelic dictator, this enlightened despot who acts against us for our own good and from whom we avidly await the orders, scoldings and adorable severity. The desire seizes us occasionally to muzzle the vampires and to reveal ourselves as we are. Nobody listens; they are waiting for *Them*. In the face of disappointment or general indifference, we say to ourselves primly, "If everyone is agreed . . ." And then we get rid of the monsters. It always ends badly. In the first postwar days, I became friendly with a foreign painter. He was from London. We talked in a café. Another Traitor, that one, or who thought he was. He had so little liking for himself that people detested him: it was his name they liked.

I found him charming; arrogant and weak, suspicious and naïve, mad with pride and shame, cruel and kind. Fascinated by his fame and harassed by it, he was still astounded to have a considerable production already behind him, which he, nevertheless, disdained. This Don Quixote could only have acquired self-respect, had he won, in another domain, a battle in which he knew he would never even engage. Indeed, two years later, everything ended with bursts of laughter. Unstable, miserable, romantic, he was entirely dependent on the hour, on the light, on a note of music, on women and above all, on men, on all men, *on all of us;* we could have saved him. Lacking this unanimity, he oscillated between arrogance and a disarming kindness. Sometimes, to forget that neglected gonorrhea, his Treason, he let himself be devoured whole by that marvelous being which he represented for others. Then, there was nothing left of him but a glow worm.

At other times, fear, kindness and good faith changed him back into himself, into just an ordinary man who painted. On one of those days, a little old man, seated at an adjoining table, was devouring him with his eyes. I knew him, he was one of his compatriots, an expatriate like him, but who had had no luck. Finally, when he could contain himself no longer, the old man rose and introduced himself to my companion, who, off guard, ingenuously returned his smile: glory and genius were extinguished together: there only remained two exiles, who recognized without knowing each other and who spoke to each other with affection. It was the unluckier of the two who rekindled the aureole around the head of his interlocutor: there had been a misunderstanding, it was not the man to whom he spoke, but the Painter.

One shouldn't ask too much of artists: summoned by too-overt respect, by a few obsequious inflections, the Great Man appeared. He was perfect: understanding, modest, so genially simple that he put his compatriot to flight. The latter hastily gathered up the papers which were spread out on his table and left the café with an embittered and disappointed air, without understanding that he had been the artisan of his own misery. We stayed on alone, and after an embarrassed silence, the great man murmured these words which I shall never forget: "Another failure." And this meant: "*He* said that he would forget about his name, his reputation, his voluminous presence, that *he* would be just an exile confronted by a companion in exile. But since they expected the Incomparable Artist, *he* resigned himself, *he* lent his body and voice to this Other who isn't even his personal parasite, who sucks, at the same time, the blood of thousands of people, from Peking to Valparaiso, going by way of Moscow and Paris, and he heard him speak with his own voice, with that terrible softness which meant: But, it's nothing. I'm nothing, I have nothing more than you, fortune just smiled on me, that's all." And he realized that, once again, he had missed his chance, and that should it appear every day, at every hour, that every day and every hour, he would miss it again.

The test is not over; we have not finished scurrying around the laboratory; the voice hasn't finished speaking. These tourists, these mercenaries who lodge in us by the month or by the day, the investigation doesn't concern them: no one is going to ask us for an account of the furnished rooms on Venus, or about the sitting rooms with a hundred mirrors that we rent to transients: everyone will be allowed to leave after their identity has been checked, except one mysterious and rarely visible guest, usurper who claims to be the gatekeeper, but who is, in truth, only our oldest tenant. The personage whom the voice persists in calling "He" is precisely *that one there*. Moreover listen to it— already the voice isn't quite the same. At the beginning, it limited itself to criticizing the movements of the occupant, it next revealed that this person was under observation, it described the tests to which they would subject him and gave the results. Now, hardened, tenacious, sometimes brutal, it *interrogates*. The inhabitants of Venus have changed into police and the rats into suspects. At first, naturally, they persuade us that we are merely witnesses in a judicial inquiry. No one seems to bother about us. It is a man named Gorz who is on the culprit's bench. His name has just been pronounced: they question him relentlessly, they shake his alibis, he is forced to contradict himself: what was he doing in Vienna on a particular day in the winter of 1936? And before that, in his earliest childhood, and later on, at the time of the Anschluss. He admits to having frequented young Nazis, to having admired them. Why? He claims to have broken with them subsequently; is this really true? Can he say, "I broke with *them*"? Wasn't he forced to do so by circumstances, by his *objective nature?* And where does it come from, this nature? From whom? From what? Mute, embarrassed, we are present at the interrogation and we do our best to feel indiscreet. What luck if we can say to ourselves: I wasn't in Vienna at the time of Chancellor Dollfuss, that business doesn't concern me. But no, we are cornered and we know it. At that moment when we shall point out to the guards that our presence in the torture chamber is explained by a simple misunderstanding, we have long since been reduced to confessions. Torturer and victim, as always, it is we, the police, who are giving the traitor the third degree. But as soon as he sits down at the table, as soon as this doomed dwarf denounces his first inhabitant, we suddenly remember this little cripple who inhabited us for a long time and we try to reconstruct the mysterious circumstances of his disappearance. In 1920, I existed and *he* still existed. Then *who* was it who mutilated him so horribly? I remember that I didn't at all like him. Then I didn't see him anymore. There was a murder, I think. But which of us has killed the other? The voice is still speaking. It has found words to designate the break which tears us apart. The first guilty parties have left their fingerprints on a knife. It won't be long before we identify them.

It would seem, in fact, that there are still savages to be found on earth who are ignorant enough to see their reincarnated ancestors in their newborn infants. They wave the weapons and necklaces of the dead elders over the suckling baby. If it moves, everyone shrieks. Great-uncle has been resuscitated. This old man will nurse, befoul the straw under him, they will call the infant by his name. The survivors of his generation will delight in seeing their old comrade of war and hunting wave his little legs and bawl. As soon as he can speak, they will inculcate him with memories of the defunct, a harsh training will restore his former character. They will remind him that *he* was ill-tempered, cruel or magnanimous, and he will remain convinced of this, despite the denials of experience. What barbarism—taking a living brat and sewing him into the skin of a dead man. He will suffocate in this senile childhood with nothing else to do but reproduce exactly his uncle's gestures, with no other hope but that of poisoning his future children after his own death. After all that, should we be surprised if he speaks of himself with the greatest caution, in an undertone, often in the third person: this wretched creature is not unaware that he is his own great-uncle.

These retarded aborigines are to be found in the Fiji Islands, in Tahiti, in New Guinea, in Vienna, Paris and Rome, wherever there are men. We call them parents. Long before our birth, long before we were even conceived, our family had defined our person. They spoke of us as "He" years before we were able to say "I." We had our first existence as *absolute objects*. Through our family, society assigned us a situation, a being, a group of roles. The contradictions of history and social struggles determine in advance the character and destiny of the generations to come.

Algeria 1935: the parents are exploited, oppressed, reduced in the name of racism, to a poverty which refuses them the quality of man, the Arab language is learned like a dead language, the French schools are so small in number that the great majority of Algerians are illiterate. Rejected by France, without rights, culture, past, they find help only in religion, only in the negative pride of a mounting nationalism. Aren't their sons, the *fellaghas* of 1957, prefabricated? And who made them, if not the colonists? Who, since Bugeaud* prescribed for them this destiny of rage, despair and blood? Who constructed these infernal machines which one day had to explode, carrying colonization with it. The role is

* Bugeaud de la Piconnerie, duc d'Isly (1784–1849), contributed largely to the consolidation of French conquests in Africa where he was named Governor of Algeria in 1840. (*Trans.*)

there, everywhere, awaiting its man. For this one, it is the role of the Jew, for that one, the role of the landowner. But these functions are still too abstract: we particularize them within a family: we have all been forced to reincarnate *at least one* defunct, in general, it is a child-victim of his nearest relatives, killed at a young age and whose desolate ghost lives on in adult form—our own father and mother, these living dead. Hardly emerged from the womb, each child of man is *taken for another*. They push and pull him, forcing him into his role, like those children whom the *comprachicos* cram into porcelain urns to prevent them from growing. At least those, we can say, were not the sons of their torturers. Sometimes they purchased them, often they kidnapped them. Doubtless. But who is not a kidnapped child, more or less? Kidnapped from the world, from his neighbor, from himself? The custom has perpetuated itself. From kidnapped children are made kidnappers of children. We knew all that, we have always known it. A solitary voice told us this relentlessly, but we prefer to pass over it in silence. It spoke in the desert, *our* desert. *It* did this or that in our place and we were its straw boss, we proclaimed, through cowardice and compliance, it was me that committed the crime: and everyone will pretend to believe us—on condition of reciprocity. And thus humanity, ashamed of having ceded, since the millennium, to fear, to blackmail, hides from itself the whirling and turning racket which lives on it: happily, someone is coming to take the rap, a traitor, a guy like one of those American longshoremen, who, disgusted by their own cowardice, denounce the gang of their exploiters, and are found soon afterwards in the Hudson between the tides. A traitor: a guy full of holes like all of us, but one who could bear duplicity no longer. He shattered the silence, refused to assume the acts of the intruder who paid for him, refused to say: me. With one stroke there they are, naked, the Others, the Zars, the loas, black angels, sons of Cain, all of our parasites. Naked but not dead: we are torn between shame and dread. From one minute to another, we expect the syndicate's next move and the execution of the informer. But we have gained nothing from this. We find our own chinks and discover our occupants, that is all. But we are stripped of our illusions; this little gnawing sound—we thought it came from our ears, but no, it was born in our hearts. This time we have recognized the universal muttering of enslaved consciences, the Human Voice, and we are not about to forget it.

This is not to say, of course, that the Traitor does not belong to a very particular species. He has his own way of being just anyone at all. Neither Mad Doctors nor Conquering Heroes have chosen him as their residence. If he speaks of himself in the third person, it is not through excess, but by default. These judicious acts that we commit in his name, he would assume as his own, if he could only find motives for them; he has made a hundred inquiries, always in vain; we shall conclude that he cares for nothing. *He* travels without wanting to travel, he meets people and visits them, he invites them to his house without liking their company. At other times, he goes underground, he holes up with no desire whatever to be alone. Is he blasé, perhaps? Certainly not: to detach oneself from the things of this world, one must first have been attached to them. Above all, do not reproach him with "having returned from everywhere, without ever having gone." Because there is nothing of the ghost about him. He never left, that is his real trouble. Why? Because he did not want it enough. His heart, moreover, shows no traces of that arrogant discontent which has served as alibi to three generations of our men of letters. The infinite, the eternal Elsewhere, the Dream—thank God, he does not give a damn for any of that. I know certain people who give themselves the right to disdain the world by comparing it to some perfect prototype. But the Traitor disdains nothing and no one. Is he then that "empty suitcase" of which Drieu la Rochelle speaks. No. The suitcase routine works for the periods between wars. They opened it, and asked the spectator to satisfy himself that it contained nothing except pajamas and a toothbrush. Today we know that the suitcase had a false bottom, and that it was used for running guns and smuggling narcotics. Gilded youth easily hid there everything of any use in destroying mankind and hastening the advent of the Inhuman. But the Traitor will carefully restrain himself from blowing up the world. The Inhuman is *already his lot* since he doesn't share the goals of men. In a word, I would class him among the Indifferents. This subgroup is of recent origin; its representatives are no more than thirty; no one knows yet what will become of them. But it must be noted from now on, that we rob ourselves of the means of understanding them if we ascribe to them an aristocratic nonchalance. They are distinguished by their eagerness. Gorz practices a profession, cultivates his mind and body, is married. You could see him in the law courts or the Stock Exchange where, carrying his elegant leather briefcase, you would take him for one of yours. Punctual at his job, even fussy, no one is more affable. He manifests only the merest shadow of reserve in his daily encounters, which his colleagues smilingly explain as shyness. One has only to ask him a favor, for him to fly to perform it more quickly. The more superficial consider him innocuous, given that he has too little to say. *He seems like everybody else*, and this perfectly imitated effacement and resemblance will assure his popularity. But when we examine him more closely, this impostor is unmasked by his zeal. Most people, convinced from father to son of being men, treat their human nature with a certain carelessness. Their title to it is of such long standing, and has been so little challenged, that they calmly follow their personal inclinations, sure of peeing, if they so desire, or of killing most humanely. But the Indifferent does not know himself by inclination. Whether he takes a drink or fights, he has to bring himself to do it, to drink without being thirsty, to avenge without anger an insult which he has not resented, *to do as others do*. His first impulse is not to have any impulse: that is what must be constantly hidden, denied. This strange product of our societies, through fear of falling to the level of angels, or that of trained beasts, forces himself to imitate the Adamities in everything; he loses himself; Jean Paulhan called himself the "conscientious warrior" in an excellent little book in which he recounts his war experiences. The Indifferent renders himself suspect for the simple reason that he is a conscientious man.

Too conscientious to be true; if he wants to pass for my fellow creature, it is just because he isn't. Does the human community contain counterfeit men? And who cannot be distinguished from the real ones? In that case, how do we know whether there are real ones? Who will verify their claims? I have heard it sometimes said that man was the future of man; at other times, that he was his past; never his present. We are all counterfeit. For the second time, the Traitor has let the cat out of the bag. By the ardor which he puts into *making himself* human, he reminds us that our species does not exist. The author of this book is a rat, how could we have doubted it? And what is more, a rat possessed. But possessed by what? By another rat? By the rat within himself? Precisely not. This Other of whom a solitary voice speaks to us incessantly, this pure object, this disappearing line, this absence, is Man, our tyrant. Here we are unmasked—rats in the prey of Man. And with this, the mad undertaking of the Indifferent becomes apparent. It is our own. We are all pursuing a phantom through the corridors of an experimental labyrinth, with Gorz in the lead. If he catches and eats this parasite who, for so long, has fed upon his anguish and weariness, if he absorbs it into his own substance, our species is possible. Somewhere, between rats and men, it is in the process of being born and we shall emerge from the labyrinth.

Once again, the subject matter of the book has transformed itself: it is not a question of knowing oneself, but of changing one's life. It is not addressed to us yet, but willing or not, it is of us that the fundamental question is asked. By what activity can an "accidental individual"* realize the human person within himself and for all?

This work, as I have said before, is organized like a machine with feedback. The present incessantly metamorphoses the past from which it issues. In the first pages of the book, it seemed to us that the voice was gathering words at random, anywhere, in order to escape from anguish, and

* This is a term of Marx (*German Ideology*.)

in order for there to be *something, anything* behind it, but silence. And this was true: It was true *at that particular moment.* But the question of man was raised: the beginning of the undertaking appears in a new light. It is a metamorphosis. *Before the voice,* Gorz already existed, he already suffered from his indifference and he defended himself against it with the means at hand. Abruptly, he changes tactics and inverts his relationship to himself. This rupture constitutes an absolute event in itself, but we would be wrong to see it as an interior adventure whose principal merit would be to have produced a book. For in fact, it is *within the book* that this takes place. It is through it and by means of it that this venture develops and becomes conscious of itself. *The Traitor* doesn't intend to *tell us the story of a conversion.* It is the conversion itself.

Gorz is thirty-two years old. For thirty-two years, whatever he did, it was immediately apparent to him that he could just as well have done the opposite, and that the results would have been the same, which is to say, nothing, or worse yet, meaningless. For thirty-two years, his existence has escaped him; he has no other proof of it except an insurmountable boredom. I am bored, thus I exist. But he struggled, he searched, he thought he found the band wagon. He said to himself: "Since I belong nowhere, to no group, to no undertaking, the exile of all groups and of all undertakings, there is only this alternative; to be on the margin of society and history, the supernumerary of the human race, reduced to the boredom of living, to the sharp awareness of the contingency of everything surrounding me; or to raise myself consciously to the absolute, that is, to establish everything philosophically as a moment of spiritual adventure.

and by so doing, rediscover a taste for the concrete by means of this speculative interest. . . . I can only rejoin the real by beginning with the Idea." In other words, as he is so constituted as to experience no particular desire, he is going to profit from his indifference; for lack of being able—or of being willing. Nothing is decided yet. To be a man named Gorz, he will make himself into *Universal Man*. He will determine his actions by concepts and will establish this rule for himself: always act in such a way that the circumstances and the moment will serve as a pretext for your acts, in order to realize from within and without, the generality of human kind. For this reason, at the age of twenty, he set about writing a work on philosophy. When one has been immunized from birth against the rages of fear, of lust and of anger, one must either do nothing, or found everything upon reason—even the gesture of opening an umbrella when it rains.

Now, everything is explained. No one will wonder any longer at his treason. He is one of those guys whose head is full of words, who analyzes everything, who always has to know the why and the how, a critical and destructive mind, in a word, a dirty intellectual. I would not dream of denying it, and that is even why I like him. I am one too. A literary paper asked the Prince of Base Currency what he hated most, and without hesitation, he replied—"Intellectuals." I have a certain affection for this counterfeiter. He is a real poet and a kind man, but I wonder what got into him that day. Everyone is well acquainted with his hunted manner, his monologues on destiny, on time, on life, selected pieces from an endless and imploring apologia, these bottlenecks of words in his throat, his charming hands which are still more words and which turn, palms upwards, to beg for mercy, his weary and played-out thoughts which still run on, leaping from one idea to another, unaware that they are running around a cage, his flashing improvisations whose finished canvases are found among his writing of the day before, and which, when extinguished, reveal the incurable sadness of a frozen stare. This man is seeking a tribunal in the sole hope of corrupting it. If he meets you, it is to make you both judge and jury. He will not spare you a single detail of his actions and will not let you go until you have acquitted him. But do not be taken in: he knows everything. This sentence which he is trying to avoid, he knows he has inflicted upon himself since the beginning of the century. He knows that he is a thief who has been serving time for fifty years. For he has condemned himself to plead until his old age the cause his adolescence judged. What would you call this devil's advocate, if not an *intellectual?* There are others, of course, who oppose this babbling with the great silences of the earth. But when you open them, what an uproar; their mind is howling with words to describe the silence of others. Gorz is, I believe, the first to have formulated the problem concretely, and for this I am grateful to him. Small matter whether they speak of language or of silence, about the confused intuitions of the poet, or about clear ideas. The point is that these talkers are compelled to talk. The man of base currency has invented more reasons to defend the shadows of the heart than Kant needed to establish the laws of Reason. He was forced into it: speeches, concepts, arguments. This is our lot, and why? Because intelligence is neither a gift nor a defect, but a drama; or if you will, a provisory solution which is most often changed into a life sentence. Someone once said to our Traitor, "You stink from intelligence the way people stink from armpits." And it's true: intelligence stinks, but no more than stupidity. There are smells for every taste. This one smells of wild animal, that one of man. First of all, certain individuals, torn apart, exiled and condemned, try to surmount their conflicts and solitude by seeking the mad image of unanimity. This is what shines in their eyes, what is timidly suggested by their smiles. Apropos of everything and nothing, the appeal is there, permanently inscribed in their faces. Whatever it may say, the voice demands universal agreement, but people, weighed down by particularities, by dense layers of self-interest, by passions, hate it when you try to dissolve their differences and hatreds by the purely formal harmony of assent.

And then, intelligence is so petty. It wants to take everything from the beginning, even what each one thinks he knows how to do. It decomposes and recomposes walking and breathing, it teaches us how to wash and blow our nose according to principles. This is what gives intellectuals that air of disabled soldiers in a period of rehabilitation. But we must try to understand them. Each one of them has had to reinvent intelligence to compensate for that rummage sale which liquidated every impulse and every infatuation within him. They have to replace those signals which have not been inscribed in their flesh, the habits they have not been given, the roads they have not been shown, in short, they need it *to live*. I remember seeing a puppy after the partial removal of the cerebellum. He moved across the room, rarely colliding with the furniture, but he had become thoughtful. He established his itinerary carefully. He pondered before going around an object, requiring a great deal of time and thought to accomplish movements to which he had previously paid no attention. In the language of the time, we said that the cortex had assumed for him certain functions of the lower regions. He was an intellectual dog. I don't know whether this made him very useful or harmful to his kind, but we can quite well imagine that he had lost what Genet, another exile, has so well named, "sweet natal confusion." To sum up, he either had to die or reinvent the dog.

So we others—rats without cerebella—we are also so made that we must either die or reinvent man. Moreover, we know perfectly well that man will make himself without us, through working and fighting, that our models become obsolete from one day to the next, that nothing will remain of them in the finished product, not even a bone, but that also, without us, the fabrication would take place in the dark, by tinkering and patching, if we, the "debrained," weren't there to repeat constantly that we must work according to principles, that it is not a matter of mending, but of measuring and constructing, and finally, that mankind will be the concrete universal, or that it will not be.

We are struck by Gorz's intelligence at first glance: it is one of the sharpest and most agile that I know. He must have had dire need of this tool to have ground it so well. But as soon as he sets about writing his philosophic treatise, he does not, for all that, escape the contradiction inherent to all intellectuals. He only wants to act in consequence of the human condition, but the act, through being realized, buries itself in the particular. What remains is the fortuitous realization of one possibility among a thousand. Why just *that one?* The worst is that it compromises him. He cannot even breathe without adding a new touch to this portrait without a model which is none other than his self-portrait. He must become, at the same time, every possible Gorz for these foolish equivalences to cancel themselves out, in order, *finally to be only man* by becoming *every man*. But no. "We are born several and we shall die a single one," says Valéry's Socrates. Gorz is neither able to prevent himself from living, nor from shrinking with use.

His universal intelligence overflows his personal adventure and looks with disgust at the emerging physiognomy of this Gorz who will be *a single one*. It rejects him, refuses even to recognize him. It would have gladly accepted him as just anybody, but he is not even that. A sequence of accidents has given him a defined individuality which is distinguished from others by nonsense.

We all know this vacant and sugar-coated anguish—that is to say, we intellectuals. We believe ourselves eternal because we play with concepts, and then, suddenly, we see our shadow at our feet. We are *there*, we are doing *this* and nothing else. Once, in Brooklyn, I thought I would lose my mind. Through my error, I was taking a walk. This is not done in the United States. Thus, I crossed streets, I strolled past buildings, I looked at the passers-by. And from one street to the next, buildings, passers-by and sidewalks, everything was the same, or seemed so to me. I went to the left, to the right, I turned back, I rushed ahead, only to find the same brick houses, the same white steps in front of the same doors, the same children playing the same games. At first, I enjoyed it. I had discovered the city of absolute equivalences, universal and ordinary. I had no more reason to walk on *that* sidewalk than on the same one where I was, a hundred blocks further. Repeated a thousand times, the stone wave carried me along, forcing me to participate in its inert rebeginning. What tired me, little by little, was constantly going forward *in order to go nowhere.* I quickened my step, I almost ran, and I stood still. Suddenly I was conscious of a nameless rejection. All these mass-produced objects, these stumps of streets aligned side by side, all looked even more alike in that all were equally devoid of me, save just one, which could in no way be distinguished from the others, where I had no more reason to find myself than in the neighboring segments, and which, for an unknown motive or for no motive at all, tolerated my presence. At once, my movements, my life, my very substance seemed to me to be illegitimate. I was not a real person since I had no particular motivation for finding myself on *this* point of the 42nd parallel rather than another, but I was still singular, irreductible, since my position in latitude and longitude rigorously defined me as such. Neither everyone, nor someone, nor quite something: a spatial determination, a guilty and contagious dream which haunted in spots the overheated asphalt, and error of being, a misfit. An obstinate body in motion, my presence in the mechanical universe became brute accident, as idiotic as my birth. Ubiquity might have saved me. I should have been legion, striding a hundred sidewalks at the same time. That alone might have allowed me to be any walker in any street in Brooklyn. Being unable either to leave myself or to multiply, I tore into the subway, finding, in my hotel once again, my usual *raisons d'être,* not very convincing, but human.

There is no subway for the young Gorz, no hotel, no

raisons d'être. Even within his bedroom, he is on the out-side, and thus everywhere illegitimate and everywhere be-wildered to his marrow. He thought he could escape his innocuous person by proclaiming the disgust with which it inspires him, but it is this disgust, first of all, which particu-larizes him; the particularity of intellectuals is nothing else than their vain yearning for universality.

But he has just completed his treatise on philosophy, he stands back to survey it, and all the bewilderment disap-pears. The reflections on the universal have tightened and condensed, they have taken on physiognomy, they look like him. At one and the same time, they are the source of this supernumerary object—this bundle of typed sheets of paper —and imprisoned within it. For a long time now, others believe they find him whole in his most ordinary actions, in his manner of eating, of sitting down, of opening a tele-gram.—"Ah, that's just like you, exactly like you, I recog-nized you so perfectly just now, what you are doing there is pure Gorz, the spitting image of him." God knows this irritated him, but what exactly was he just doing, if not making a voluminous gesture which then closed in on him? The others will be only too happy, they will lean against the transparent walls of his prison and they will *recognize him*—"That way of writing, old man, of correcting your-self, of entering into the subject little by little, of dabbling your toe before plunging in, why, it's you, of course, it's you, all you, and those ideas, you poor fellow, they are Gorz, the spitting image of him." A devil inside a bottle. He has but one and the same gesture for opening jars of jam; the thoughts of another; his umbrella; only one gesture to penetrate the ideas of a seventeenth-century philosopher and to enter a friend's or a young woman's apartment. One by one, he examines the phrases of his book again. Gestures! Gestures! Gestures! Gorz is right there, before his eyes, he stretches out his long neck, purses his thin lips, just as he does within himself. . . . In all, he has tried to live and he has failed. He knows now that he was doomed to fail and that, moreover, he had been secretly resolved to do so.

At this precise moment, the Voice began to speak. An almost unintelligible little mumble, born of anguish and re-crimination, and which ruminates this surprising and fore-seen defeat. The Voice makes a simple statement: it is certainly him, it is the spitting image of him. That suffices to sway everything. It was the others who claimed to know this parasite which fattened upon his acts, the universal gaze of the Indifferent passed through him as light passes through a pane of glass. Suddenly he is there, heavy and opaque. Confess! You saw him, spoke to him, we know it; your system of defense won't convince anyone, we know the place and date of your meetings; you're trapped. The voice moves on to confessions: "Well, yes, I know him better than anyone else. I have always known him and I will tell you what I know about him."

Was I not right a while ago when I said that one should speak of oneself in the plural? There are two of them living on this one wretched creature. There is universal man, this elusive and heavily-armed tyrant, and then the other, his cast-off. He makes himself into *a man named Gorz* by trying to be only Man, and to tell the whole truth, he wants to become *everyman* because he refuses to be a man named Gorz. But just who is refusing to be Gorz except Gorz himself? This refusal explains and defines him. If he agreed *to be,* in other words, to have been the miser with the long neck who wants to preserve his foolish universality; if we talked about him constantly, enumerated all his particular obsessions; if, instead of going through him, the intellectual look saw through him, would not this "original"* disappear along with the stubborn negation which constituted his originality? It is certainly not future man who would come to take his place, but another fellow whose fundamental obstinacies would only risk being more positive. What would be gained by it? Is the game worth the candle? But in fact, it is too late to begin counting losses and profits. The voice speaks, the undertaking has begun. The Traitor has taken his own particularity as his object.

It is neither a question of knowing it, nor quite that of changing it; but of first of all changing himself by the will to know it. The indifferent has no stupid project of painting himself; he wants to modify the fundamental relationship which unites him to Gorz. When he turns towards the child, towards the adolescent that he was, when he interrogates his person, the inquiry is already an action; he halts abruptly in his frenzied flight, he forces himself to regard himself without disgust, he transfers his taste for reckonings to himself and, for lack of being everyman, he tries first to become, for himself, *every Gorz*.

This is not so simple: by neglecting himself for so long, he is in the midst of himself like Robinson Crusoe in the middle of a desert island. How will he find the lost roads? Brambles and creepers cover everything. He reaches for

* In French, *original* has both the meaning it has in English as well as that of "eccentric." Thus, the writer is playing upon the two meanings of the word. (*Trans.*)

some memories, but what is a memory? What is the truth of this small inert picture? And of what importance is it? Is it the past which explodes like a bomb into the present? Is it the present disguised as the past? Or the both together? He must answer these two questions: *who* is the Gorz which I am? who has so made me that I am Gorz and that I refuse so ferociously to be him? But how to decide? Where are the tools? To be sure, offers abound. There are proven methods which hasten to assert themselves and which even make little exploratory demonstrations to prove their efficacity. One says: "Your class is in complete decay; without principles and without hope, it is exhausting all its forces to maintain itself and hasn't enough heart, or if you will, naïveté, to try anything new. Your indifference only reveals its anxious uncertainty. Existence seems pointless to you because bourgeois life no longer makes any sense. As for your philosophic uneasiness, don't seek its origins any further. The bourgeoisie no longer even has confidence in its antiquated idealism, trying to disguise it under tinseled rags. You have held this shredded cloth in your hands, you have seen its woof and been disgusted by it, powerless either to content yourself with these obsolete ideas or to find a new system of thought." He listens approvingly, but he is not entirely convinced. He has no difficulty in agreeing that he is a young bourgeois. Without needs, wholly abstract, a "pure consumer of water, air, bread, others' labor, reduced to the acute consciousness of the contingency of everything around him." But he knows many other bourgeois of his age who do not resemble him in the slightest degree. Surely, without abandoning his method, he could find the historic and social circumstances which might explain his singularities. He tells us himself that he is Austrian, half-Jewish, that he was forced to leave Austria at the time of the *Anschluss* and that he lived in Switzerland for several years. He is convinced that these factors are not without influence upon his present attitudes. But the question is *What influence?* And how was it exercised? And still more generally, is there anything more surprising, more mysterious than the action of people, events or objects upon the development of a man? All around him, everyone is agreed: we are conditioned. You would find no one who doubts the existence of this conditioning, or who questions himself as to its nature. These are things known from father to son. The disputes arise when they try to classify the conditions and to determine their importance. But all these people are heirs. These presuppositions, this supposed evidence, form part of an old legacy which each generation palms off upon the next, and of which no one has ever made the inventory. The Indifferent, on the contrary, has inherited none of their convictions. The Exile of all groups must also be the exile of all ideologies. When he comes to consider at the same time, that he was "born of a Jew" and that he has an "acute consciousness of the contingency of all things," he admires the isolation, the opacity, the irreducible loftiness of these two so different facts. Looking at them ingenuously, one would call them two miniature cities, circled by ramparts and moats. Each of them was painted on old canvas enclosed by a frame. Both of them hang on the chimney piece. *There is no visible road* between them, since they do not exist in the same world. He is not unaware, however, that people come and go in their little personal museums, passing from a Circumcision to a Flagellation, without even looking up the names of their authors, and that they say: *"That* is the cause of *this.* I am the unfortunate product of my race, of the Judaism of my father, of the anti-Semitism of my classmates," as though the real link between the mysterious images of himself was simply the wall around the paintings which contain them. When he thinks of the calm certainty of these heirs, it is only to sink into the most profound amazement.

It is then that the other method suggests itself, this strange dogmatism which is based upon an absolute skepticism. Does he remember his first years, the aversion which his mother felt for the Jew whom she had married and which she imparted to him so perfectly, the unbearable tension of the family group, the severe upbringing to which he was subjected as soon as he could talk? Why does he not simply ask himself whether he was not the victim of a castrating mother, and whether he should not date from this time, from this oppression undergone in terror, the appearance of the "complexes" which sever him from the world today? Wouldn't "He" definitively be *the Aryan of Honor,* this personage whom an outraged wife wants to impose upon her son because she cannot stop reproaching a certain Jew for being the only husband she could find? The docility of a contrived child could live on in the adult in the form of apathy.

To which he replies that his upbringing has, in fact, given him complexes. His mother did want to make this Other out of him which he, in part, became. He suffered, in his earliest years, as he does now, from a zealous and uneasy indifference. But he does not succeed in understanding how these famous "complexes" perpetuate themselves. He was apathetic at the age of eight, and he is today. *Is it the same apathy?* But he cannot so easily believe in human passivity. His every experience rejects this convenient idea as well as the metaphysics upon which it is based. Will he admit the contrary—that he fed and coddled his complexes, that he takes care of them and fattens them, that the adolescent and the adult resumed, underlined and enriched the first characteristics of the child by a sort of continued act of creation? It would be he, then, who is responsible for it all, who, from day to day, made himself indifferent. But he cannot reach a conclusion so quickly. None of these interpretations is completely satisfactory, none of them quite clear to his eyes. Like the child in the Anderson tale who sees the king stark naked, he is, once again, a Traitor, who, making the inventory of our philosophical heritage, finds the coffers empty and ingenuously says so. Why, moreover, should he be interrogated according to others' methods? Why should he turn himself over to a Marxist or Psychiatric third degree? On the contrary, it is up to him to challenge these procedures in the question that he asks of himself. This Oedipus brings his investigation to bear upon his own past and the validity of his memories, upon the laws of experience and the limits of reason, and finally even upon the legitimacy of the prophetic gifts with which our Tiresias credit themselves. But he turns his back on the universal. He invents the method by reflecting upon his own case: it will prove itself by its success. To emerge into the light of day as a particular totality, he must isolate himself within the experience of his own particularity. He must invent himself by inventing his own interrogation and the means of answering it. The Traitor, erasing all, begins himself anew. And this is what gives us today the opportunity of reading a *radical* book.

We have listened to "His Master's Voice" for a long time. At present, it is Gorz who speaks: The end of the monologue turns back on its beginning, envelops and absorbs it. The meaning of the work emerges in its full clarity. At first it was a question asked *by nobody* in the darkness. Under what conditions will the one named Gorz be able to say "I"? But immediately following, a still-indistinct being appears out of the night. The book does not simply set out to determine these conditions, it becomes the living effort of Gorz to fulfill them. *He* knows now that *he* will have done nothing if he does not strangle the vampires who wash him, dress him and fatten him so that they may, in turn, fatten upon him. The first act which will be born of my hands alone—which will depend only upon himself and the obstacles to be overcome, which will fall back upon itself, to gather its forces steadying itself, is the one which will speak my first "I." This imperceptible sliding of an action against itself, *will be me.* And what prevents him from acting? He knows that too. It is the too-premature desire to be universal too soon. Now he repeats to himself that his future action will necessarily borrow *his* eyes, *his* mouth, *his* arms, will have his stubborn manner, and above all, will be each day, more rigorously defined by the ephemeral agitation which it will communicate to the surrounding objects. Seen from the outside, a man is no more than this—an anxiety which works matter within the limits of a rigorously defined area. Old singular undertakings impose their singularity upon a new undertaking which retracts all of them to singularize them further. *Me,* I am this ceaseless coming and going. If he is able to act, he will be *himself*, but he must *accept* himself in order to act. What prevents him from doing this? What is the reason for his vain yearning for universality? He discovers a heap of rubbish crammed into his heart, his childhood. He attempts to dissolve it, but that is not enough. He can hide from himself no longer the fact that, at each minute, he reinvents his illegitimacy, the burden of his old privations, infirmities. For not being everyone, it is he, today, who falls into a proud passivity. To make everyone understand that he receives his determinations from the exterior and without assenting to them, it is he who obliterates, or at the very least, absents himself, leaving the habits which others have made for him, the natural and social functions of his body, to hold the fort alone. It is he who, in full freedom, has decided, like a St. John of the Cross without mysticism, to do nothing, ever, in order, freely, to "be nothing in nothing."

Then is he free? Of course, for he never doubted it. They have made him, signed him, molded him in plaster *and* he is free. Yes, slave will, free will, are in him, one and the same thing. How can that be? He will try to tell us, to tell himself, but his goal remains a practical one. For him, it is a problem of inventing the dialectical movement which can sum up the changing rapport of the past, present and future, of the objective and subjective, of being and existence, of machinery and freedom, in order to be able, at the same time, to affirm and dissolve himself constantly, until finally, a true impulse arises in his heart which ravages it, surging from his heart into his hands, realizing itself on the exterior through that holocaust of objects which we call *an act*.

Such is his task. He only just begins to understand it. He

puts down on paper what he has understood, and in that same moment, he perceives that his most intimate desire leaves his heart through his hands, that he is *already* embarked on an undertaking, that today's, yesterday's, and last month's words come together and fall into order, reflecting back to him his new face, that he is in the process of unmaking himself through words, in order to be able, one day, to make himself through acts, that this destruction creates him, determines him irrevocably, that little by little he is transformed into that incomparable and ordinary being which each of us is, when our Vampires are sleeping, that he is "wet" at last, he has "taken the plunge," condemned now, whatever he does, to never again having any other springboard but himself. This is the moment: *hic Rhodus hic salta;* the undertaking turns back on itself, giving itself the thousand coils of conscience, the thousand rings of reflection, it touches, feels, sees itself; the undertaking was the Voice. The voice recognizes itself. Through it, action unfolds and says "I." *I* am doing this book, *I* am seeking myself, *I* am writing. Somewhere, a fellow with a hollow eye is sighing, intimidated: "Speaking in the first person is so pompous," and then he fades out. Gorz appears: I am Gorz, it was my voice that spoke, I am writing, I exist, I make and sustain myself, I have won the first round.

Is this worth a cry of victory? After all, who is Gorz? "A boy with no social significance whatever," a "reject" of the Universal who has left abstract speculations aside to delectate upon his own innocuous person. Where is the reward? Where is progress? I imagine that Gorz will not answer this question. But we can answer in his place. For step by step, we have followed this fantastic Cuvier who, finding a bone, begins to reconstruct the animal from this minuscule vestige, and realizes, when he has finished, that the reconstructed creature is none other than himself. The method only works for him—he has said this and repeated it a hundred times. He could only prove it by his own case. But we have followed him, we understood the meaning of his acts at the same time he did, we were present at his experiments and saw the muscles reborn around the bone, saw the organism reconstruct itself bit by bit, saw the author and the book create each other. And what we understand belongs to us. The Gorz method is ours. When he tries to interpret his life according to Marxist dialectic, according to psychoanalysis, without ever *quite* succeeding, his failure concerns us, we shall know how to attempt the ordeal and know the result in advance. And when he asks his own object, that is, himself, to create his method for him, we immediately seize the significance of this singular endeavor. For we are his fellow creature in this. Each of us, like him, is a unique anybody. And what exactly is this object which, in the name of method, makes itself into a subject? Gorz or you and I? You are not the Indifferent, you have other questions to ask yourselves? Gorz, by inventing himself, has not absolved you of the duty of inventing yourselves. But he has proved to you that the totalizing invention was possible and necessary. As he closes the book, each reader finds his own underbrush and the poisonous trees of his own jungle. It is for him to clear the land and make his way, alone, to put the Vampires to flight, to smash the old steel corsets, those worn-out actions, where fear, resignation and self-doubt have imprisoned him. Could we have found the universal by betting on the particular? No, that would be too beautiful.

We are not quite animals any more, without quite being men. We have not yet profited from this catastrophe which was loosed upon a few representative members of the animal kingdom—the power to think. In a word, we shall still remain stricken mammals for a long time to come. This is the era of rage, of fetishes and sudden terror, where universality is only the dream of a dead man, in the womb of separation and fear. But for some decennials now, our world has been changing. Reciprocity reveals itself in the depths of hatred. Even the very ones who want to outdo one another in their differences, must be willing to conceal themselves under a fundamental identity. This new movement, this modest but relentless attempt to communicate through the incommunicable, is not the dreary and always foolish desire for a universality which is already finished and inert. I would call it, rather, the movement of universalization. Nothing is possible yet, no agreement is in sight among the laboratory animals. Our universals separate us, providing the permanent opportunity for specific massacres. But if one of us, gnawed by anxiety, would turn away from the Idea, if, rejecting abstract thought, he would retrace his singularity *to transcend it*, if he would try to acknowledge his solitude to escape from it, throwing himself, for whatever it might be worth, into a strange empirical language, like those reinvented by aphasiacs—the first bridges between our archipelagoes—if he could replace our intransigent loves, which are only masked hatreds, by conscientious choices, if in every singular and given circumstance, he would try to unite with others, of whom he does not approve and who do not approve of him, in order that the reign of Injustice will be a little less unjust, he will oblige others to reinvent this same tenacious effort, to unite through recognition of their diversities. This is what Gorz has tried to do. This Traitor has smashed the tablets of the Universal, but it was in order to discover the movement of life, this slow universalization which realizes itself through affirmation and through transcendence of the particular. The immediate consequence: at that same instant when he can finally say *I* am doing this, *I* am responsible for it, he perceives that he is speaking to us. For today, there are only two ways to speak of oneself, the third person singular or the first person plural. We must first know how to say "we" in order to say "I." This is indisputable. But the converse is equally true; if, to establish the "us" first, some tyranny deprives individuals of the subjective reflex, all interiority evaporates with one blow, and reciprocal relationships along with it. *They* will then have triumphed forever, and we will never cease running to and fro in the experimental labyrinth, mad rodents in the prey of Vampires.

Gorz's book concerns all of us. If he stammers at first, if he does not know where he is going, if he transforms himself incessantly, and if we feel his icy fever in our hands, if he contaminates us without ever having seen us, and if, to finish, he speaks directly, intimately to every reader, it is because he is penetrated through and through by the movement which quickens us, by the movement of our times. Radical and moderate, vague and rigorous, banal and inimitable, this is the first book *after the defeat*. The Vampires have had a memorable massacre, they have snuffed out hope. We must catch our breath, play dead for a while, and then stand up, leave the charnel house, begin everything again, invent a new hope, try to live. The great slaughters of this century have made a corpse of Gorz; he has risen from the dead by writing an Invitation to life.